Hippie at Heart

(What I Used to Be, I Still Am)

by

Lynne Zotalis

Hippie at Heart, What I Used to Be, I Still Am is creative nonfiction. Some of the events described happened as related, and others were expanded and changed. Some of the individuals portrayed are composites of more than one person, and many names and identifying characteristics have been changed as well.

Dedicated to Chuck

1

Our last sunset together

Flying back from Mexico with my husband's body entombed in the cargo hold, I grip the arm rests as if I'm hanging onto sanity. The word, *casket,* presses into my thoughts, echoing. Vaguely familiar, I can barely make it out. *Casket.* It's calling from another dimension, a shock wave pulling me down, away from reality. There's music, a beautifully ethereal melody speaking to my psyche. I recognize it: Thomas Otten's "Qualitati Umane." Someone, something is drawing me away. *Casket.*

Babe, is that you? Where are you, my love? Blinded by iridescence I search luminous clouds in vain. I can sense you just beyond reach. Are you out there?

I can't get any air. Instinctively, I double over gasping for breath, contractions tying my stomach into a knot. You're twenty feet below me, your body in a *casket*. I can't breathe. I cup both hands over my mouth.

Come on. Hang on. You have to keep it together. A few more hours and I'll see the kids, our four adult children for the heart wrenching reunion. *Casket.* With my eyes tightly shut, following the word, I try to envision it.

Are you speaking to me? I sit upright, inhaling deeply as if in labor. I'm drifting back to my roots, to the beginning . . . imagining . . .

* * *

"Casket," I repeated the word my daddy said, copying the sound, "cas-ket, casket," practicing like any four year old learning a new word. Organ music droned.

"Why is Grandma in the box?" I asked Daddy.

"It's a casket," he explained, choking back a sob.

I was in his arms, where he held me up to look at my dead grandma Lydia lying in state in the church. I loved her. With such tenderness she'd pull me onto her lap humming a lullaby or a hymn as she snuggled me into her cushiony bosom. It felt safe, secure, and so different. The navy blue dress she wore was slippery and smooth, like I could slide right off it, but her affectionate embrace gently wrapped around me. She was a fairy godmother.

"Why's she in there?" I asked, pressing Daddy for an answer, "Why are you crying, Daddy?"

Daddy was trying to be strong, gently explaining, "Grandma is asleep... for a long, long time."

"Why won't she wake up?"

"She's going to heaven."

"Why are you crying?" I asked, beginning to sob.

All he could say was, "Daddy's sad," almost whispering.

Her face was just like it had always been, sweet, softly creamy with wire rim spectacles. Do dead people really need their glasses? My parents were going to name me Lydia Anne, after her, but decided against it as too aged, too old fashioned; instead, I was Anne.

Years later I would bemoan the lack of glamour in such a boring, mono-syllabic name, thinking if I could have been named Sandy, life would be much improved. Even Lydia trumped Anne. A-n-n-e, the name everyone misspelled as A-n-n.

In my experience, certain early memories made the most profound impression based on their level of pain. Others were fleeting frames projected against my subconscious: mercurochrome painted adhesive taped fingers to cure my forbidden sucking habit; a blackened jacket, filthy from sliding down the steeply pitched coal dust coated driveway; paper dolls balanced against the riser, their demise irreversible as the staircase crevices swallowed them up.

One year prior to Grandma's death, my earliest recollection was imprinted from a bicycle accident. Sitting on the thick metal rear fender, legs dangling in the cool breeze, arms clenched around my babysitter's waist, a jolt ripped my tender flesh to the bone as we jerked to a halt. Searing pain pierced my twisted ankle as it tangled through bike spokes. She carried me home screaming for help, as I howled. It took weeks for the swelling to subside, purple and blue to return pink. The emotional trauma healed much more slowly than my battered foot. Miraculously, no bones were broken.

"No, I don't want a bike!"

It was my chronic answer whenever my parents, Jack and Edith, asked what I wanted for my birthday. I wanted a tractor like my grandpa had, like the one I showed Mommy from the catalogue. Two wheelers resurrected the dreaded experience.

Jack and Edith led me to the front door, "Open your eyes."

There it was, sitting on the walkway, in all its shiny red glory: my brand new miniature riding tractor. It was my fifth birthday and I was so unaccustomed to getting what I asked for, the second daughter of a hard working pharmaceutical salesman-father and overwrought housewife-mother that I thought, "This is a dream." Wondrously, unexpectedly, it appeared. It was the best day of my life.

They gave in, even though my mother continuously felt it her duty to remind me, "You think we're made of money? Money doesn't grow on trees; waste not, want not; there are children starving in China."

The epithets were meant to instill utility, a standard response to deny anything new. My chubby build resulted from guilt over the unfinished plateful that murdered Asian children, who'd fare better if I were fat.

My very own tractor

* * *

Did I expect any other response? From Mexico, the first call to my folks was a trial run before I attempted to break the news to our children.

"Hello," Edith said.

"Mom," I could barely get it out.

"Anne? What's wrong? What happened?"

"Sit down," then I blurted, "Nick died."

"What? Nick? How?"

The other extension clicked. Dad said, "What's going on?"

Edith told him. Then the third click.

My sister, Cynthia was visiting them, "What's the matter? Who?"

Jack and Edith lived in the Sun City retirement community where they golfed and partied like it was a job. Constantly on the go, they maintained this unbelievable pace of social activity. Anyone under fifty visiting, had strict rules as to when and where they could swim, golf, practically be seen. The Association policed and reported regularly any infractions. Such as someone leaving their garage door open or hanging clothes outside even on their back patio. You weren't allowed to have a car parked on the street longer than a day; not too stridently enforced but understood having a car sitting in the driveway, not in the garage with the door closed, was frowned upon. Raising our four children in the country was as far away as Mars! We had visited them once in all the years they were growing up more so due to financial constraints but probably as much because of the bizarre lifestyle my parents chose.

Peppered with questions, crying, I could give no understanding. Not willing to waste any more precious minutes with the salvo, I pitched the impossible, "I need money, Dad."

ZZZip. He took on businessman mode, clearing his throat, "Oh, well, what are you talking, how much?"

"I need $10,000 to make this happen. I have to have ready capital for persuasion, to work this system and buy my way out, if necessary. I need help."

Edith interjected, "We don't have that kind of money sitting around. We're not made of money."

"Ahhhhgg," I groaned, feeling my stomach knot.

Even now, I had to beg. I had no energy to argue or convince. Their refusal was the cruelest blow.

Slightly conciliatory, Dad said, "I'll have to see what I can come up with. It will take some time, juggling some things around."

"Forget it. Don't bother," I spewed, hating them.

"Well, now, don't be like that. We'll see what we can do," Edith whined.

"I have to go. I have to call the kids and tell them their dad died!" I snapped, sinking down, down, down into panic.

I sat, shaking unable to put two thoughts together, swaying side to side at the edge of the bed. Who else can I ask, where, how am I going to get him out of here? One deep breath, sit up straight, think.

When I called them several hours later my sister and Dad tried to explain the prudence of charging me the current interest rate on whatever monies sent. Stunned by such a callous contingency I refused the offer.

There was the slightest satisfaction in hanging up on them, telling myself, "I **will** get through this without you, goddammit! **I don't need you**. And I will **never** ask you again."

* * *

2

Homemade creations

On Halloween, Christmas, and Easter, Mom would sew new dresses and costumes for Cynthia and me. The matching outfits with strange, scratchy fabric, taffeta? were thrifty, if anything. Containing dozens of oddly shaped pieces, the patterns took hours to lay out and pin together. Mom was somehow able to talk out of one side of her mouth while the other adeptly commandeered thirty or so pins. Standing on a chair for the interminable fittings, I could always count on a few flesh sticks. Maybe it was the dropped waist style, that sailor collar neckline, or my figure but whatever the end result, you "made do." Eager to slough mine as soon as humanly possible, I was cursed with the cloned outfit for an additional year after Cynthia outgrew hers. Shoes with her imprint shaped my feet.

Maybe it was the whiskey and Coke, knocked back after we kids were properly packed off for the night that made those creations so bizarre. Through her black cat's eye glasses, Mom would squint in the poor light, puffing a Salem while revving that foot peddle like a race car. I dreaded the finished product.

Mom climbed the domestic ladder of success vying for the cleanest house in town, waxing the linoleum kitchen floor a half inch thick with fresh coats until she'd eventually have to scrape it all off. Religiously, she'd start the process all over again, barring traffic for at least three hours until it dried. Thank God for the bathroom in the basement or we'd have had to pee outside. The only other route to the ground floor bathroom was through the living room, and God strike us dead if we came through the front door onto the vacuumed carpet. OCD, she would vigilantly hover close enough to all activities policing but never participating. No energy or inclination. I don't have a single memory playing a game with my mom or anyone else's mom, for that matter. Moms were a nebulous domestic machine.

If I was washing dishes while she dried, and there was a smudge left on a plate, she'd push it right back into the scalding, soapy water, remarking, "You call that clean?"

But if she was washing, I was drying, and tried the same tactic, her defense was,

"A good wiper would get that off."

Crumbs were the bane of her existence. I thought everyone ate a cookie hanging over the kitchen sink. There was no pleasing her.

12

Frazzled after another relentless day of exhausting maintenance, she'd dismiss us, wincing as I tried to hug and kiss her, "Off to bed, get out of my hair."

"Take your shoes off, don't track that in, wash your hands, hang that up, sit up straight," Mom pelted, never letting up. "Seldom was heard an encouraging word."

"When are you going to get it through your thick skull?" she'd fire at me, slicing my confidence into small enough pieces for her to chew up and spit out.

My attempts at cleaning always failed inspection. Guaranteed by the eccentric double standard to fall short, discouraged by failure, I longed for affirmation. But positive reinforcement was a foreign language. Not practiced in the 50s, at least not in my household.

Daddy was my ounce of human kindness, what scant time he spent at home. When I could settle into his lap for tender moments, I'd bask, I'd soak, unaware of my desperate need ameliorated slightly by this phantom father.

"Daddy, can I comb your hair?"

He'd fish the four inch black ACE comb out of his pocket handing it to me. Sliding it through the luxurious blond waves I tried to smooth them into any other style except the one they never relinquished; naturally permanent ripples gently tumbling over his head like waves on the sea. Parting it on the opposite side, I'd try to contain it with my chubby fingers.

"It won't stay, Daddy."

"You'll just have to hold it then."

"How long?"

"Well, forever, if that's how you want it to look."

"That's too long," I said, in my most knowing perception.

"What's this?" I asked, touching my index finger to the rippled skin on his neck.

"That's a scar."

"Why do you have it?"

Touching it as softly as I could, I ran my finger along the five inch remnant of his courage. It was a different texture than the rest of his skin, extremely thin, sort of loose, but not so much as to hang. I was afraid I'd poke through it if I wasn't careful.

"Does it hurt?"

"No."

"Can you feel this?" I asked, barely perceiving the delicate graze of my own fingertip.

"Yes, barely."

"How did you get it?"

"I was shot in the war."

As a preschooler, I didn't know what else to ask but was left with a tremendous curiosity. Every time I tried to get more information, I was met with the same resistance. Eventually, I quit asking.

Ricky, me, Cynthia

The morning Mommy and Ricky were due to return home from the hospital the house was aflutter with activity. Readying the room, bassinet, and formula left me in a mass of feelings ranging from excitement and confusion, to fear. The night before with Mommy in the hospital, Daddy made a special supper turning hot dogs into cars. With toothpicks for the axle, carrots stuck on the ends for wheels, we colored our models with mustard. Pickle slices, onions and thin strips of cheese garnished the creations. No recollection of taste but no matter.

My tender heart was so conflicted sensing the shift. No longer the baby, the youngest, now I was just the second daughter. If I'd been a boy, Jack and Edith would have quit but after four years and three miscarriages trying, my baby brother, Ricky, had arrived. I hid under the piano keyboard behind the bench not even wanting to look at my baby brother, wondering why no one noticed I was gone. I wanted Daddy to scoop me up and sing my song, the one he made up using my nickname, Bunny. Instead of "My Bonnie Lies over the Ocean", he'd substitute, "My Bunny Lies over…"

Finally discovered, Mommy cajoled, "Come and hold your new baby brother, come and hold Ricky."

I thought, "Hold him? Give him to Cynthia. Can't you get him to shut up?"

That squalling little bundle of spit-up and poop was nothing more than an intrusion into my world.

"Who's going to hold me?" I asked Mommy.

"You're too big now, you're not a baby anymore," her disconcerting reply, cementing my dislike, multiplied my fears.

Buck up. Hugs and kisses and laps were over! The baby everyone was hoping for, waiting for, praying for was here.

A full two teams' worth of kids

Our neighborhood in northern Minnesota was a square block teeming with young families; kids running, biking, roller-skating, hollering everywhere. All summer long we engaged in yard games, week-long Monopoly marathons, and ball games at the field, with ample children for two teams. Without fail my sister and I would be the first ones called home. Barely 8:00 o'clock, we'd hear Mom screaming our names out the back door. In the summer! Lying in bed, shades drawn to make it dark while the sun wasn't yet set, the laughter and fun we were missing floated through the screened windows. Captain May I, Red Light-Green Light, and Kick the Can still continued for another hour until reasonable parents called their children in. From my bed, I'd hear the pop and fizz of the Coke bottle opening, ice clattering into the tumbler as the evening cocktail was mixed to tranquilize the fading day. We were allowed pop maybe once or twice a year. It was like nectar of the gods. The six packs of green bottles were carefully sequestered on the highest shelf of the pantry. Along with the tin Red Dot can of scrumptious potato chips.

Bruce gets lucky

Love came early to my five-year-old heart. Bruce was the adorable, funny object of my affections. With his ash blond crew cut, goofy jokes and rambunctiousness I couldn't get enough of him. Our parents played Bridge while we played house setting up the scene in the basement with baby dolls, rooms cordoned and defined with blankets strung on chairs. He'd willingly be Daddy—me, Mommy, serving up juice and cracker meals, tending the children while Bruce went off, to work. We'd dress up and mimic our parents in a make-believe world. Typically, we kids would have to lie down until the adults were finished with their game, whereupon whoever was visiting would carry out the sleeping children for the ride home. I loved the little dishes of colored mints and salted nuts on the corner of each card table. These were for adults only. We were lucky to get popcorn.

"Bruce is going to sleep with me," I announced innocently enough.

19

"Well, that's not a good thing to do," the instant reply from both sets of parents.

We whined, "Whyiiii nahhht? We want to."

"Because only married people sleep together," their sage rationale.

Without the slightest hesitation, I burst out, "Then we'll get married."

Daddy phobically asked, "Who will marry you?"

"You can marry us."

"Well, you don't have any wedding rings. You see, you have to have wedding rings (they held their hands in our faces proving it) to get married."

My brain worked on the dilemma for a few seconds, and wham, I blurted out the perfect solution, "Just let us use two of your rings."

Our parents were stumped and anxious to get on with their game so right there, in the living room, Bruce and I were joined in semi-holy matrimony. Daddy said a few lines while he placed the rings on our fingers. Repeating I do's, they hustled us off to bed.

"Go right to sleep now," Daddy said as he tucked us in bed.

With the lights out, this honeymooner got an eye-popping education. Boys of all ages get hard-ons.

Proudly, Bruce exposed the teeny, taut member with a hushed, "Look at this."

I didn't know what to make of it, but did wonder aloud, "What's that?"

"My wiener," Bruce explained.

"Oh," just, "Oh."

What else could be said about it? That was all it was... but I was curious.

20

I fell asleep thinking, "How does he pee with his wiener pointing straight up?!"

Barely two years older, but so above me, Cynthia rarely answered or spoke to me. She didn't like me, for being born, I guess, taking the baby place or for having blond hair. I could never figure out what I'd done to earn such disdain.

"Why is Mom so mean?" I asked Cynthia.

No answer. Cynthia would face the wall in our shared bedroom, feigning sleep, pretending not to hear me. We slept side by side in identical twin beds. If you scratched the gray flecked vinyl headboard it sounded like sandpaper. The running jump from our bedroom doorway didn't give the ogre a chance to grab my ankle. It was a certain fact that a gnarly brown paw would yank me into the abyss if I wasn't lightning fast. That's probably why I peed the bed and suffered Mom's wrath rather than the certain grasp of the arm waiting under my plaid dust ruffle. Unreasonable superstition also dictated that my covers had to completely cover everything up to my chin, leaving no neck visible insuring protection from vampires. Your face was safe, independent of the rules.

The message Cynthia emitted to me was, "Be invisible, be a shadow, don't mess anything up and, NEVER dare touch me or my stuff."

3

My homely hairdo

Cynthia got to wear her fine brown hair long, Mom pulling it tightly back into a bouncy ponytail feeding our ever-present competition. Mine was white blonde, a Dutch boy, chopped just below the ears with thick, unevenly blunt bangs.

"You have too much hair, you wouldn't look good with long hair," Mom candidly explained as she buzzed my neck with the electric clipper.

"I look like a boy," I'd whine, after being shorn, imploring her with puppy eyes.

"Just sit still," she'd snap, grabbing my hair, yanking my head around to the front.

Torn between the love/hate feelings, I'd try to tag along with my sister, but she'd easily ditch me racing away on her bike.

"Wait up!" I'd holler to the deaf ears, the eyes that refused to notice or acknowledge my tears squeezing out. "Please!"

The wind pummeled furiously peddling limbs as the distance spread between us. Longing for love, a morsel of affection, some semblance of human kindness, I was the pathetic underdog trailing behind my disinterested sibling. She had this pickiness, a finikiness about her that I could never get away with. Fearful of setting Mom off, I tried to insure exemption from the next barrage by eating everything put in from of me. Cynthia could have cared less. Callous and indifferent, she refused practically everything Mom cooked. Round meat sandwiches were one of her staples, consisting of bologna on plain white Wonder bread. No butter. She never had to have sauce on her spaghetti, or gravy on mashed potatoes, as blah as possible. For a snack she'd chew incessantly on ice cubes.

It didn't faze her thick skin hearing Mom chide, "Why can't you eat like Anne? She eats everything."

I'd gloat, feeling self-important, better than Cynthia, consuming every vegetable, meat, and always dessert. It didn't matter to Cynthia the energy Mom put into her culinary efforts.

Mom would heap another helping on my plate, urging, "If you have room for dessert, you can eat more brussels sprouts."

Well sure, fatten me up. That will help my self-esteem! The more I ate, the happier Mom was. It made peace, kept her quiet; not that it was difficult to wolf down Mom's cooking. Her tasty pork cutlets were so tender, smothered in luscious gravy, flawless every time; they would practically melt in your mouth. I savored the tuna casserole bubbling with creamy mushroom sauce topped with a crushed layer of potato chips. A freshly baked angel food cake hanging upside down on an empty Coke bottle made my stomach growl. That was her secret of success, letting the warm cake cool while inverted. We had to tip-toe past the oven, careful to close the screen door ever so softly, or the cake would fall. The frosted creation was a work of art. My favorite sandwich was reserved for the first day of any family vacation. Mom would pack a picnic for us to enjoy after Dad logged a few hundred miles. She'd combine egg salad with tuna fish, topping it off with cheese. Then she'd wrap the filled buns in tin foil to bake. Nestling the piping hot sandwiches in an air tight container, we'd feast on them several hours down the road.

When Christmas rolled around our house burst with the delightful aroma of cookies. It's a mystery my chubbiness never ballooned into obesity. There were rosettes, sugar cookies, krumkake, spritz, sanbakels, and lefse. Her baking skills were a gift from her mother. The flip side, however, was the Lutefisk that threatened to ruin the entire holiday. With a smell that gagged, the slime-coated fare handily overpowered any cookie. I could never get close enough to even try the lye soaked fish. The adults lapped it up like a delicacy.

Three weeks out of four, traveling salesman Daddy was on the road, leaving overwrought housebound Mom to 'cope' (using the word ever so loosely). He drifted into my life on the weekends for a few hours spending all Saturday doing bookwork in his office. Why he snapped that afternoon I have no explanation for. A bunch of us were playing tag in our back yard, me ignoring a prior request Daddy had made. I'd hauled a large empty box out of the garage for us to take turns being enclosed in and now finished with that game I'd been told to put it away. In a mischievous mood I whipped it up onto the garage roof. It got a huge laugh from everyone. But when Daddy came out and saw it he grabbed me by the arm jerking me in through the back door and down the basement stairs. Breathing heavily he didn't utter one word. His anger as he unbuckled his belt scared the bejesus out of me.

"Put your hands up against the wall," he commanded, "and lean in."

I obeyed as I felt the belt sting, pelting my backside. Determined not to cry, my mind raced to the kids still in the back yard. Could they hear the blows? Would they know what was going on? The embarrassment of them witnessing him acting so wildly was almost as painful as the belt. Off the deep end over a box made no sense. And I didn't cry. I wouldn't give him that.

Sunday after church, he'd regroup, packing his car for the next trip. The atmosphere on weekends was generally tense, even electric as they released a week's worth of stress attacking each other. Dad infuriated Mom countering her screaming with either sarcasm or indifference.

The neighbors were well aware of the contentiously caustic, even explosive nature of our household, given the close proximity of small lots and thin walls as she spewed vitriol either at him or us kids, not even sparing the neighbor kids.

Hollering out the window, "Play in your own yard," or, "You've got your own yard."

And these gems hurled at us,

"Wake up and die right."

"You can't do anything right."

"Numbskull."

"You oughta be horse whipped!"

"Were you born in a barn?"

I don't know what I hated more; the angry harangue, loud enough for the neighborhood to hear or the insidious mocking tone, hitting the target as my tender sensitivity shrank.

When I tried to get away with the same lingo, my sass was handled promptly with a bar of soap ground into my teeth while Mom twisted it adeptly making sure she didn't miss a single tooth. It wasn't hard to figure out why no one wanted to come over. They'd all heard or been there to see her face poke out the back door, barking orders about the grass or flowers, killing our play with acid-tongued remarks.

Being faithful Lutherans, Jack and Edith volunteered one of their bedrooms to house unwed mothers. Each year, for three years, one teenage girl having been booted from her home, stayed with our family. She'd deliver the baby, give it up for adoption sparing her family shame and disgrace, and promptly go back to her life. Modern Cinderellas, they did cooking, cleaning, laundry and cared for baby Ricky. When their watchful eyes were absent, Cynthia and I teamed up, teasing Ricky, sometimes scaring him witless in unreasonable vent to our jealousy. So envious of his position, we rarely had much to do with our brother, but watched for unguarded opportunities.

If one of the unwed mothers had been living with us at the time, things probably wouldn't have gotten so out of control that Saturday; maybe the angst had something to do with a hangover. Emblazoned on my soul, certain battles went far beyond the usual bickering. The scorching fight between Mom and Dad began with jabs and barbs, quickly escalating with screaming, yelling, too loudly, too out of control this time to ignore by playing louder behind our closed bedroom door or by turning up the volume on

26

the morning cartoons. Hearing the word "gun" Cynthia and I inched our way into the kitchen where Mom and Dad, tears streaming, fought over a rifle. Dad stood by the back door, shoving the rifle toward Mom.

"JUST SHOOT ME; GO AHEAD, SHOOT, SHOOT ME, DO IT!"

Cynthia and I pleaded hysterically, "Please stop, please, don't do it, Mommy, Daddy, please don't! Stop!"

One year old Ricky was sequestered in the living room in his playpen. As if they'd completely snapped, they didn't even acknowledge our presence. I doubt they even heard us or could feel our arms pulling at them. Suddenly, our neighbor, Jim, walked in. Without knocking, he just came through the back door like an angel sent to save us. Daddy fell into his arms, sobbing. Mommy slumped onto a kitchen chair, hanging her head down on her arms resting atop the table. Cynthia and I just sort of leaned against her sides, waiting, wanting her arms to enfold us, to reassure us. That didn't happen. Jim talked, settling them down; diffusing the threats, bringing sanity and diverting disaster. It was just another day, another Saturday morning of cartoons and verbal abuse that was never spoken of again by anyone. How does one account for the permeating atmosphere of words that wound spirit and soul? There's no way to calculate the damage done to my fragile, young mind or measure the hurt that was inflicted. It was life, just life, or its appearance.

I didn't know if everyone's household operated in this manner. It didn't seem like it. I didn't witness anyone else's parents going at it like mine. Jack and Edith didn't allow time for fun except in their own week end social circle. Somehow they fit in Bridge club, adult parties, awash with cocktails and boisterous camaraderie, of which we were rarely a part. Rolling her rubber

27

girdle up to flatten hips and belly the snapping, crackling noise made me clench my butt cheeks as I watched the pains she went through morphing from hausfrau to Loretta Young. It wasn't like she was overweight but that was the standard hitch for nylon stockings. I adored the transformation achieved with a tube of red/orange lipstick desiring the glamorous blotted kisses on the Kleenex to find their way to my face. If children were included in the parties, it was a peripheral locus. We devised our own entertainment trying to gauge our antics to stay under the radar. Developing my best line of defense, I mixed liberal doses of comic relief with deceit.

No wonder the Three Stooges were my favorite actors, always providing that raucous, hilarious escape helping me survive my hostile environment. Pirating their material, I employed my sassy comebacks exuberantly with tough bravado.

In Sunday School one morning my teacher wanted to know how much time she had remaining for her lesson, so noticing the brown leather band on my wrist she asked me, "Anne, what does your watch say?"

I knew Curly's answer to that same question, which I delivered with a straight face,

"It doesn't say anything; you have to look at it."

Well, it brought the house down. That desire for the high note, the crack-up got me into tons of trouble but it was worth it. Mrs. Severson, the Sunday school teacher, had a spectacular sense of humor that I'd experienced at our parent's parties. The Seversons, Charlene and Ted, lived across from a golf course with their three boys, Jimmy, Tim, and Bill, typically referred to as "the hellions." Charlene was the antithesis of my mom, having a household that looked like a cyclone struck it. With a narrow pathway winding down the center, the landfill decorated rooms were jammed from floor to ceiling with junk, clothes, mail, and dirt. How my mom could have a friend like Charlene was a complete mystery. Even more puzzling was how Edith could have such a blast at these gatherings but be so permanently pissed off at home. Charlene commissioned the two younger boys, Jimmy and Tim, to find dried out, white dog crap out in their back yard so she could play a gag on my parents. Our family was invited to a barbeque, the menu; bratwurst and knockwurst, the white variety. Emptying out one of the Styrofoam trays, Charlene filled it with dog crap, rewrapped it in cellophane, and placed it in the fridge. When the dads opened it to put on the grill, the reaction was priceless. Sick, gross, and twisted, I loved every minute of their parties. While they were getting profoundly snockered in the back yard the kids stole the golf balls that had just been driven down the course across the road from the front yard. We'd hide behind trees, giggling as the poor suckers looked, in vain, for their ball. Tiring of that, two of the boys dared each other to lie in the road to see what the oncoming traffic would do. No one bothered to give chase so after a few lackluster encounters we proceeded to the next shenanigan; convincing the youngest brother to take a ride in the clothes dryer. Tim, although a bit banged up, was too thankful for the reprieve to tattle, knowing such an act of sedition would guarantee him a worse fate.

Swollen headed Ricky

"Open wide," Mom said, dosing us kids with Dramamine, a thick, syrupy yellow liquid. Before any road trip, we choked down the perfunctory spoonful of lethargy to ensure everyone arrived alive.

"I hate it; I don't even get car sick."

Mom countered, "It tastes like cherries."

"Are you nuts," I thought, "It makes me gag. Yuck!"

Box after box of pharmaceuticals lined the basement walls. The clutter drove Edith nuts burying kitchen counters until the sorting out phase could be rearranged into Dad's trunk. Tons. Samples, in those teeny, child-sized bottles. As enticing as those were there was only the occasional stomach pumping. Four year old Ricky and his friend, Kathy, ate a jar of flat pink pills resembling M & Ms requiring one such trip to the hospital.

My little brother proved to be a walking accident suggesting maybe the pink pills weren't the only incident of drug tampering. Ricky fell through a railing, plummeting nine feet, smashing against the concrete floor face first. Dad, dripping from the shower a foot away, pulled on his clothes, using his towel to soak up the blood. Holding inert Ricky over his shoulder, driving his blue '55 Studebaker 80 miles an hour with one arm, Dad blasted across town to the hospital. Ricky's concussion abated after a few days but his appearance scared us for weeks.

The cough syrup so liberally doled out, was banned years later. I guess formaldehyde didn't prove to be quite as healthy as it was effective. Named Hydraline Compound, it knocked us out cold, not to mention its one-two punch silencing the cough. Quiet nights and car rides. The key to lights out!

Instead of earning sympathy I envied Ricky's attention from all the stitched gashes and wild rides to the hospital. Cynthia and I continued our torment, picking on him, but I swear I didn't intentionally hit him. Fooling around whacking a golf ball in the back yard, the club careened to a dead stop in the top of Ricky's head. Standing behind me he caught my follow through. At least it was the weekend and Dad was home with our one vehicle.

Mom wasn't as lucky on another gruesome occasion. That horrifying accident punctured Ricky's knee. He'd tripped, running in a field landing on an old rusty pitch fork. His friends dragged him across the road and up our driveway where Mom bandaged him with a dish towel tourniquet.
"Stay with him and hold this tight," she commanded, tearing off to borrow the neighbor's car.

Blood running down his leg onto the driveway where he lay, the sound was spine tingling as he howled with agony. Stitch after stitch, he began to resemble a rag doll.

There was a gang of neighborhood boys, four, five, some even six years older than my eight years. Big and tough looking, cigarettes rolled up in the arm of their short-sleeved white tee-shirts, tight dungarees defining their manhood, they towered over us. Careful not to be seen, my friends and I would spy on them from behind a garage as they hung out on the corner. We were fascinated by the graceful smoke rings gliding from their mouths. I scavenged one of their cigarette butts so a couple of us could experiment with the illicit habit. Filterless snubbed out, absolutely disgusting, I took a drag, choking, eyes watering. Excitedly, I determined then and there, someday I'd be a smoker declaring the same to my pals.

We knew them as hoods with their Brylcreemed D.A.'s. Our neighborhood was separated into new, aluminum-sided, pre-fab houses; theirs, the ancient, remaining farm type dwellings stubbornly hanging onto history. My single story rambler had flamingo colored siding and fake brick trim that I thought very modern. When you tapped on it with your fingernails it resembled the plastic drinking cups we got as premiums with a gas purchase. Contrasting this were outdated two story, wood-sided homes that sprawled on over-sized lots occupied by the families of these strangely alluring hoods. Two of the boys, Jimmy and Lonny, had in common the distinction of being born youngest and only sons, after several sisters, in traditional Catholic families. Some of those adult sisters, whom we watched smoke and drink coffee on their screened-in porch, seemed as old as our mothers.

Fourteen year old Lonny enticed me into his backyard pup-tent one summer day.

"Wow, you really want me to play with you?" I said.

"Yeah, I want to show you something," he said casually.

I watched him unzip the bulge in his pants.

"Give me your hand."

Unwittingly, I obeyed as he squeezed my chubby, little hand around the bluish, pink erection. Under the smooth, soft layer throbbed rock hardness. I was speechless. I knew this was so wrong, so very naughty, worse than anything I'd ever done in my life: worse than pulling my pants down with my pals, much worse than looking at the bare-breasted, pin-up girl playing cards tucked away in one of the drawers of my parents' desk. Taking a spring type clothespin, Lonny clamped it onto his penis.

"Yikes, doesn't that hurt?" I gasped, wincing.

"Nah, I can't... even... feel it, here... try it," he strained.

Robotically, I took the clothespin and slowly, carefully, attached it to his now, purplish penis.

Abruptly, mustering courage, in a squeaky voice, I whispered, "I have to go home," and scrambled through the flap, running, running, running until I was out of breath.

It was only a few houses away, but far enough from his perverse game. When we crossed paths again in the neighborhood, I flatly refused his invitations. To my relief, he quit asking.

All of us neighborhood kids knew about the gravel pit a mile up the road with its reservoir where the hoods swam illegally. Rightfully scared enough to ever disobey my parents' edict against it, resignedly I watched Lonny and Jimmy lead the pack as they rode off on their bicycles, towels rolled up and tied with twine to the rear fender betraying their destination. All I could count on to relieve the 100 degree heat and 90 percent humidity was a stupid foot-deep, plastic pool in our backyard. As the boys disappeared over the hill I thought, "What I wouldn't give for the guts to pedal out to that pond."

In their poor, Catholic families, having a boy seemed to be of particular importance, especially for the father, who would not be happy until there was a son to carry on the family name. Lonny's run-down old farm house on the corner was so in need of repairs and siding, (it had those dull brown, tar paper shingles that were supposed to resemble bricks) but the factory where his dad, Mr. Jessup, was employed only provided for the barest necessities. We'd watch him walk past our house (they couldn't afford a car) in his dark brown, threadbare, wool pants and jacket, dirty and tired after a long, sweltering afternoon. It was odd, seeing this old man, who was probably only in his fifties, walking with his black lunch pail. My dad went off to work in a suit and tie, driving his shiny Studebaker. We never said "hi" to Mr. Jessup; he didn't either. We just stared, curious about their life. Catholics were like aliens to us Lutherans, with confession and Friday fish days. Mr. Jessup's whole existence, in my mind, was a mystery comprised of walking down the sidewalk in front of our house several blocks to the factory and then returning, every single day of his life.

Sirens grabbed our attention like fireworks on that oppressively hot July day. Fire trucks had never whizzed down our residential street. The entire neighborhood, Lutheran and Catholic, spilled out every member of every household to see the spectacle of squad cars and rescue vehicles; an ambulance trailing after the fire engine. Blaring, honking, the noise thrilled us to a fever pitch.

"What's going on?" the query was heard from everyone's mouth.

All of the mothers were counting heads, taking stock, making certain their child wasn't involved, wasn't the victim. It took on a circus atmosphere. Rumors filtered back to us. It was at the gravel pit. Someone went under. The boys tried, they searched. It was too deep, too cold. No one said the unthinkable truth but the word "drowned" formulated like a cartoon bubble in my mind. From up the block a hush fell upon the carnival-like crowd as if a silent hand covered our gaping mouths. Each individual took a step backwards, like parting the waters of the Red Sea, as Mr. Jessup stumbled past, his eyes wet, glazed, trying to see his way home. The black lunch pail was held against his chest, where he cradled it, as if it were a child.

There was dead silence, realization striking when we heard his shattered voice crack with emotion, "My boy... my boy... my boy," he sobbed.

Nothing more. That's all he could say. Every mother, every child waited on the boulevards, what seemed like hours, for all of the vehicles to retreat, slowly and silently, like a funeral procession. My mom sat on our front step, apart, inaccessible smoking a Salem. I stood with my friends, surrounded but alone, feeling a piercing sadness in my heart. I overheard Mom discussing it later on the phone. It took several attempts dredging the dark, muddy pool before they finally employed a diver to recover Lonny's body. They said he went in too soon after lunch, suffering cramps, disappearing under the frigid water. We couldn't get enough of the story, imagining possible scenarios, discussing what drowning must feel like, how scared they were when they couldn't find him. If they knew what he'd done to me, they might have said a lot more. We didn't see any of the boys hanging out on the street corner for some time and when they did reappear; their edge had been noticeably sanded down.

4

Why was I such a little thief? I blame candy. Life was so beautiful with candy, like magic. Candy made life so much more enjoyable. Candy made me happy. A few blocks away from my house, the store was a delightful oasis on the twelve block walk to school. The metal signs hawking Coca-Cola and Wonder Bread rattled as I banged the green screen door letting Mr. Wagner know I'd arrived. Weathered shiny, the smooth wooden floor boards, the grooves separated by years of ground in dirt, squeaked under my feet as I inched sideways, peering through the glass at the choices. Crammed shelves of canned goods along with a fresh butcher case escaped my notice in the abridged supermarket.

With eyes singularly fixed on the luscious confections, my daily mission was to find a few pennies, even a nickel securing that sugar fix. Mom's billfold was my usual target pilfering a few cents for my discretionary spending. We got an allowance but I was obligated to purchase weekly savings stamps at school. Not such a bad thing, a U.S. savings bond. You'd lick the little stamps, requiring the entire five years of grade school to fill up your book. It must have been about 200,000 stamps!

I studied the candy case, laboriously pondering dozens of affordable choices: black, creamy licorice people that were four for a penny. Three pennies, twelve pieces. And if you ate them in three bites; the head, the body, and the feet, you could stretch it even more. The huge candy bars, namely Three Musketeers cost a nickel but the savvy shopper in me didn't like to blow the whole wad on one item. My all-time favorite was a Slo Poke; the caramel, butterscotch sucker, also known as an 'all day sucker.' Keeping my stealing and cache secret from tattletale Cynthia only added more flavor to the sweet spoils. When I couldn't get candy

I had a stash of brown sugar tucked away in my dresser drawer. I preferred the hard lumps that best resembled voila, a piece of candy.

Bullying my younger friend, Denise, she became my pawn to evade Cynthia's inquisition. Accosting us in the garage, I attempted to swallow before she noticed.

"Denise bought it," I lied, defending my chocolate coated lips.

With my back to Cynthia a few feet away, I mouthed to Denise, "Don't tell."

Cynthia knew I didn't have money to buy candy so her mind was calculating how to rat me out if she could get Denise to corroborate theft. Sweet, innocent Denise didn't know what to do, so she just stood mute. I lucked out that time. Feeling Cynthia's stealthy surveillance growing ever more vigilant, I got sneakier. I would not be denied my habit.

* * *

What had they put Nick's body in? Was he in a casket or some flimsy wooden box? What were the regulations that made it seemingly impossible to bring him home?

"Would you like something to drink?" the flight attendant asked the passenger across from me.

I have to open my eyes. I will have to nod, at least acknowledge her question, so I can go back into my trance. Panic seized my thoughts; fear consumed me, threatening the barrier that enabled me to keep control.

"Breathe, Anne. Breathe. Slowly, in. All the way, concentrate. Out."

"No," I shake my head to the attendant.

38

She asks the couple next to me, "Can I get you anything to drink?"

They both order gin. I think they're still partying from the previous night the way they're acting. I can't open my eyes. I can't be in reality. I have to stay in control. I can't lose it. I can't be in the present. My thoughts continue to swirl. Not eating or sleeping for three days I know I'd pass out if I had to stand up.

Don't think about Nick. Think about the kids. Zelda, Aaron, Chloe, David. My kids. Our kids. I will see them. I will hold them. They will be waiting for me. I will be there, soon, out of this goddamn nightmare.

"Are you out there, Nick? Are you in the atmosphere? Those clouds, glowing in the sunlight, hanging, effortlessly out the window… are you there? Nick, my love, where are you? Don't be gone. Don't leave me. Nick…" There's no wrapping my head around it. Can't.

Casket. Again, I see it through gauze. It's more like a sense of the shape. What's that organ playing? Nearer My God To Thee? *Casket.* It's like hallucinating. The jet engines hum.

Where am I? My breath exudes steadily, as I slip from consciousness.

* * *

My best friend, Sallie Bauman, was also my fiercest rival, typical of childhood relationships. One day perfect harmony, the next, choosing up sides for a second grade enemy hit list. So volatile, so honest and spontaneous, Sallie was half bosom buddy, half arch nemesis.

Facing off on the playground, Sallie's thick braids swung as sharply as her tongue, "I thought you were my best friend."

The words stung, piercing my heart for betraying her, telling secrets about her. Jealous, insecure, rash blabbermouth, me.

I charged back fiercely, "I hate you! You always get everyone against me."

Sallie sputtered, "You lied about me. You said I liked Jeff Severson, which I don't on account of his elephant ears and he smells."

Sallie flapped her hands back and forth against the sides of her head as she demonstrated the potential flying ability of Jeff's uncommonly colossal ears. And the smell; like sour, crusty week-old underwear.

"Maybe I'll just tell him you said that."

"If you do, I'll get my big brother to beat you up," she countered.

Before I could think, I lunged at her, pushing her down on the ground, wrestling, grunting, pulling those all too available braids. Immediately, kids rushed around to cheer their favored opponent.

Just when I had her pinned, knees on her arm muscles, "Do ya give? Say it. Give," I taunted tasting victory and damn.

Mrs. Kalinky yanked me off, choking me by the back my collar, marching us both off to the principal's office for a humiliating lecture on appropriate, young lady-like behavior.

This day it had progressed beyond the usual competition of name calling and attention getting to outright physical aggression. Even so, we made up, declared a truce, and walked home hand in hand, the day to day cycle of bratty, strong-willed girlfriends. Best friends.

The see-saw, love/hate ended suddenly when illness invaded, penetrating our routine childhood existence. Sallie was absent for days, then months, the invincible force of kidney disease making her an invalid. Like a beautiful living doll, her chestnut brown braids gently flowed down the pillow as she stared lying there with sad, almond eyes. Living just one block up the street allowed me to visit every day, but only for an hour while she mostly sat up in bed. She was able to get out of bed, able to play somewhat but tired so easily and quickly that her bed became the playground. I envied her fresh store bought pajamas, the cute bear and princess patterns that her wardrobe had become. Tutors would come and go, as would hope of her ever again running, skipping, and riding a bike.

Why? How could they not try to help me understand? Nobody informed me of the seriousness, even the probable terminal elements of that disease in the mid-1950s. What were my parents thinking that entire year, not trying in the simplest, childish terms to prepare me or help me through the difficult ordeal? When school dismissed, I'd walk to her house toting homework in my book bag, which she rarely did, along with birthday treats and party favors from all the missed events. I felt so important and special to have her undivided attention, me, the star of the show welcomed by Sallie's mother so graciously, thankfully.

Sallie and I would set up dollies, games, and paper dolls; dress-up, all on the bed playing almost normally, even delving into 'doctor' scenarios which caused me extreme guilt when she didn't recover by the beginning of third grade. God was the all-knowing, all punishing deity of my childhood. Sallie wasn't getting well because we were naughty. Maybe it was the drugs, the medication that gave her the tiniest bump of a nipple and the soft mossy patch of pubic hair. It was too much of an attraction to resist. Soft little breastbuds on an eight year old. I was so jealous. It was wonderfully exciting, stimulating to play the husband to her wife, calling her 'dear' and 'yes, honey,' what's for dinner?' She had her mom serve up treats for our meals, telling her to shut the door on her way out. Our private little make believe world revolving around her bed, her room, and her piles of toys which increased weekly, showered upon her as substitutes for a terminal existence. While spring brought hope of new life, it faded away with my best friend.

There was surprisingly, gratefully a rare bit of kindness, even gentleness when Mom sat down on my bed that August morning. She didn't even comment that the mess of covers wasn't made yet.

"Sallie died last night."

Her words echoed... died last night... died last night... died last night... bobbing, looking for cohesion. I gazed at the wall, pastel blue, my closet door, open, the bare bulb with its string pull, the tiny, bell shaped metal piece attached to the end. Eyes glazing white I couldn't comprehend if Mom was speaking. Staring at the bulb it was as if I'd looked into the sun. Blinded. But I couldn't look away. I didn't ask what happened. No more explanation was offered. Lonely, separated, Sallie 'died last night.' Why? Died? Now who would be my best friend?

I remembered the Bible stories from Sunday school of miracles, Jesus raising Lazarus from the dead. So couldn't Sallie come back like that? I would pray earnestly for just that to happen. Every night.

"God, please if you will bring her back, I'll never fight with her again. I'll be a good girl. Please God. I'm sorry I was naughty. I'll never be bad again. Please."

Of course, I had to pray to myself because if Cynthia heard me she'd tell.

I couldn't see Sallie the entire final week she was alive. They'd taken her to Mayo Clinic in Rochester, Minnesota, where she'd been treated many times during her year-long battle. With her family at her side she passed from this world. Was she conscious to the end? Did she suffer terribly? I did hear from her brother that in the final coma she bit her lip bloody. Why? What was her actual treatment? The questions I couldn't fathom at that tender age haunted me for years. Why didn't anyone see the anguish, the confusion or fear that engulfed me? You didn't talk about it. Period.

Amid hushed voices, my dad and I entered the dimly lit funeral home, our steps silently cushioned against the burgundy carpet. I grasped Dad's hand tightly as he led me past rows of chairs filled with blank-faced mourners. It was stuffy, close. Even scary. The room was a foggy haze, blurry eyes spilling tears down my cheeks. In the softly cushioned casket Sallie's was the only face that registered. How could I grasp it? Her dear, precious body, forever nine. Turning around, choking with sobs, I pushed into Dad's waist, my forehead pressing into his tie tack. His unintelligible words, in raspy anguished tone, the murmured explanation meant to comfort with some small, ineffectual effort attempted to make it right. It was useless. Lying in the pure white satin-lined casket, my senses were captivated by her frail, delicate beauty, an ethereal aura surrounding her. A hymn playing softly in the background, barely audible, was one I sang in church. Peace and the slightest smile graced her doll-like face as long, soft braids settled down the ruffles of the brand new, pastel pink dress. I thought it strange they had to buy her a new dress to wear in her casket. Even though she was sick, she had outgrown all her other ones. Except for Disney movies like Sleeping Beauty and Snow White, I'd never seen anything like that. There was Sallie, serenely still, a fairy princess, lying dead, my best and closest friend for half my life unbelievably gone from me, forever.

The following week, Sallie's mom asked my sister and me to come and get some of her belongings; toys, clothes, whatever we would like. I wanted it all. Standing there, waiting in the doorway, my eyes traveled around the room coming to rest on the empty bed; covers flat and bedspread smoothly tucked in. Perfect. Sallie's playroom had been the pillows and blankets piled strategically to prop up paper dolls. The bedroom walls were lined with toys, dolls, and games, some still in their original packages waiting to be unwrapped. Frozen in time, my throat tightened as the space around me constricted. How could I decide what to pick? How could that snot-nosed Cynthia be allowed to take anything of Sallie's? She'd never even been in her room before that day. I wanted everything that had anything to do with her; her fingerprints, her smell, her braids. I wanted Sallie. My mind whirling with thoughts of our hours together, telling secrets, plotting, and planning, I could only choose two small mementos before fleeing from the heaviness in her room. I intentionally avoided her special favorites fearing her mom needed those. I couldn't even thank her. No words would come.

God wasn't Santa Claus. Sallie wasn't there at the foot of my bed in the morning where I beseeched God to deposit her. Every night I cried myself to sleep praying for a Lazarus miracle. Where was she? Where was heaven? Did she miss me? Was she playing and having fun? Was she growing? Did she have toys? Did she eat or go to the bathroom? Who was taking care of her?

Jack and Edith never said a single, solitary word about it. I had to lock up my feelings pretending everything was alright. Life

44

went on with new pals in fifth grade, but no new best friend. In the 50s you didn't dwell on it, you bucked up. You didn't have counseling, you didn't discuss problems, you stuffed them. You didn't really even grieve, you pretended everything was fine. That message, though never voiced, was loud and clear.

"How are you?"

"Oh, I'm fine. Fine."

This was Midwestern, hearty stock, sturdy and staid. So where does a nine year old go to hide, to figure it out, to deal with it? To an imaginary place, a world of lies, deceit and fantasy. Anywhere but reality.

My report cards brought the admonition, "You can do better than this, you're smarter than this."

No one seemed to connect Sallie's death with my obvious disinterest in school.

"Anne needs to try harder; she isn't working up to potential. She's disruptive, behaves badly and is generally the instigator."

In the 'habit' category, a pejorative 'N' was written, ranking "uses time wisely" as— Needs improvement. Uses time wisely? What was I, an accountant? I was nine with growing emotional problems, trying in my juvenile way to find relief from the pain of a shattered heart.

A red transistor radio that I got for Christmas became my comforter. The 4x5 inch plastic box with the plug in ear piece, gold dials and switches rescued me. Listening to the crackly rock and roll station, singing along, the lyrics assuaged ceaseless churning thoughts. Monitoring the volume so Cynthia wouldn't hear—Mom didn't approve more than fifteen minutes—the sounds of Chubby Checker, Brenda Lee, Bobby Rydell, the Everly Brothers, Gene Pitney, and the most gorgeous of all, Fabian, serenaded me to dreamland. After school, every chance I got, I was glued to American Bandstand imagining the spectacular life those teenagers from Philadelphia led. I begged Edith to sew me a straight skirt which she attempted to fashion but wasn't remotely form-fitting like the Bandstand girls wore. It was a dismal failure. With one of Mom's silk scarves around my neck, the ends tied pointing out to the side, standing in front of the full length mirror, I copied the cool teenager's expressions and mannerisms trying to figure out the Stroll and the Bop. I even stole one of Cynthia's training bras so I could stuff it with tissue, my breasts having not yet made their appearance. No boys in their right mind would consent to my invitations, so I improvised, dancing with girlfriends, or a broom or sashayed around the steel beam that supported the ceiling in our basement. Entranced by his passion and disdain for convention, immersed in his energy and reckless abandonment, I watched Elvis Presley gyrate on the Ed Sullivan show. Reality, awakening, fireworks. I was thunderstruck.

5

Family at Grandma and Grandpa's farm

Every summer my family traveled 250 miles to my grandparent's farm to visit Mom's folks. Her sister lived nearby so our cousins Jean and Kari joined us. Jean was Cynthia's age, Kari, mine so pairing off accordingly, we spent a week trailing after Grandpa like Labrador puppies. Kari and I loved donning Grandpa's work jackets, well-worn hats, gloves and even boots. His small feet weren't much bigger than ours. Emulating him, Kari and I would clomp along, trying to help him, as he fed and bedded down the animals. With rapt expectation, Grandpa's exploits were regaled in hilarious detail, either by him or one of my aunts. My favorite was the trick he played on some teenage boys one Halloween. Typically, a rural prank was to tip over the outhouses which Grandpa had been victim of for three years running. This year he rigged a booby trap so by leaning into the structure the boys would lose their balance. He'd spent hours getting it just right and then hid to await his revenge. Leaning into the side, sure enough, when the outhouse gave way, two of the boys went with it down into the shit. It never happened again.

The outbuildings, providing imaginative expression, were transformed with crayons as we drew household furnishings—dressers, stoves, and cupboards—on the barn walls, partitioning rooms with bales of hay. Not concerned with the sweltering heat, we'd bring our lunch, eating it in the pretend kitchen, ignoring the aroma of manure wafting up from the cows on the ground floor.

Hay forts in the mow became the landing pad as we swung the length of the barn from the pulley rope that ran along the support beam. We didn't realize that the pulley could have actually run right off the end of the track if the upper door had been open. Fortunately, it was always closed and we didn't plummet to our deaths. For hours we'd swing around Tarzan-like destroying Grandpa's neatly stacked bales.

I was petrified of the laying hens as they sat on the eggs we were sent to retrieve. Not fond of the 'adoption' process, they'd peck at me, one time even drawing blood. That was the end of that. Fearing blindness, my eyes gouged out, I couldn't go near them.

Grandpa would always warn, "Don't go in the pig pen!"

It was probably his way of daring us to. The kind of pigs that charged at you, crashing into the fence trying to get a nibble, we'd sneak ever so near, afraid to climb the fence fearing they'd chomp our toes off. After shoving some corn from the crib into our pockets, we'd throw it in amongst them, one measly half ear at a time, and watch the wild scramble ensue. Squealing, nipping, stomping, dust billowing, one lucky pig scarfed it down. Grandpa could always tell if we'd fed them but usually didn't make a big deal out of it, him the worst prankster of all.

Grandpa, with his close cropped hair slicked back with greasy pomade, western snap shirt, rough and tumble spirit, had a mystique emitting danger. Verging on wild. Never quite knowing what was coming next. When we were younger, he'd motion us cousins over to him, saying, "Do you want some candy?"

Innocently, I sidled up to his huge green vinyl arm chair expecting candy, only to have a pinch of snuff shoved up my nose. Just enough to make me sneeze my brains out as he cackled mercilessly.

Grandma would pause from her kitchen, peering over the top of her steam fogged glasses, admonishing in an exasperated tone, "Oh Walter!"

Riotous to be around once a year, I could only dream of what every day with him would be like. I imagined no better place on the face of the earth.

I don't know how the idea occurred to us or how our parents consented to it, but alcohol, most likely, played a large part. Jean, Cynthia, Kari, and I took our parents' cars into one of the fields to blast around the bumpy terrain. At nominal speeds, we cruised from one end to the other pretending to be Indy race car drivers. Barely tall enough to see over the steering wheel or reach the pedals, we exercised restraint while the grown-ups drank and played penny ante poker knowing the slightest mishap would insure we'd never be out there again.

And the food Grandma prepared. Wonders and delights. With her ample bosom somehow corralled into the bib type apron, tight curls pulled back, her spectacles hanging off her nose, she orchestrated the boiling pots on the stove like a conductor. Each day she made three full meals of meat, vegetables, and dessert from scratch. Tender, flakey deep-fried sun fish, potatoes fried in bacon grease and batter fried chicken, expertly basted eggs and bacon, and freshly picked raspberries to top our cereal. Taking plastic containers out to the berry patch, we'd pick one for the bucket, one for the mouth; plump, juicy red raspberries so ripe, they fell off the bush with the slightest encouragement. We topped ice cream, cake, and even cookies with them and never got tired of sprinkling sugar on a whole bowl full. And we got glorious soda pop. 7-Up in tall green bottles. Sometimes a whole bottle. Our own bottle. I never got pop at home! Never! Grandma rarely left that kitchen, except for the card games which she treated quite seriously. Peering out from behind her cards, she'd declare, "pot stinks!" whenever anyone forgot to ante. She'd keep track like it was high stakes when actually there couldn't have been more than a buck pot in a really great round. Grandpa got totally out of control after several whiskeys, Seven and Seven, laughing and swearing, getting rowdier and bawdier with each drink. It was so wickedly arousing to hear those forbidden words. Grandma tried to shut him up with her, "Oh Walter!", but he couldn't be bridled. Like a wild stallion, rearing and snorting.

Grandpa and Grandma farmed their entire life, supplementing the income with construction for him and J.C. Penney's for her. How they managed the never-ending work year after year with one part-time hired hand was a marvel. Adding to the allure and excitement of the visits was Grandpa's cantankerous edge. Always slightly out of control, too coarse occasionally, he pushed the envelope making for some strange encounters. The farm provided a welcome departure from my controlled, sterile home life. I couldn't wait to arrive after the long boring drive; Mom trying to blow her cigarette smoke out the vent window of the front seat, nauseating us with her failure. Of course, Cynthia was allowed to sit up front because she got car sick, which was ridiculous, Dad having dosed us with Dramamine prior to departure, making the ride bearable; that coupled with the spectacular rewards of the farm.

I was eleven when my idyll was shattered. Putting his jacket and hat on to go out and do chores, I took my cue, tagging along. Repeatedly filling the scoop shovel with meal and corn, he'd bring it to the trough, strong arms and taut muscles responding to the routine. His barn clothes had that smell of sweat, tobacco, manure, and dirt in an acrid blend that didn't diminish my desire to be with him. Walking out of the pole barn farthest away from the house, farthest from sight, he stopped for what I thought would be a breather and a smoke. I stood next to him, dutifully waiting for direction when his hand brushed the hem of my bermuda shorts. Paralyzed, frozen, the danger was palpable. Panic and fear locked me in time, in space, in a vacuum as Grandpa deftly slid his fingers up the inside of my shorts and inside my panties. I stood, petrified, my feet cemented to the ground.

Feeling my virginal prepubescence, he showed surprise, questioning, "You have hair down there already?"

I stared straight ahead, numb, screaming in my head, not knowing what to do. How do you not know what to do? How is something so shocking that you stand immovable, you don't run, you don't even say, "Stop it!" or "Don't do that!"

He continued feeling around, with his hand, the finger going where no other had. He didn't speak. Maybe it was a minute, maybe a year, a lifetime. The curtain veiled my heart as my mind blocked out what was happening.

I would never trust Grandpa again. I would never be alone with him again. I would never love him again. I would never again think he was the funniest man I ever knew.

He pulled his hand out, shoved it back into his grimy tan leather glove and warned, "Now don't you tell your mom about this."

Not your mom and dad. Just 'your mom.'

I wondered why? And I didn't tell. How could I? What could I say? That was the most awful part after the actual fact, that I couldn't tell. Not because he said not to, but there was something that wouldn't let me even think about it, let alone verbalize it to Mom. The only sympathy or compassion I'd ever felt from her was when Sallie died. I couldn't come to her with this. Where were her maternal instincts buried? What made her so closed, so distant, so averse to touch? Probably her father, but I didn't come to that hypothesis until many years later.

I simply walked back to the house and stayed in my room as much as possible, coming out only for meals. Mom and Grandma thought I had picked up a bug of some kind. Some kind alright. Sadness overwhelmed me. It was as if I was mourning the death of my best friend again, grieving my lost childhood, my innocence, and my sanctuary of fun. It was all gone in that moment. I was robbed, raped as it were, not in the technical sense of the word, but in having security stripped away, having to bear the secret, ashamed, betrayed, humiliated and afraid. All I wanted to do was go home, and never see him again, but I still had to give him a hug before getting into the car. Grandpa acted fine, like nothing was wrong, joking irreverently. It was all so puzzling, so confusing. Did he think it was okay to molest his granddaughter, a girl of eleven? Did he simply forget about it? Wasn't he the least bit afraid or worried I would tell someone, my mom or my dad?

As a defense mechanism, I fabricated a fantasy inventing a boyfriend with whom I did touchy-feely things. I made the mistake of confiding to my cousin, Kari, the next time I saw her.

"You can't tell a soul. Promise?"

"Yeah."

I reiterated, adamantly, "No, I mean, cross your heart and hope to die!"

"Yeah, I will!" Kari vowed, making an X over her chest.

"Well, this boy, Robbie and me went out to the woods and took off all our clothes and ran around like cave people. It's way down by the creek where no one ever goes and then we laid down in the grass and let the sun beat down on us."

"Wow," Kari said slowly, in awe.

The story did what I needed it to do. I was exciting, I was bad, but *I* was in control. Though not apparent to me at the time, my coping mechanism was a way to feed the demons and keep them at bay by providing inner titillation. I did have a crush on Robbie Perkins in reality, but nothing ever developed beyond bike rides. He was the star pitcher on the Little League team so I waited for him after the games and we'd talk. That was as much thrill as I knew in reality.

Kari was so impressed that she told our other cousin, Kathy, a devout Catholic, but she must have forgotten to swear her to secrecy because soon afterward my parents confronted me with the whole story.

"We got a letter from Aunt Netty saying you were in a cave somewhere with boys and you were not wearing any clothes," my dad began.

With heart pounding intensity, my mind raced to figure a way out of this. It really was a lie but now they wouldn't believe me. After all, Aunt Netty had it in writing, a bona fide document. That sealed it!

I tried to convince them that it was just nonsense, dramatizing to the best of my ability, "I was just making it up to get a rise out of Kari. I never even said anything about it to Kathy. Kari told Kathy and Kathy exaggerated it and she's wrong. It's not even what I said. Aunt Netty has it all mixed up."

In my mind I knew Aunt Netty had me going straight to hell but I couldn't worry about that now.

"Well then what is the truth?" Mom asked.

[Oh, you mean the truth about your dad sexually molesting me six weeks ago, about him shaming me into secrecy?] I didn't say that. I couldn't. I lied some more.

"I have never done anything like that, honest. It didn't happen. I'm sorry, really, I am."

"We don't know what to believe. This doesn't make any sense," Mom said.

That's when my friend arrived at the front door, knocking loudly, interrupting the awful interrogation. We were supposed to go bike riding.

Mom said, "Where are you going, out to meet those boys?"

Thinking of Trudy standing within earshot, I did my best to stymie the embarrassing conversation.

"Please, can we talk about this after I come back? Trudy's right out there. Please," I begged.

Dad said, "Yes, young lady, but we will continue this. You can count on it."

Yeah, like you'd forget about it! That was truly my wish, my hope, but I knew them too well. So here I was, the slut, with accusations hanging over my head, around my neck like a noose. A wild rendezvous with my boyfriend, such wanton behavior, giving my mortified parents enough ammunition to condemn me to eternal guilt. And now I could agonize over it until a later date. What a rotten twist. The story that I used for a scapegoat turned into additional trauma. It was all a ruse, made up. I wasn't doing anything with Robbie Perkins besides watching his lightning fast curve ball sometimes throwing a no hitter. With that white flannel uniform, red trim, red baseball cap. Such a crush on him. All I could think of was how I was going to kill Kari when I got a hold of her! I know she was trying to impress Kathy possessing that intimate knowledge of my 'love' life.

With Dad on the road so much we didn't get back to the topic for a couple of weeks. I avoided it as best I could, even attempting a lame runaway one night. Where do you go when you're eleven in 1961? I went to the end of the block, turned around, walked back and stood at the corner of the house waiting for Mom to find me. She didn't come. Getting Ricky to bed and whatever else was pressing, she was too busy. Cold and dejected, I gave up after an hour or so.

She ignored me at first, me standing right around the corner from the living room. She heard my footsteps creeping down the hallway as she sat watching T.V.

Trying to wait me out, after a few minutes she asked, "Where were you?"

Oh, you did notice I was gone? But you didn't care enough to come after me.

"I just walked around. Up the street. Nowhere."

I could tell she was a bit unnerved, like, "what the hell is happening to this girl?"

Her only comment was, "You shouldn't worry me like that."

No hug, no affirmation, no help. Here I am, acting out, dying for acknowledgement, for love and this is it? I went to bed, crying into my pillow, holding the transistor. My salvation. I pretended they were singing to me, personally: "Tell Laura I Love Her," soothing, comforting, but when Bobby Darin serenaded me with "Dream Lover," I sobbed feeling my heart split in half. "I want a dream lover, so I don't have to dream alone."

"What's wrong with you?" Cynthia questioned from her side of the room, overhearing my sighs. Exasperated, she berated, "I think you're nuts."

"Shut up," I shot back, "I hate you."

"I'm telling," as she stalked off to the living room.

"Shit!" Turning my transistor off I feigned sleep.

I didn't need to see Mom's face in the door; enough of her for one night.

The next day Cynthia moved her bedroom to the basement which wasn't really a room, but she partitioned off a corner using her dresser and bed. Fine. Good riddance. I can't stand you either. But why won't you love me? Why is it your mission in life to tell on me, to hurt me and be as cold as you can? The subject of my so-called sex life evaporated because of lack of evidence. My word against theirs. They wanted to believe I wasn't that bad. Sheesh, I was only eleven.

The curse. That's what my mom called it. That dreaded word: menstruation. For years its memory fired up waves of humiliating anger. God, does every woman recall her introduction to menstruation that way? It was 1960, not exactly the sexually advanced advent yet, and certainly not in conservative Minnesota. This was well before the days when young minds became desensitized by countless TV ads for feminine protection, S.T.D.s, birth control, and E.D.

In compliance with curriculum, we fifth grade girls were scheduled to endure a filmstrip presentation along with a lecture about our reproductive selves. With no advance notice, herded into a separate room sequestered from the boys, we were acquainted with the intimate details in the most confusing ambiguity.

This was my introduction to female functions, having a mom whose reply to all sexual questions was, "What do you want to know that for?"

Never the most encouraging or open atmosphere.

As the school nurse delineated each aspect of the diagramed uterus and fallopian tubes I was struck by the peculiar similarity to a ram's head. So removed, so not personally vested in the topic, along with the other twelve, flush-faced girls, we kept our eyes straight ahead, asking no questions or volunteering any information.

I heard noise at the back door of the room, faint whispering and scuffling feet. It didn't signify until later. I thought I would die if anyone walked in, anyone of the male gender!

So the instruction continued, boringly, while we prayed for the speedy conclusion. Those stupid little pamphlets, distributed by Modess, (pronounced, Oh Yes), you're thinking HELL NO, and Kotex repeated every detail the nurse had made. Nothing would have made that awkward situation comfortable but I thought it was better hearing it from her than our regular teacher.

I didn't want to have to see her every day in class and think about it.

When she finished, the inevitable query was, "Does anyone have any questions?"

One brave little voice asked, "How will we know when it happens?"

After roughly forty-five minutes of education about that very thing, we weren't even clear about what occurred.

She answered, "You'll notice a spot of blood on your panties."

EEEwwww, was all I could think! Quickly, with furrowed eyebrows, I scanned my memory to try to find the part in the filmstrip that told us about that. Nothing. Could it have been any more vague? Confusing? Strange.

I didn't talk to any of the other girls about it, none of the usual giggling or twittering. Probably because it just didn't make any sense at the time. We were sent back to our regular classroom, with pamphlets hidden, jammed under our armpits. God, if any of the boys saw them! Narrowed eyes scanned us as we took our seats. At recess, the boys asked what happened, but it was unutterable.

My cheeks burned under their prying questions, "Oh c'mon, tell us."

Not a chance. I squirmed with bafflement. This very private, personal information was connected to the shame my grandpa had inflicted on me.

I wanted to run, screaming.

"Leave me alone," I said, spinning on my foot, heading in the opposite direction.

It hardly seems like there would have been enough time for the whole conspiracy to develop, but I was the target of a brutal plot. PERIODGATE. The little shits had spied at the door (the noise I heard) and gotten the gist of the topic. They told some of the girls that *I* told them about the filmstrip. So these girls, righteously indignant, ratted me out to our teacher saying I blabbed the facts of life to the boys. I had no clue what was going on until after school but the whispers and looks before the bell rang bespoke trouble. My teacher, Mrs. W, asking me to remain while everyone filed out, informed me with baffling censure that what I had done was very unlady-like.

"I don't know what you're talking about," I stated, so sick of that catchword.

"You weren't supposed to discuss the filmstrip with Jimmy and Robert," she accused, haughtily.

"What!!" I gasped.

"You know what you did," she countered, stoically.

Accused and prejudged before any discussion, I despised Mrs. W. I had a reputation as "trouble," always cutting up, so the verdict was unequivocal.

Adamant on this occasion though, I argued, "That is a big lie. I never said a word to them. Honest. Who said that? I'm telling the truth."

Mrs. W was an old maid who wore either navy or black shirt waist dresses, matching pumps, nylons and a tight dark brown coiffure exactly the same each and every day of the year. A cardigan was the only thing that mixed it up when weather demanded. Her demeanor indicted me before the year had progressed more than a few days. She suffered no insubordination, required strict adherence to each and every rule and definitely favored the book worms. It was obvious she'd be gunning for me by that first week's end. This was her big moment. Time to put this cheeky brat in her place. But without a confession, she really couldn't do much more about it. Instead with obligatory words proceeded to impugn my character, manners, discretion, blah, blah, blah, pronouncing her belief in my irremediable corruption. Patti, my best friend, was the only one who believed me, having spent the entire recess and lunch hour by my side. But that wasn't enough to combat the overwhelming wave of mass hysteria the whole topic produced. My God, you'd think I'd had sex or gotten pregnant! Patti waited outside to walk home with me, her deep set chocolate eyes, soft and sympathetic, drew me right into her as she took my hand in solidarity.

I couldn't discuss the bogus accusations with my mom so, suffering in silence, I determined never to get my period. My decision solidified after witnessing Cynthia's visitation. She had discovered the dreaded spots after school one day. Hysterically, crying her eyes out, sitting on the toilet, she ordered me to get Mom who was at the neighbor's having coffee.

I tried to find out what was wrong, figuring she was close to death, "Are you hurt? What happened?"

She just kept repeating, "GET MOM! Just Get Mom!"

So I ran and got her. Mom showed us both where the sanitary napkins were kept. What an awful name, sanitary napkins. "Pads" was better, but still, who wanted to say it?

I had shown Mom the pamphlet the day of the filmstrip, receiving her standard, "now if you have any questions... "

Yeah, yeah, I know. [You won't answer them].

My will wasn't enough to stave off the onset. Shit, there it was, THE SPOT. Shit! The torturous elastic belts with the metal hooks that dug into your tail bone took about a half hour to attach the pads. Trying to find a comfortable position sitting was hopeless, the hook slicing right down your butt crack. No Stayfree or New Freedom in those days. It was punishment and incarceration all the way. Certain my classmates could detect the bulge in my clothes, the thought of them finding out made me nauseous. My first period went okay but when it arrived the second month I was dismayed to find the pad box empty. No way was I telling Mom so I improvised with wads and wads of toilet paper, going to the bathroom as frequently as I could. I hid my badly stained underwear in the pockets of an old bathrobe and tucked it into the back of my closet. To my chagrin, they were discovered, when my sister's overnight guest needed a robe. Since it had been weeks, I'd conveniently put it all out of my mind.

Cynthia toyed with me, skirting the facts, snidely teasing, "Jolene forgot her bathrobe last night. I gave her yours, the one hanging way back on the hook. Guess what she found?"

She had that shit eating grin plastered on her face, locking her hahaha eyes on me.

"Oh great," my stomach turned.

Having the goods on me, she exacted many bribes to keep the secret. For once Cynthia didn't rat me out. I wondered if Mom noticed half my underpants were missing. My body seemed a mystery shrouded in secrecy. Mystery bred more questions that only fueled my insecurity. When I was twelve, staying overnight at Patti's house, she told me, surreptitiously, that her mom was "on the rag." I was curious about the term. Following her into the bedroom, she opened her mom's dresser drawer to show me two stacks of neatly folded hand towels. Not wanting to let onto my ignorance I didn't question her. After much thought I concluded that this was their improvised pads. They were Native American by heritage and maybe that was a carryover from olden ways. I never did find out for sure.

* * *

In the entry for my journal, October 2000, I wrote:

"Wish I didn't frequently have this sense of foreboding or guilt or something—whatever it is. Just can't enjoy myself without thinking something's going to happen. I try to ignore it or pray for peace and rest—or try to put it out of my mind and be busy. It's kinda stupid, like worry, which I say I never do. So stop it."

I tried to discuss my fears with Nick but he was so pragmatic, so sensible that he ultimately told me to quit bugging him about it.

"Get a grip, Anne, why do you have to bring in that negative energy? Do you think something is going to happen, really?"

I was too afraid to say that I actually believed something was imminent, thinking that I would bring it upon us, so I forced myself to let it go.

"I'm sorry," I said, "It doesn't make any sense."

"Well, then, don't talk about it anymore."

While raising the kids, we had this philosophy: Do everything in your power to get them on their way, to help them be successful, so they wouldn't come back home. So far, it had worked. College expenses for our four children left nothing extra. Putting that aside for once, we decided on an extravagant fling for our thirtieth anniversary four months after I wrote those words in my journal.

Fuck me! How could I do this? How could I get his body out? From the motel room in Mexico, talking to Edith on the phone, I learned that Meryl's brother was prepared to send his private jet to bring me home if commercial flights were too problematic. My longtime friendship with Meryl dated back to seventh grade. Her offer gave me courage knowing I had people like that Stateside working on my behalf. Phone calls flooded in as word spread about Nick's death. Friends and family were too far away to be of any tangible assistance.

There in the hotel room, staring at Nick's suitcase, I picked up his green velour bathrobe, cradling it, burying my face in it, inhaling his scent.

"I'll forever miss the taste of you, your smell… come back. Christ. Utterly alone."

Closing my eyes, I imagined my arms reaching around to his shoulder blades, feeling the skin compress as I pushed into his back with my fingertips.

And now this nagging accusation, "Shit, had I made this happen? God, help me."

* * *

6

Dad standing in front of plastic covered, gold brocade chair

When I was twelve my dad received a coveted promotion rewarding him with a sales territory in the big city of Minneapolis, Minnesota. So in July 1962, the family packed up and said goodbye to small town life. The two story house, built in 1948, was a huge upgrade from the cracker-jacks box neighborhood. Two bathrooms was one of the luxuries, along with a dining room and my own bedroom. Edith kept her new furnishings immaculate with thick clear plastic coverings, the kind your legs stuck to. I loved the setting with its two forty foot pine trees straddling the walkway up to the front door. It had white wood siding with genuine red brick trim. Shrubs and fruit trees filled out the yard enclosed by a white picket fence.

The junior high and elementary schools were three blocks away so after a few days I ventured down to the playground to see if I could meet someone. The city kids had some bizarre deviations from the innocent neighborhood games I was accustomed to. Outdoor contests of 'kick the can' turned into thirteen year old vandalism and 'tag' with a twist that included boob grab wrestling. My new-kid status gave me cache and instant acceptance. Not aware of the boundaries, or lack thereof, I'd go along with the thrillingly wild grabbing and touching for a while, in my desire to impress, but after taking painfully direct hits, I'd flee for home. Jack and Edith would have never let me go out again if I'd revealed to them what was going on. Even though I felt guilty and afraid, I wanted to hang out with someone and make friends. The playful cat and mouse game crossed the line when seven of us (three girls and four boys) decided to take our game into Mick's house. His parents must have worked nights or were deaf because no one came to my aid. All four boys pinned me down, pulled my shirt and bra up, and ogled my budding breasts as I fought to free myself. I couldn't believe this was happening. Outside, in the dark with hit or miss ineptitude, everything maintained a degree of anonymous modesty. But now I burned with embarrassment, groaning with every ounce of strength to escape their grip. Suddenly, my playful naiveté was shattered by their raging hormones. The two other girls in the mix stood on the fringe and watched, either glad it wasn't them or maybe disappointed they weren't the object of all the attention.

"Let her up," I heard them say, "c'mon you guys, knock it off!"

They didn't try to help, jump in, nothing.

And the boys paid no attention to their pleas. I was trapped, immobilized under glaring light, completely vulnerable. Scared and humiliated, I started to cry. That broke the fever pitch.

One boy, the one sitting on my legs, took pity on me and said, "That's enough!"

I could have stayed inside at night, could have played it safe, but I needed to figure out the way things worked in the city, this new neighborhood. How else was I supposed to learn? Assault was my initiation into junior high morality. No one apologized for the incident but it didn't happen again. We all seemed to understand that it had gone too far. Turning the focus to disgusting pranks, we quit the groping altogether.

We'd fill a brown paper bag with dog shit, set it on someone's front steps, and then light it on fire. With everyone hidden around the corner of the house, one person would ring the doorbell. The occupant would fling open the door, stomping the bag to incur a shit storm. That wasn't nearly as dangerous as scaring the hell out of passing drivers. When it got dark we'd hang a string across the street, tied to a tree on either side, with a five by five inch piece of aluminum foil attached in the center so it looked like it was dangling in thin air. When a car came along, the headlights caught the foil, and the startled driver would screech to a halt. Some jumped out in hot pursuit when they heard the robust laughs in the distance. No one ever got rear ended or injured in the idiocy, and equally as fortunate for us, we never got caught.

As if puberty wasn't frightening enough, immersed into city life, my insecurity was multiplied beginning junior high in strange surroundings. When school started I set my sights on the 'in' clique, the popular, cool kids. Obviously not part of this crowd, my neighborhood friends were history. No more small town dork, I was taking control of my destiny.

After changing into the gym uniform of navy blue short shorts, white button-down short sleeved shirt, white socks and tennis shoes, thirty-five seventh grade girls formed four columns behind the red border line. P.E. introduced me to my first friend, Meryl. By some screw up on my part I was in a single-file line of one.

Meryl, noticing my embarrassment, slid over to join me as she introduced herself, "Hi, I'm Cav," she smiled, her dark, almond eyes, warm with welcome.

It was a shortened moniker coined from her last name, and she was. Short, that is. I was one of the tallest in the class with white blond hair, contrasting our disparate lineage; hers, French with lovely olive complexion, mine, washed out, Scandinavian. I felt no less than saved from mortal humiliation by her gesture. We sat next to each other in three classes, our names following alphabetically, giving us ample time to learn each other's character. Both silly, goofy cut-ups, we had little time for academics earning laughs from classmates and the scorn of our teachers.

The city kids all seemed so with it, so sophisticated with their slang and hip style. Copying the dress, the hair, and the make-up, I absorbed every detail. Out of Edith's critical, disapproving sight, I applied blue shadow and eye liner in the girls' 'can.' I also kept a vigilant watch out for my ninth grade sister, who'd be just too thrilled to inform Mom. Rolling my skirts up two times made the waistband an inch thick but achieved the desired length, above the knee.

Meryl was my inroad with the clique. She introduced me to the other six girls that made up our core. I endeavored to hold onto that esteemed place of popularity by any and all means during my high school years. The wilder, the better. Shop-lifting, school suspensions, skipping school, car crashes, drunken bashes, drug experimentation, and sexual promiscuity gave Jack and Edith many gray hairs. On Saturdays, we'd rope an unsuspecting parent into driving us to the mall where we'd wreak havoc. It was so simple to don clothes underneath our own in the dressing room, not to mention the make-up, records, and whatever else our hot little hands could spirit away. Dana, Nancy, Georgie, Rebecca, Bev, Lana, Meryl, and I made up our brat pack. We'd dig the cigarette and cigar butts from the round sand ashtrays placed outside the store entrance and vandalize the mannequins, sticking smokes in their fingers and mouths. Darling baby mannequins were the funniest with a gross brown cigar butt crammed into their mouths. If a security guard gave chase we'd just split up and outrun him, to regroup in our designated 'can.'

Almost all my girlfriends' parents were more lenient than mine so I spent as many weekend nights as possible at sleepovers. We got cheap thrills being outrageous, feeling each other up, talking about sex, boys, periods. I liked our code name much better than Edith's 'The Curse.' My girlfriends and I called it 'George.' Who knows why? Somehow I knew of this passage from the Bible that described how periods were handled back then. The woman, having an issue of blood, was sent to a place outside of the camp for seven days. On some level, that made perfect sense: alone, away from hassles, responsibility, hangin' out.

"Wouldn't she get attacked by wild animals?" one girl queried.

"Maybe that's why the women were sent out there," I laughed, "it took care of the entire issue."

Late into the night, we'd be laughing hysterically or scaring the shit out of each other performing séances, using a Ouija board, whipping ourselves into a frenzy of other-worldly visualizations. A few of us daredevils raided the fridge using carrots and wieners for dildos. It was blissful freedom to be so reckless, feeding inner demons at a safe distance from my stifling home life.

The best stroke of luck was having periods so heavy and excruciating that my gynecologist, whom I dubbed Count Speculum, prescribed a "cycle controlling" remedy.

Threateningly, he adjured, fixing his stare, "Now these aren't effective as birth control, they're simply a way to regulate your cycles."

What a crock of shit. It was my ticket to promiscuity. I was euphoric over the liberty that came along with the Enovid birth control pill. Cycle control, my ass. The brand was one my dad sold. I dug into his G.D.Searle literature assuring myself of the truth. It was clearly stated: birth control, a bonafide green light to do whatever the hell I felt like doing! Initially, sex was nothing close to satisfying. My boyfriends were wham, bam, thank you, ma'am, but that didn't deter me. I'm sure none of them had heard of a clitoris or if they did had no clue where it was. I put out to get love. Boys gave love to get laid.

A few months later when I returned for a check-up, Count Speculum reiterated his warning, this time in a distinctly condemning tone, "It appears as if you are having relations. You better not rely on this pill to prevent pregnancy."

Stone-faced, I denied everything. Society's rigid method of scaring young women into abstinence had no impact on me.

My boyfriend and I were having a ton of sex in the luxurious back seat of his '57 Chevy.

The next time my best friend, Meryl, stayed overnight, I convinced her to sneak out after Jack and Edith were asleep.

With my usual bravado I ratcheted it up a notch.

"Let's steal the car," stating, "I can drive. What's the big deal? C'mon, we won't get caught."

"What if we crash, though?" Meryl questioned. She was the most conservative member of the group while having the most lenient mom making her house the most coveted sleep over destination.

"We won't crash," I whispered as we tiptoed across the basement floor. I recalled my grandparent's farm, blasting around the cornfield figuring that was enough experience to master city driving.

"Now come on," I reassured boldly.

We climbed on top of the piano; the old upright stood just under the egress window. Figuring my parents were well into deep sleep or stupor at 2:00 a.m. we inched out. It was a feat to squeeze through the narrow opening, holding back giggles as we slid onto the lawn. Stealthily, silently we raised the garage door, listening for the slightest sound. A light. A neighbor. I put the gear shift into neutral so we could roll the car into the alley, then forward all the way to the street. At the end of the block, turning it over, I took it slowly, to get my bearings, 'sea legs.' We couldn't use so much gas as to be noticed; no stations were open at that time of night, so our joyride lasted only an hour or so. The exhilarating thrill, worth every risk!

When Meryl started driving legally she was definitely challenged, having profound difficulty developing her skills. As if I was much better, neither of us scatterbrains had any business behind the wheel. Smoking added another hazard, occupying a hand that should have been at either ten or two o'clock. When navigating the blinker and steering wheel in the process of executing a right turn, she'd have to throw the cigarette on the floor or out the window. Barely maintaining control one time, the cigarette ricocheted against the door and back down her sleeve. I grabbed the wheel guiding us to the curb. Screaming in panic, howling with laughter, we fished it out, leaving a small hole in her blouse and arm.

Maneuvering my heap of a vehicle with faulty brakes around the streets of south Minneapolis was even more challenging, not to mention lunatic. I'd keep the speed below thirty, down shifting, furiously pumping the brake pedal, using the curb to stop, if required. The emergency brake worked if all else failed. Even more blockheaded was this favorite stunt: one of us would control the steering wheel; the other, lying on the floor, worked the foot pedals with her hands.

We'd call out directions, like, "Brake, gas, more gas, brake, brake, BRAKE!"

Repeatedly, hands were stomped on, an eyelash away from impact. Brazen stupidity steeled our nerve.

Meryl and I entered the job market together at the end of ninth grade. It took some whining and convincing before her brother, Teddie, would consider us.

"We can do the job. We won't goof around. We won't screw up. Give us a chance," Meryl and I argued.

Her brother, who detested us, was head of the design department at Bachman's Floral. Meryl's mother, Tillie, our loyal, indulgent advocate, ran interference with Teddie. He was eight years older than Meryl and saw us as uncontrollable, spoiled juveniles; an accurate description. Honestly, loathe to let on, we thought he was so beyond cool with his brand new, yellow fiberglass, Corvette Stingray and wardrobe straight out of the latest fashion magazine. We'd die before we let him know that, instead, coming up with derogatory names, teasing phrases to torture him with, carrying on until he wanted to murder us.

"You're such a peanut," we'd taunt, "Maybe you should try eating a little something. Try to put on some weight."

"So I can be a blimp like you two," Teddie would retort, scoring a direct hit.

We weren't fat but had the typical teenage insecurity about weight. Drinking Diet Rite Cola, we'd try to starve ourselves into losing ten pounds, only to turn around and sabotage the effort with a binge of potato chips and pizza or French fries and tartar sauce from Porky's, a popular drive-in, the kind with order taking speakers on the pole.

"Teddie called us blimps," Meryl whined, tattling to Tillie.

"You're all a bunch of dumasassoles!" Tillie responded, her cigarette dangling from the side of her mouth while hands worked fabrics into stunning custom made outfits.

Widowed when Meryl was eight Tillie worked fourteen hours a day minimum to keep her household running. On the side she did catering and certainly didn't need any more grief from us.

"Just SHUT UP. **CAN'T YOU SHUT UP ONCE!?**" Teddie yelled, slamming the door to his bedroom.

We laughed, having gotten a rise out of him. He knew we'd be just like that in the design room at Bachman's. Little shits making fun of him.

"I won't cause any trouble," I promised.

"Me neither," added Meryl.

Meryl's mom won the day and against better judgment, Teddie hired us. The positions were assistants in the wedding department, managed by Rosemary, one of the sweetest dear-hearts we ever met. That curtailed any mean-spirited shenanigans but wasn't enough to tame the silly foolhardiness. Rosemary would crack up, thinking we were delightfully good humor. The design area adjoined the wedding department in one huge open room. Teddie couldn't miss my buffoonery echoing throughout the cavernous expanse. Meryl dubbed me "loud-mouth lime"; she was "rootin'-tootin' raspberry," as in the soft drink ads. Rosemary taught us how to make bows and tape leaves as well as tiny buds and flowers which would then be incorporated into the bouquets and corsages. Not requiring much concentration, this left our minds free to jive, joke and mimic our workmates. It was like a stand-up act, our co-workers applauding the antics. When the tasks were completed, Meryl and I would saunter off to the bathroom, hide out in a walk-in cooler, or sneak down to the delivery/ loading area. Teddie kept track of these absences but rarely reprimanded us in front of everyone. A fabulously talented designer, professional, and unparalleled in artistic creativity, he had too much going on to be babysitting us. But Meryl heard about it at home, which she'd then relate to me.

"He says he's going to fire us if we don't pipe down and stay in our department! As if!" she said, mocking his tone of voice, rolling her eyes.

"What if he does," I said, "can he really do that?"

"If he does, I'll get Tillie to make him hire us back."

She was so confident, I felt fairly secure. With a half-hearted attempt at detente, Meryl and I toned it down. But the next week, having learned a new trick I had to try it out on the staff. I went into the cooler while Meryl got everyone in the department to look my way. Practiced to perfection for this performance, pressing my lips against the glass window, I blew my mouth out. It looked like the G-force effect, causing explosions of laughter in my audience. That called for an encore. The uproar brought a curious onlooker from the administrative offices located just above the design room. It was none other than Ralph Bachman himself, owner-extraordinaire. He caught the second mouth blow, gave a forced smile, turned and went back upstairs. It hadn't escaped Teddie's watchful gaze. He walked over and reamed me out.

Meryl stepped in, "Oh, come on, it wasn't so bad. You laughed."

Teddie enlisted Tillie to secure an apology and with feigned submission we continued, albeit gingerly, in the wedding department.

He detested the asinine name we made up to torment and mock him. Arnot Peadvark. It was really a clever play on his diminutive size. We thought he was a peanut, tiny. An ugly animal we'd come across in the dictionary was an aardvark. So in musing, mulling over ways to harass the evil ogre, we exchanged a few letters: peanut Aardvark; Arnut Peadvark; Arnot Peadvark. Perfect!

"God, you are such complete idiots," Teddie responded, fuming.

"Well, you're Arnot, that's what you are. Don't you get it? You're an Arnot Peadvark," Meryl said, explaining the peanut reverse, like he would get the humor.

We were sitting next to each other on the couch in her living room. Teddie leaned over, put one hand on the outside of

74

our heads and smacked them together. He might not have known the force of his anger or maybe the K.O. was his intended outcome. For a few seconds, our heads slumped. We woke up bawling like babies.

"Oh, quit faking it, you weren't knocked out," Teddie chortled, hurriedly trying to make his case, knowing Tillie was within earshot. He really was surprised, pleasantly, in a 'serves you right' attitude. For sure!

"Mohhhhhhmmm," Meryl moaned, as she pulled herself up slowly, shakily, from the couch. Teddie trooped right after her, to counter her arguments.

"Dumassassoles!" I heard from Tillie's sewing room.

We got him back by broadcasting his demeaning name all over the design room. He probably could have beaten the rap on grounds of justifiable homicide.

What drew me to Darla was her dark side. With bright red hair she personified the Irish temper stereotype. God, what balls, I thought, the first time I witnessed her verbally attack her mom. How the hell did she get away with that? It impressed me no end. Replete with swearing, I envied how she summarily dismissed her mother from the kitchen where we sat sipping Diet Rite cola. She'd fried up her favorite sandwich, grilled peanut butter, and we wolfed it down hashing over details of our school day. When her mother simply walked through, Darla commanded her to get out and quit eaves dropping. Instead of a reprimand her mother would go upstairs and pray for us! That was a new one.

Meryl didn't like Darla, probably for those same reasons that I admired her. Tillie was a sweetheart. Why would you ever act like that to her? God, how I wanted to swear at Edith. One day after school, in Darla's bedroom, we circumvented Edith's stricture against pierced ears.

"Whatdaya mean, she won't let you get your ears pierced? It's simple."

"Really?"

Explaining how it worked, she bullied me into compliance.

"First, rub your ear lobe between your finger and thumb to numb it out. Then we'll ice it for 30 seconds."

Boldly, without a second's hesitation, Darla jammed the thick needle through my ear lobe as I held a potato slice behind it. God, it killed bleeding just a little.

"Now be sure to wear your hair down over your ears until they heal. Then they'll stay that way and your mom can't do anything about it."

I lapped up her edgy, demanding, even intimidating personality.

Home life with Jack and Edith hadn't improved with our move to Minneapolis. On the contrary, due to Dad's reduced time on the road, tensions escalated, fueled by continual conflict. I hated my home life, its dark atmosphere stifling like a heavy cloak. Static permeated the air when they occupied the same room. One welcome development that made life bearable was my newfound friendship with Ricky, now a teenager. Following my rebellious lead, he and I formed a bond of solidarity against Cynthia and the 'rents' (our parental nickname). I still teased him but he could hold his own, throwing it back at me with good-hearted humor. While Edith was at work, Ricky and I would blast the stereo, eating wherever and whatever we felt like, rough housing and playing tag until something broke or one of us got hurt.

Chasing him out the back door, and down the steps I rapped him, "You're it," spinning around, and running back inside.

Whipping the door around to lock him out, I heard the glass shatter.

"Yeeooww," Ricky yelled. I saw his arm poking through the window, a deep gash opening across his elbow.

Blood soaked the sleeve of his shirt as I grabbed the dish towel hanging on the oven door.

"Sit down here," I commanded, pulling out the kitchen chair as I tightly wrapped his arm. "Keep pressure on it."

I dialed Mom's work number. She told me to call the neighbor who drove Ricky to the hospital. Five hours later, I hugged him, very carefully, as he walked through the back door. His arm was bandaged from the hand up to the shoulder, having sliced through to the tendon.

Ricky's luck saved him another time when he graduated from high school. His friends traveled to Taylor's Falls for a drunken night of celebration. Jumping off an embankment, Ricky was knocked senseless in the shallow water they'd neglected to examine. Either he was so snockered that he bent like a rubber doll or it simply wasn't his time to die.

Another expensive hospital visit gave Mom more to fume about.

"I work and I work and what thanks do I get?"

We heard that so many times it was second nature to tune her out.

Incessantly on Jack's case, she'd nag, "Pick that up. Leave that alone. You're leaving crumbs all over the counter. Get out of here."

Finally, he'd blow, retaliating with caustic darts. Lashing back and forth, the two of them verbally shred each other. I wondered why they stayed together. They detested each other but would go to sleep at night in the same bedroom… in the same bed!

Upstairs, in my room, I'd try to block them out. Edith still smoked making it easy for me to camouflage my own habit. First, I'd get a damp washcloth and turn on the window air conditioner to vent the air out. As I blew the smoke through it, I'd swing the washcloth overhead to break up any lingering smell.

"Fuck you, God, how I hate you, I can't stand you!" muffled by the air conditioner, I was fairly certain they wouldn't hear my tirade.

God, if I could charge downstairs and let them have it like Darla.

The Ozzie and Harriet mentality of perfection countered by the upheaval in the late '60s and the malevolent example at home contributed to my confusingly insecure teen years. 'Leave It To Beaver' and 'Ozzie and Harriet' were popular T.V. shows depicting idyllic families. Ozzie and Harriet cared for each other. They didn't berate one another, ever. Raising the children, teaching by their good example of respect and modern psychology, it was sheer fantasy, an existence I couldn't imagine.

Jack and Edith used 'grounding' as a desperate attempt to control me. Feeling like a caged animal, it was the ultimate punishment being confined in that household. I couldn't run, couldn't escape. What made me so frantic that particular Saturday, I don't know.

A few months into my sophomore year, everything: school, boys, zits, George, cramps, weight, everything overwhelmed me. Cynthia told Mom and Dad she smelled smoke from my room so the vigilantism curtailed my habit. I wanted to kill her.

The response didn't surprise me when I asked to go out.

"No, you can't have the car. You don't always need to be going somewhere," Dad argued.

I did though. I did need to be out of there. I needed to keep running, not sit still or be alone with my thoughts.

"So can't I go if someone picks me up?" I queried, my logical solution.

"Why can't you just stay home?"

I didn't say it, but thought, "Because I'm smothering here."

Dad went out to do some yard work while I retreated to my room. Nobody else was home. I snapped. I got up from my bed, walked across the hall to the bathroom, and sat down on the toilet. The razor I used for shaving my legs was lying near the edge of the bathtub. I kept staring at it, focusing. Sitting. Focusing. Picking it up, I unscrewed the top and took out the double edged blade. Dad's head, just beyond the window, was visible as he trimmed an apple tree. I could hear the schoot-schoot, schoot-schoot of the saw back and forth. Not cognizant, holding the blade between my right thumb and two fingers, I sliced across my left wrist laying open the tender flesh. As red colored my hand, I watched, mesmerized, the pool forming on the floor. Reality registered in my brain as searing pain jarred my torpor.

Jerking upright, "God, what am I doing?! What do I do now?! Shit, shit, I gotta do something quick."

I wrapped a towel around the gaping skin feeling nauseous, my knees buckling. Get to the phone in my room, call my friend, Darla, tell her to get over here, tell her what I did.

Meryl could never handle it. I couldn't lay this on her. How I surmised that? But knowing it would take too long for Darla to get here, I made my way back to the bathroom. Holding my wrist, rolling the crank a quarter turn to open the window, I rather calmly told Dad he needed to come inside. My request, a confession, was more excruciating than my bleeding wrist, but I knew I didn't want to die.

"Why did you do this?" he questioned, after examining it.

"I don't know."

He could see I needed stitches but his curious way of proceeding left me baffled. Being a pharmaceutical rep, he had lots of doctor acquaintances so pulling out his list of contacts, he started calling them. One by one it was evident they wouldn't be in the office on a Saturday afternoon.

The doorbell rang. Darla.

"I'm not answering it," he said.

"I called Darla. I have to let her know I'm alive. She'll call the cops or something."

He was so pissed, at me, knowing this couldn't be kept under wraps. At the door, he curtly informed her that the situation was under control and she could leave. And NO she couldn't talk to me. I sat at the kitchen table applying pressure to my arm, my head spinning. Why weren't we going? When he realized the only way to receive treatment was to go to the emergency room at Fairview, he finally acquiesced.

In the car, Dad broke the palpable silence with his blistering comment, "What do you think your mother is going to think about this?"

Well, lay it on. Heap it on. I couldn't trust my voice, choking back tears, so I shrugged my shoulders.

"You're going to have to tell her yourself," he said.

My God! Isn't that comforting? That's all ya got? If I just open the door and throw myself out, will that help?

The young doctor who stitched up my wrist was quiet, gentle, and appropriately concerned.

"What led up to this?" he inquired.

I had no answers, saying, "I don't know. I just did it. I don't know why."

Not satisfied, he questioned Dad with equal lack of success.

"We'd like to keep her here overnight for observation. We'd like to talk more about it," he said, trying to get through to Dad.

Nothing doing.

"We'll take care of her at home," he replied, dismissively.

With obvious shame he brusquely refused the offer, ignoring my cry for help. I was mortified thinking about Mom, the conversation, how it would go. Riding home in vacuous silence, crushing shame petrified me the entire twenty minute distance, wondering if he could hear the throb of my heart. I waited until she was in bed that night, sitting on my bed in darkness, listening to the hum of my alarm clock, watching the red hand tick the minutes by. Making my way down the narrow, carpeted staircase I felt as if I was heading for the gallows. How many times had I hurried down, lost my footing, and slammed against the closed door with my books and folders flying everywhere? Go slowly, don't slip. Almost tiptoeing to the last step, I turned, walking through her door. The light was off; she was lying there under the covers, relaxed. Moving toward the side of the bed I stood by her head.

"I have to tell you something," whispering, barely audible.

Chest aching where my heart pounded I stood stone still as she waited. Thoughts were a jumble, forcing my breath to move, in, out, how to say it, how to,

"I slit my wrist today."

Eyes closed, my breath stopped while tears squeezed out. Complete silence. For one second the thought flew through me, like those dream sequences you have feeling like it's hours but it's probably less than a minute, like the flick of an eyelid; should I walk away, should I try to say something else, fade to nothing, disappear? Flick.

Her question was abrupt, "What did you do that for?"

I willed it out, the same thing I'd said all day, "I don't know."

"Well, that was stupid."

* * *

Softly, the flight attendant asked, "Can I get you anything?"

I couldn't respond.

"Sorry," she offered, gently.

If everyone would just leave me alone, if they would stop bringing me back to the present, I would have a better chance of avoiding hysterics before touchdown. I realized that some on my flight knew. The resort area where we'd stayed was so intimate that news of death reverberated throughout the hotel complex. With black outfit, head to toe, garish dark under eye circles, flat unkempt hair, my appearance was telling.

I was given the first row aisle seat, closest to the galley, within reach of the attendants, who were apprised of my situation.

It did give me some small comfort to know that someone was watching out for me. In my entire life I'd never felt so alone.

God, Nick, how could you be dead? What happened!!!?? What the fuck?

A couple of months before our wedding anniversary I went to travel agencies and researched Mexican vacations, bringing home brochures for Nick and me to pore over.

"God, Anne, this is a lot of money that we could put toward so many other things," Nick reasoned.

Nothing came before his kids. Family was uppermost to both of us. He was a mathematical genius, keeping bills paid, providing for us on $40,000 a year. Methodically, he'd sit at his desk, and carefully work his accounting magic. College tuition, house payments, still paying off the previous year's Christmas presents, stretching every dollar, Nick had to be convinced to splurge on this excursion.

"I know it'll be tight, God, when is it not, but we've always denied ourselves everything. Isn't it time to be crazy, impractical? Isn't it time for us? It's our thirtieth anniversary. We have to do something big. What if we're not here next year?"

He didn't say anything, just sat there pondering. The wheels were in motion and I understood his need for space. This is how it worked with us. Thirty years figuring it out. If I pushed, he'd dig in his heels. His method of always looking at situations more slowly as he weighed every detail had taught me patience. In the early years I would get so frustrated feeling like I was being ignored but after three decades, I had it down; plant a seed, zip it, and wait.

Nick was a gentle man, and a true gentleman, warm and soft spoken like his Greek dad. Inviting and open, his dark eyes

83

had a magnetic attraction. I wanted to get inside, behind them and figure out his deep secrets. He wasn't gregarious, the way I was, but possessed an ease that caused people to feel comfortable around him. Nick's thoughtful nature was an excellent balance to my spontaneous, bawdy personality. He explained that growing up an only child had a lot to do with his demeanor.

The first time my cousin, Kari, met him, she told me, "I like him. He makes me feel like I'm an old friend."

When I brought up the Mexican vacation over dinner a couple of nights later, he laid his fork down, giving me one of his penetrating looks. Reaching across the table, he took my hand.

I loved his affection, his smile, as he squeezed tenderly, "You're right, we need to do this."

He automatically pushed his chair back seeing me rise. I straddled his lap planting kisses beginning on his forehead, continuing with his nose, cheeks, tongue swirling the velvety soft earlobe, tasting his neck. Dinner was over. Dessert.

As we discussed the trip over the next few days, the travel insurance made sense. Knowing how brutal Midwest winters were, we had to be prepared in the event a snowstorm hindered our three hour commute to the airport. I thought we'd covered every contingency.

Remembering our initial conversation, how I had persuaded him, the one question tormented me, "What if we're not here next year?"

I shuddered.

* * *

7

My prit'near perfect flip senior picture

It was 1968. I felt like my life began the year I graduated from Washburn High School. We'd drifted apart over the last two years, but Meryl and I'd planned our groovy excursion since eighth grade. She had relatives in San Fran, me in LA, so we set our course and escaped parental control for a month. From the bland Midwest to sunny, happenin' Cal, we were flying to another planet. Three days with my LA cousin, several years older, he convinced me to try out his royal blue Corvette Stingray. Creamy white leather interior. Convertible. Holy shit. The sheer power! Content to just sit behind the wheel, I was completely freaked I'd wreck it, if given the opportunity. His approbation persuaded me to give it a shot. Learning a stick shift on a Vette was no easy task. After many trial runs back and forth on his side street, I was ready to "head out on the highway, looking for adventure." God, I couldn't believe it; driving his 'Vette! Well, trying to. Having extreme difficulty with the tight clutch, I killed it at every stop light, cheeks blazing red from embarrassment as the horns blasted. My destination was Riverside Park where the hippies hung out. I wanted them to see how cool we were driving a Corvette. Such naiveté. All I knew about hippies I'd gleaned from Time and Life magazine regaling pictures of communes, Haight Ashbury and dropouts. Instantly attracted to their rebellious attitude I was intrigued to discover the new philosophy that veered so far from middle class America.

The flower-child epoch on the West Coast was light years ahead of the Midwest. As the park came into view, the appearance of beautifully free-spirited young people, their disdain of materialism evident, was a stark contrast to my Barbie doll persona. Sitting lotus on the grass, passing a joint, they looked so peaceful, eyes closed, swaying to guitar music, a harp chiming in, another thumping bongo drums. Some sang, others danced barefoot, in see-through, madras print skirts, their long hair flowing. Couples embraced, making out, right there on the lawn, in front of everybody. Freedom. Love. Rebellion. I was enmeshed, eager to jump right in. During my junior and senior years, I'd dabbled in marijuana, downers and speed, but hadn't yet been initiated into hard core LSD and other hallucinogenic substances. Piqued by news reports of draft dodgers and hippies, my attraction was solidified seeing them first hand, feeling an immensely appealing aura. It was the coolest thing I'd ever seen. Not so much for Meryl, the barometer of reason. If she would have had the same reaction as me I may never have come back from that trip, both mentally and physically. All I needed was the slightest encouragement, a partner to bolster me, and I would have stayed in California. Much to my disappointment, unconvinced, and unimpressed, she didn't buy any of it.

We kept to our schedule, visiting the pedestrian tourist attractions. Disneyland, Knott's Berry Farm, and then onto Frisco. On the flight home, Meryl and I were in agreement, however, concerning the upcoming school year.

"I'm not even into college," I bemoaned, sipping my vodka tonic. We weren't even carded, flying unaccompanied, trying to come off so sophisticated.

Lighting up a Kool, she laughed, exhaling, "Yeah, like I am."

"I only signed up for Normandale to get Jack and Edith off my case. Always with the 'why can't you be more like Cynthia, she never gives us any trouble. why do you always defy us' bullshit! I can never measure up in their minds. Not that I want to be anything like her. Perfect Cynthia."

Meryl asked, "What else would you do?"

"Work, I guess. I don't know. Go back out to Cal. You know I hate school. Now it's right back into days and weeks of class? God, I'm depressed. Give me one of those, will ya? And your lighter."

The noose seemed to tighten the closer we got to Minneapolis.

After one year of extremely boring, innocuous junior college, I decided to quit. My inner voice said, 'change direction.' The weekend beer bashes, the same people in popular cliques, still teeny boppers, were making me sick. So unhappy, frustrated with my classmates, not doing anything different since high school,

God, really? What was the point? It was time to follow my heart. I wanted to drop out [of society] ever since California but didn't have the nerve. The seed had been planted. I felt hooked. Churning, stirring, the questions compounded. What was my life about? Who was I? What did I want to be? What was truth? Love? Reality? Purpose? Did anyone have answers? Where could I find meaning?

After many hours of contemplation, I came up with my rationale for quitting school. I imagined the scenario with Jack and Edith, their angry faces, frustrated as I laid it on them: I was moving out, I had to find myself, didn't know what I wanted to do, where I'd live or any other question I knew they'd ask. I shouldn't have bothered, their understanding so limited. Instantly I hit a brick wall, attempting to ease their incredulity. With the conversation revving to a full on crazy screaming match, to say it ended in an impasse is putting it mildly. Sometimes I wondered if they had any idea or even cared about what was going on inside of me. I didn't know *who* I was but was sick of being her.

A life changing wave had rushed into my spirit that day in California and I was ready to be swept out to sea, swallowed whole. Needing to discover, to understand what the hippie movement was all about, I ventured in. My wardrobe blossomed with baggy bell-bottoms, tie-dyed shirts, and the ultimate declaration, free-flowing breasts. It empowered me to wear clothes that aligned me with certain people and, at the same time, made others stare in disgust. I wanted to freak everyone out. My soul was screaming, "screw you and all your middle class values." Finally, a depth of existence I could relate to.

Picture of JLL's in the Star Tribune. I'm far right, top. Meryl, in long dress, standing on right. Tommy, second person to the left of Meryl.

We got jobs at JLL's, a trendy boutique on Chicago Avenue in South Minneapolis. Both Meryl and me. Some good friends, Tommy, Meryl, and a dozen or so eighteen to twenty year olds worked together, managed by two audacious entrepreneurs. Their idea was to have an eclectic selection of clothing that appealed to counter culture types, I think. Who the hell knew? God, it was fun! The vision was blurry, at best, which explains the shop's demise in about a year. What were they thinking? It was so wild! I dropped my first mescaline right there in the 'can' one lovely summer day.

Tommy said, "Anne, you gotta try this. It's fabulous."
"What is it?"

"A yellow submarine," he answered.

"What does it do?"

"Oh, it's real mellow. You see colors, far out shit, you'll love it," handing it to me.

I dropped it (swallowed it). Just like that my life took another sharp left turn. After about a half hour I was 'coming on,' feeling woozy, drunk-like. This was one in the afternoon. What was Tommy thinking, giving me hallucinogens at work!?

"I can't stay here. Tommy, I'm feeling too weird. I don't know anything. What's happening? What's going on with my eyes?"

Trying to be coherent, trying to keep it together I had to grab the edge of the counter in an attempt to keep my balance. Walls were wavy, like a fun house, lights flashed, depth perception completely altered. Taking my arm, Tommy led me out to his car where I slid along the seat leaning back feeling the fabric graze my fingertips. I kept petting it like a cat, the sensation was so unbelievable. Everything was amplified. Utterly astonishing and debilitating.

I know he wasn't prepared for the marathon aftermath. You were doing everyone a favor by turning them on. That's what we thought. The consequences were usually manageable, but the occasional freak-out added dangerous drama. Tommy made some lame excuse to the manager to get out of our shift and we split.

I laid my head back against the front seat, so out of it, so high, the scenery swirling, changing in the most bizarre way. My eyes wouldn't focus, my perception off, my hearing strangely affected. This was my immersion, my initiation into psychedelics.

Tommy, who, wisely, hadn't dropped any, tried to explain what was happening, "Just let yourself go. Relax. Enjoy it. Don't try to figure it out."

He turned up the radio to enhance the atmosphere. I wasn't exactly scared, being such a dare-devil, but my mind was getting more out of control by the minute. Maybe he knew or was reminded after I reacted so intensely, but Tommy had given me a four-way hit. It was supposed to be divided between four people! He could have said, good luck, or whatever and bailed on me, but he was really a true friend, attentive, and very responsible (for a drug dealer) in the way he became my guide.

Thank God for the lakes a few miles away. We hung out on Thomas beach, lying in the grass watching swimmers, children, dogs scampering. The day-glow sun hung dreamily amidst a vibrant blue sky, peeking through clouds that provided amazing pictorials for my personal entertainment.

At about 7:00, it was apparent I was going to be doing an all-nighter, pretty much a given with hallucinogens. We picked up Darla, enlisted to help with the rest of my endless trip and drove to a party that included a strange mix of straight, former high school friends, some Normandale students that definitely weren't into the drug scene. This made for some odd conversation. When only every second or third word he was saying registered with me, I accused one guy of messing with my mind. Extremely paranoid, reasoning that he was deliberately jerking me around, I became combative. The disbelieving look should have told me he didn't have a clue, but my mind wasn't working with any logic. Tommy shielded me, diplomatically running interference, as he ushered me into the bathroom. That was probably a mistake as well. My otherworldly reflection in the mirror responded like modeling clay as I touched it. Imagining indentations, I could push my nose over to my cheek. And my eyes; so dark in color, so vivid, so bright, I thought I could look past them into my skull.

"Wow, this is so very FARRR OUUUT! Tommy, can you see my face?"

He could but wasn't sure what I was talking about.

"You look great, you're fine," he tried to reassure, smiling.

Darla and Tommy decided I'd fare better away from the crowd so the three of us took off in his car. Four hours later, having driven from Burnsville to Stillwater and back, somehow I possessed enough cohesion to know I had to let my mom know my whereabouts or she'd be flippin' out. But what? No planning, no story, no agenda, no brains! I was expected home by a certain hour. I still had a curfew, midnight, which was fast approaching. So they coached me.

"Just go in, say as little as possible, head up to your room and try to sleep."

That was the sage advice. Okay? Yeah, right. I had to do it, pull it off. I couldn't call at that hour and try to convince her of a sleepover. Aggh, shit! How could I face her? God, Tommy, what did you get me into? What were his words?

"It'll be cool, you'll love it."

Okay, so I needed to get past my sentry mom who always waited up. Lie, lie, lie, liar, liar, pants on fire. How about creative manipulation of the truth? We pulled up and parked at the end of the block, both of them speaking calmly, coaching, words of 'wisdom', explanation, it'd be fine, you can do this. Alright, I'm ready.

Climbing out of the car, "Later," I said with a wave, planting my feet, giving them a forced smile. Walking carefully up the three steps, now the front porch, down the gangplank.

"Hi," I said, trying to keep my voice light as I walked in the front door acutely aware of the sound shutting the door, my expression, was it normal? Edith was sitting in the living room, her knitting needles clacking, watching Johnny Carson. Thank God for the distraction.

"You're late." She peered at me, looking for trouble, signs of drinking.

I smiled, keeping eye contact, offering, "Sorry."

"Where were you?"

"Oh, Darla and I were driving around. We went to Porky's and lost track of the time. Well, I gotta work tomorrow so I'm going to bed. Goodnight," I said, rushing over pecking her cheek.

Retreating upstairs, I hollered, "Goodnight."

Phew, I made it! Drugs don't leave any tell-tale odor so I passed. Basically, she wanted to believe my cock-and-bull story.

I couldn't turn my radio on because Edith would hear it. I had to be still. Silent. Asleep.

Lying on my bed, spinning, hallucinating on the white daisy print wall paper, I dialed Darla, making sure to stay under my muffler of covers, "It's 2:30," I whispered, "and I'm not a bit sleepy, now what do I do? This is so insane. Is this it now? Will I be THIS now? Fuck. I mean, how long is this going to last?"

Here's the solution she gave: "when you start feeling very warm, you'll know you're coming down. Be as calm as you can. Breathe. In and out."

So, I put on more clothes, a sweater under my bathrobe, piling on more blankets, figuring I could speed the process. About a hundred degrees later I called her back. It was 4:00.

"Just lay there, be quiet and don't let your mom hear you," Darla counseled.

That's it, I figured. I'd never be the same, convinced I'd never come down, a blathering idiot the rest of my life. Sonofabitch!

Meantime, Darla called Tommy, "You better find some Reds, man, for Anne or I don't know what's gonna happen! She's really out there. Jesus Christ. What the fuck were you thinking, man?"

Wasn't that a stellar solution? Reds were slang for Seconal, sleeping pills.

After Mom left for work, in the FTD department at Bachman's around 8:00, I showered, dressed and waited for Darla and Tommy to pick me up. They scored some Seconal and a place for me to crash till I slept it off. I woke at 4p.m. with at least a semblance of reality. The story we came up with to tie it all together was a whopper and that evening back at home I should have won an award as I justified my previous night's odd behavior.

"I know you thought something was wrong last night but I couldn't explain. We saw this thing in the road, like an animal, a cat or something. We stopped to discover it was a dead puppy. The poor little thing. He had on a collar with a tag so we wrapped him up and took him to the address where we broke the awful news. I was just so upset that I couldn't even talk about it, you know, Peanuts having been run over."

(He was our own miniature poodle that met the same demise two months prior.) My nose should have been a foot long, but Mom seemed to buy it. I wanted to garner support, sympathy to keep her suspicions in check. It was a continual effort to stay one step ahead, to not be thwarted in my search for self.

After that experience I vowed no more hallucinogenics. That lasted all of a month. Vacating my parents' house where I had to pretend to be straight became top priority. While they were on vacation to the Black Hills, I hauled my belongings to Lana's one bedroom apartment she shared with her sister in a great old red brick building on 36th and Girard. It was my ticket to freedom. Bolstering my resolve, I planned to confront the 'rents' upon their return.

I toyed with buttressing the living room with friends to buffer the encounter like my brilliant defensive move at sixteen. After I totaled Edith's car, again while they were on vacation, I had four of my friends sit with me in the living room as I confessed. It was drama but they didn't kill me on the spot, having to maintain a modicum of temperance. This time I intended to face them alone, like an adult.

"I have some news," I said trying to sound confident, calm, mature.

Bracing themselves, immediately jumping to the worst conclusion, Dad asked, "What's going on?"

We sat in the living room, sticking to the plastic covered furniture, sweat forming behind my knee. I reached forward wiping it away, curling up my toes feeling my heart pound.

"I moved into an apartment with Lana. It's a two bedroom down on Girard. I'm working and have enough money saved up and I have all my stuff there."

I talked faster and faster seeing they were not in the least convinced.

"You don't think we're just going to let you do this?" Dad said.

"Why not?" I countered, incredulously.

Mom asked, "What about school?"

Not softening it, I blurted, "I'm not going anymore. It's not what I want to do."

"What? Since when? Well, then what *are* you going to do?"

"I'm not sure. I have been doing a lot of thinking and I need to figure things out. It isn't working for me. School. I don't belong there."

"Figure what out?" Dad asked, raising his voice in exasperation.

"Life, I have to find myself, find meaning, my purpose." I was getting more frustrated, squirming with each question. This was not going well, spiraling downward. I clenched my fists behind my knees digging my fingernails into my palm. Don't scream. Don't bite. Why didn't I wait until they'd had a cocktail?

"So when do you think you're doing this?" Mom asked.

God, weren't they listening at all. I already told them I moved my stuff down there.

"Tonight. Now," I said, belligerently.

"We can't let you do that."

"I'm eighteen. It's my right. You can't stop me. That's the fact. I'm going."

Dad stood up stiffly, chest out, "Well," he said, "I'm going over there with you and if I don't like it, you're coming home with me. Edith, are you coming?"

She shook her head no, in disgust, exhaling as she turned her head from me. Her head kept going back and forth, bobble like. Yeah, right! I thought, I'd like to see you try to bring me home! You don't know the first thing about me if you think you can control me like that. I'm gone, gone, gone! You're not suffocating me anymore.

So I drove my car, Dad following in his, to inspect my new place. Giving it the once over, trying to intimidate me and my roommate, Lana, he tried to act like the decision was his. Bullshit! I felt so powerful. I was such a WOMAN. This was it. I was free! Free at last! Out from under that constrictive, depressing cloud that snuffed out my true nature for eighteen years. Dad stood at the door and looked at me, waiting for some weakening, something that would give him the excuse to demand obedience. Anything.

Not receiving it, sarcastically he said, "Well, good luck, I hope you find your answers," adding, "You know you've broken your mother's heart."

I stood, defiant, not wanting it to be like this but couldn't see any other way out. I had to get away from them. So torn, so confused, it had to be.

Heaping it on, he finished with, "This will kill your mother."

Guilt is the gift that keeps on giving and I could forever count on that generous dose. And guess what? She still lived! It was a miracle. Caustic, callous? Probably, but I had to sharpen that edge, had to stand firm, not cave. Oscar Wilde summed it up so succinctly in *The Importance of Being Ernest*, "Relations are simply a tedious pack of people, who haven't the remotest knowledge of how to live, nor the smallest instinct about when to die."

What a season, 1969, that summer in Minneapolis; hundreds of eighteen, nineteen, and twenty year olds marching to the beat of unrest. Peace rallies and stoned out sit-ins were standard fare. I made tons of new friends, perma-high compatriots, searching for truth, chanting the mantra, 'make love, not war.' The atmosphere was electric encompassing the Vietnam War, unlimited sex, drugs, and rock and roll. The national climate was highly charged after the '68 assassinations of Dr. King and Senator Bobby Kennedy ushering in an unprecedented era of riots, Chicago having had the most violently brutal confrontation during the Democratic convention. In the August heat thousands of protesters, police, National Guard, and Secret Service shocked the airwaves as we witnessed unarmed citizens attacked with billy clubs, rifles and tear gas. Seeing the actual images on T.V. obliterated any remaining faith or hope in the political system, bolstering my conviction to unite in whatever way possible to resist.

I loved hanging out on Lake Street at Electric Fetus, Psychedelia, head shops, and anywhere on the West Bank. I soaked in every new truth, basking in all of the anti-establishment philosophy. We spoke the same language, had the same vibes, related, rapped, and blew straight people away.

Lana and Linda shared the bedroom, so I took the couch. Fine, glorious, beautiful. Life was superb.

The gulf between Meryl and me grew to a chasm. She had no time for my wild ideas, drugs, or lifestyle. Her mother, Tillie, was battling lung cancer and Meryl was her loving caregiver. I knew I should have been more of a friend during the torturous battle but I wouldn't be deterred from my quest. Blocking out the past, I was totally self-absorbed in my journey. Surprised by Meryl's presence at a party one night, hearing her voice, I all but flew down the stairs from where I'd been 'balling.' The punch was spiked with acid.

"Don't drink the punch. Meryl! Wait!" I hollered, leaping across the living room in one stride, grabbing her cup.

She trusted my altruistic connection to her, as she let go, "What's in it?"

"Acid."

"God, thanks. Shit," she said, her big eyes bulging out. Though bonded from the past, we were miles apart, eons apart, with nothing else to say.

98

My heap of a car having tanked, I hitchhiked, alone, all over the city, fearlessly flaunting my liberation. Bouncing braless, hair disheveled, clothes hanging off the shoulder, I had that just raped appearance. My one rule when sizing up a ride was: if the car was full of guys, I emphatically declared, no thanks. It really was relatively safe, just a way of life. I was only propositioned once by an older man that mistook me for a hooker.

"I'm just hitchhiking, man," I said, warning him. "Get your hand off me."

He had reached over to my thigh, copping a feel as he drove.

"What d'ya mean?" he argued.

"Pull over right here. Right now," I commanded.

"Aw, c'mon, I know what you want."

I freaked, raising my voice, "I mean it. If you don't pull over right now, I'll jump."

Grabbing the door handle I told myself I'd really do it.

"Alright, alright, take it easy," he said, slowing to the curb.

Lesson learned. It was an innocent bubble in some ways, a slice out of time like no other for those particular years; before the guns, the gangs, and the violence invaded our world. Music was mellow, ethereal; transporting us above and beyond the dingy apartments we rented for eighty-five dollars a month. The songs were a cultural phenomenon blasting our eardrums with the message of our generation. Johnny Winter's performance at the old Labor Temple, in '69, transcended all the others to come possibly because of the particular drugs that night, because it was my first real rock concert experience or the combination of all the elements combined.

While waiting in line I felt the walls closing in. My boyfriend, Jim, along with our friends, Teri and Bill, Stan, Keith, and Gary had driven together. All of us tried to synchronize dropping something like acid or mescaline to 'come on' about the time the music began but the line had come to a standstill. The noise, the press of concert goers, the brightly lit corridor, was freaking me out.

Teetering on the precipice of insanity, the environment had to be carefully orchestrated or a bad trip could send one over the edge. That was the perilous instability about being high. Hallucinations displaced reality with paranoia lurking ominously in the shadows. You were out of it, out of your mind, out of control, but if you could keep the circle tightly buttressed with those you trusted, the precarious balance was maintained. Even the person driving dropped acid.

On the freeway one night, Jim told me to take the next exit.

I looked at him, incredulously, "You're drivin', man!"

The danger was a large part of the attraction, blending elements of bravado with unbelievable ignorance. At the Labor Temple that night, Johnny played his soulful guitar in an entrancing performance, his magic weaving around and through the hall. No chairs or bleachers, we sat on the floor. To the audience's delight, after half a dozen numbers, Johnny surprised us as he introduced his brother, Edgar. These two profoundly talented white haired Texans balanced each other's wicked riffs impeccably, having played together since young boys. Unparalleled in my experience, the bluesy rock, coupled with the Winters' eccentricities was nothing short of a spiritual awakening. The entire audience, aglow as hundreds of lighters and matches appeared, dotted the hall in a show of loving worship. I found utopia, nirvana, wanting to float in the presence and never come down.

We sat on the floor directly in front of the stage in April at a Depot concert downtown Minneapolis where Joe Cocker's amazing performance mesmerized us. With the Mad Dogs and Englishmen and roughly 30 other odd performers on the stage, in one roll or another, his seizure-like, body jerking delivery blew my mind. Arms and hands flailing spasmodically in sheer abandon, he screeched his cover in that full throttle spit spewing blues, 'she came in through the bathroom window.' Frank Zappa blew our minds at the same venue a few months later.

Seeing people with their hands over their ears he screamed, "Is it too loud?"

"Yeah," we yelled back.

Belligerently, he cranked up the volume. It was too small an area to have amps at full blast but no one made any adjustments. When Neil Young played an acoustic solo concert at the Guthrie Theatre, cutting it short, citing a sore throat, I thought, suck it up! I paid twenty bucks for the ticket, a premium price. We tripped to The Moody Blues at Northrup Auditorium and Led Zeppelin at the Met Center in Bloomington. The music of the early 70s formed and solidified my social consciousness with messages pertaining to anti-war, rebellion, racial conflict and inequality. Anxieties, issues and culture kept our wrap sessions going till all hours of the night.

In a constant state of transition, my mind swirled as the hallucinogenic haze fueled doubt and suspicion of the status quo. During all-nighters, we espoused hip gurus; Kahlil Gibran, Herman Hesse, and Timothy Leary advising us to tune in, turn on and drop out. They made perfect sense, helping us sort out life with convincing revelations and logical arguments. I bought into the cultural phenomena of the *Whole Earth Catalogue*, the *Foxfire book*, *The Book of the Hopi*, and *Black Elk Speaks*, formulating a radical way of life, with a dismissive attitude toward all my past values. High on acid, I could figure out all of my problems, until the deflation the next day when I came down. The answer was simple: remain in the altered state. Not hard. Parties brought anywhere from ten to thirty like-minded hippies together to turn on. If that was smoking pot, dropping acid, or shooting up, we all partook. At a second floor Lake Street apartment one night, about ten of us stood in a line leading into the bathroom where a proficient needle user was giving all takers a mixture of Seconal. He never changed the needle, just filled it up over and over. Instantly, when the drug hit the bloodstream, a profound state of slow motion set in. Slinking back to the living room, totally spaced out, I melted into the floor. People were in various stages of undress, nerve endings supercharged with willing partners everywhere; the high, extremely peaceful and mellow, sensual. Hands and lips in one swirl of desire found intense release moving with uninhibited abandon. It was the most natural expression, loving everyone equally. An orgy of sensation.

The next day, my arm having turned a hideous black and blue from the wrist to my shoulder, I was freaked out enough to wise up about shared needles. Luckily, that was before AIDS made its appearance. Purplish turned green and yellow fading after a week. It must not have been my time to check out! Rife with drugs in our hippie community, I easily scored acid, mescaline, pot, hash, opium, psilocybin, MDA, you name it; it was cheap and available. We could count on the quality, before the days when lacing drugs with harmful additives adulterated such substances. Not that LSD wasn't risky, but in later years it became common practice to have other, more noxious substances thrown in for effect.

My close circle consisted of Teri from high school and her guy, Bill, my three year older love interest Jim, my roommate Lana, Stan, Gary, Keith and Bon, and Darla. We bought genuine Acapulco Gold and Panama Red from Mexico for two hundred bucks a kilo. An ounce of primo dope, a lid, went for ten dollars. We were literally floating in a sea of illegal substances. Law enforcement was, at best, two steps behind in its effort to stem the glut of drugs. Attempts at surveillance were so lame that we could spot a narc at first glance, giving us a bold feeling of invincibility. Nobody maintained regular jobs. Staying up all night, crashing at six a.m. after watching the sunrise from the outskirts of town left us in no shape to go to work! Driving around on the freeway and city streets under the influence of hallucinogens didn't pose any deterrent.

"Far out, man, right on. Heavy. Let's do a number, a joint. I'm trippin'."

You 'did' drugs, you didn't take them.

"We did the farthest out acid!"

Hippies had their own lingo. Cops were pigs. You referred to everyone as Man, even though girls were chicks. Sex was balling, as in; she's balling him or everyone. Anyone who wasn't doing what we were was straight, stupid, and a sell-out—a tad hypocritical, when the mantra was love and peace. To be honest, there was just as much hate and prejudice in my drug warped psyche as I accused the capitalist money mongers of possessing.

When Teri wanted to move in with us, we found a three bedroom rat hole on the West Bank. Located on 22nd and 22nd, the sleazy upstairs dump cost a mere ninety dollars a month. It would have been better if he'd never seen it but I made the mistake of asking my dad to help us move. The building should have been condemned, the downstairs apartment not even habitable. When Dad and four of our guy friends tried to haul the fridge up the narrow back stairway it got so wedged in that it remained stuck there, halfway up, our entire three month residency. We never ate there anyway, so a refrigerator was optional, but with a blocked exit we'd have been shit outta luck if a fire'd broken out.

"I'll never bring your mother over here. She'd throw up," Dad said.

What could I say to that? He needed a joint, desperately. It was bad enough, him being exposed to my girlfriends but the guys! With their long hair, ripped, faded bell bottoms, disrespecting attitudes. He didn't lose it. I have to give him that.

I chose royal blue marine paint with kelly green trim for my boudoir. It had a shiny luminescent glow. For some reason, all of the doors were missing to the rooms so I substituted with a groovy India print tapestry topped with strings of multi-colored beads.

Even though I didn't condemn anyone's habit or drug of choice there was a general feeling among hippies that heroin (smack) was over the edge. In all of our experimentation, I believed that if I ever tried smack, I'd be dead. Heroin had that sort of cachet shaping my opinion about its dire consequences after two of my high school friends, Mike and Johnny got hooked.

Shooting the heroin into their asses initially, in high school, a year later the downward spiral landed Johnny in lock-up as he tragically succumbed to the substance's unrelenting stranglehold. We sat across from each other at a table in the secure visiting room of the psych ward where he ended up, me trying desperately to think of something to say. Completely zoned out, communication with him was useless. Resisting the urge to take his hand for fear it would elicit too much emotion, fearing spilled tears, I tried to vibe my encouragement. His gentle soul still visible, he smiled at me with such warmth. Lost in withdrawal, Johnny was incoherent.

I wanted to say, "I love you, man," but instead, abandoning words, I sat in silence.

Life ended tragically for Johnny hanging himself not many months after his release.

Mike kept on riding high for several more years, using notoriously outrageous means to procure ready cash. Always in need of more money to supply his habit, he sold my roommate, Teri, and me a hot stereo. We were instructed to pick it up at a sleazy second floor apartment on Lake Street. A universe away from our love and peace league, this raunchy dump was a smack haven. Walking past two grimy, stick thin guys cooking the mixture over a flame, I stared as one wrapped a rubber cord around his arm watching his vein bulge from the boney forearm anticipating the needle's relief. Teri and I followed Mike into the living room where the stereo was piled. Two more surly toughs were standing guard on either side of a picture window with shotguns peering through the hazy film to the street below. What the hell was all this about? Teri and I exchanged puzzled looks. How stupid were we to be there? How fucking dumb? Suddenly the scene blew into an uproar as yelling thundered from the hallway. Bodies scrambled in confusion, rushing and shoving to escape certain arrest. I smashed the money into Mike's hand, trying not to drop our purchase as we tore out the back door and down the stairs. Ignoring the tumult behind us, we piled into our car and sped away. Not until we got home, behind locked doors, could we breathe a sigh of relief, thankful we got out unscathed. The next day we arrived home to find the stereo ripped off. That was the last deal with Mike. We never confronted him but just assumed he'd stung us. It was the smack.

8

Jim and Nick walking on 31st and Pillsbury

Occasionally, drug busts and dry spells diminished our dope market to seed straining utility. The horde of stems and seeds were swished through a strainer scrounging enough raw material to get high. Jim brought this tall, straight looking dude over to my place one night in a desperate search for a joint. One of the reasons, or the sole reason I took that apartment was because it was right across the street from Jim's place. I wanted to ratchet our relationship up a notch, maybe even to monogamy. In stark contrast to Jim's lovely, flowing red mane, the guy he brought with him was wearing tan khaki pants, a light blue button down shirt, and he had short, black hair, not the sort I was used to seeing in my bedroom. Suspect of anyone with hair above the ear, Jim introduced Nick, an old frat buddy. My attraction to his deep, dark eyes was immediate. Quiet and a little nervous, maybe even shy, he didn't say much besides hello. I gave him a pass, Jim seemingly vouching for him. It didn't appear to be his scene, acting sort of uncomfortable with all of us sitting cross legged on my bed. He sized me up; I caught his glance checking out my nipples poking through the tight tank top, blonde hair draped across my shoulders. Indulging in the attention from two guys, I lapped it up, sending out, "you want some of this," vibes. Sifting enough for a small pipe full, I watched the mysterious stranger toke away having no clue he'd be my husband within two years.

A few months later I saw him on the University of Minnesota campus. Noticing him above the crowd, the instant attraction felt providential. Jim and I, along with hundreds of other students, were in front of Coffman Union protesting the Vietnam War. When he waved at Jim I didn't recognize him from our first encounter, but something was deeply familiar. He'd undergone a definite transformation.

"Whoa, who's the guy with the legs?" I asked Jim, eyeing mystery man up and down.

Long, lean, six foot plus, dark, wavy shoulder length hair, mustache, elephant bells, cowboy boots, this sultry stranger piqued my interest.

Jim said, "We were in the same fraternity together. PhiDelts. I dropped out but he's still finishing up. Don't you remember, I brought him up to your bedroom to find some dope?"

"Him? No way, that's not the same guy!"

I thought he was gorgeous, hair now luxurious waves, a decided improvement. Would he remember me?

Making our way in that direction, out of the corner of his mouth, Jim said, "Don't say anything about the dope."

"Mmkay, gotcha."

Following Nick's lead, I feigned ignorance.

"This is Anne," Jim said, introducing me to him and his girlfriend, Cindy.

"Hi, how ya doin'?"

Smiling, thinking, oh yeah, I made an impression. He knew exactly who I was. That bit of kismet, energy exchange. Unmistakable.

Learning from Jim that Nick and Cindy were extremely involved and had been for two years, I thought, oh shit. Cindy looked like an Allie McGraw double, apparently not on board with the hippie movement being a Gamma Phi (just the most elite sorority) and pretty much had her life mapped out. They didn't seem like a good match, or so I conjured, as I devised a strategy to get to know this guy a lot better.

Over the next few months Nick became my confidante. Our respective relationships were problematic. His girlfriend didn't dig the hippie direction he was heading in and Jim's behavior was suspect, at best, overtly distant and unfaithful at worst. I knew it wasn't cool to question Jim about his infidelities so I poured my heartache out to Nick. Free love was the norm; relationships weren't often exclusive so to be bummed out about Jim's myriad of sleeping partners was not hip. But it wasn't ever that simple. It made for some ugly situations when Jim and I'd be high and he'd inform me that so and so was staying over, not me. God, you fucking asshole. Giving the appearance of nonchalance, I'd split for home to ruminate, write through the lonely night, and figure out how to get back at him. In the beginning, I thought Jim and I were exclusive. Mistaking his initial attentiveness for

109

fidelity, I soaked it up. But after a couple of months, Jim became aloof, even ignoring me when we'd be at the same party. Hurt and confused by the rejection, craving the love I was so desperate for, I'd retaliate slinking upstairs with some random guy, making sure Jim saw.

But now being friends with Nick, platonically, was refreshingly innocent. Without the sexual component in the equation, the relaxed atmosphere as we rapped, hanging out, smoking dope into the wee hours was uncomplicated. Our tight bond of friendship developed commiserating over unfulfilling relationships.

"I was slated to go into the Air Force," Nick told me one night, as we sat on the multi-colored braided rug in his apartment living room.

"Really?! I can't imagine why you'd be into that. Isn't that the last place you'd want to be?"

"Yeah, well, before I got into drugs and got my shit together I was pretty right wing. I came into college a Barry Goldwater supporter. That's all changed in the last year."

He explained how Jim and Bill were in his fraternity but had gone the hippie route, along with several other brothers. Their influence, along with dope, had altered his values.

"They flew me to Michigan for the whole Air Force orientation last year. I was pretty impressed with the pilots walking around the base in their flight suits. They're on such huge ego trips. I went through the physical, the testing, and passed everything."

"So what changed your mind?"

"I found out I could fly without planes!" Nick said, cracking up.

"How did you get out of it, then, if you'd gone up there and went through the whole process?"

"I never signed the final papers. Lucky, huh?"

"Can you imagine where your life would have ended up?"

"Ya, take a guess! Vietnam," he flatly stated.

Escaping the Vietnam War was paramount for every guy I knew.

Nick continued, in no uncertain terms, "No way I'm goin,' I'll hide out in Canada. It's too crazy. I've had ten friends from high school die over there."

"God, that's insane! No one should be over there," I avowed seeing the impact that revelation had on him. Fear, sadness, and confusion swirled through our conversation as I listened intently, trying to understand.

"Yeah, in June I was in one guy's wedding and in August I went to his funeral."

"Shit."

"I can't hardly comprehend it. What are we even doing over there? Dying for some illegal conflict? What the hell is going on? Another guy I graduated with was shot up, and after a week or so was shipped home in a bag. His dad wanted to see the body. Who wouldn't, just to be sure it was your son, right? So they unzipped the bag and he was still all bloody, covered with all of his guts hanging out, dirt ground in, just like they pulled him off the field. That's the way his dad had to see him."

"God! What a freak-out! God, that's horrible. What assholes!"

"I'm never goin'," Nick repeated, "never."

The depth I'd found with Nick was a glaring indictment exposing my partner's shortcomings. In a natural progression, we ended our current attachments in anticipation of the potential direction of our friendship.

Nick and I were blown away at how we catapulted to couple status. The catalyst was MDA. That's what we called it, known today as Ecstasy. We scored this fabulous batch from Boulder, Colorado.

"What a rush!" Nick sighed.

Flush-faced, we sat across from each other in the ratty, over-stuffed chairs at our friend Gary's apartment on 31st and Pillsbury with my ex, Jim, his new lady, and four others. In the initial stage, 'coming on' to the MDA, we laid back, immobilized as the blood stream and heart were flooded with a massive infusion of chemicals. Whatever hazard this actually posed to the system didn't concern us. The goal was to come as close to the edge of reality/sanity without going irretrievably over.

"Yaaah," I replied, breathlessly. That's all I could verbalize.

Our eyes locked with a penetrating gaze as brain waves melded together, transcending time and space. Maybe it was only a minute, but it was forever. Almost levitating, floating towards one another, drawn right inside each other, it felt like electricity: a powerful, defining jolt, instantly unifying our hearts into a single being—one soul, one psyche, one entity as our arms wrapped around in a tender embrace. There were no words, just vibes. Mind vibrations were the true communication. With mouths agape, our friends were left awestruck as they watched us flow down the hallway and out the back door hand in hand, smiling ear to ear.

The Uptown district was home to counter culture adherents as well as a hub of illegal activity. Its proximity to the lakes, and funky alternative atmosphere was unusually conducive to self-expression. It was an oasis of freedom. Just to *be*, blending in without fear or judgement, strolling the neighborhood or hitching along Lake Street and Hennepin Avenue.

We spent the remainder of the day without a care, in the most ethereal state of nirvana meandering around Lakes Harriet and Calhoun. Miles later, back at my apartment passion exploded melding into each other's body sealing our relationship with an all-night love-in. After a week of the same, MDA, love, floating in oblivion, he moved in. Along with our significant evolution, Nick and I tacitly understood the need for subterfuge with our parents. Technically, he lived with Jeff, our Vietnam vet buddy, in the apartment next to mine which was the perfect cover for our 'rents.' Living together was 'living in sin,' the universally held taboo in the 60's. There wasn't any reason to involve the 'rents in any of our life style decisions. I knew exactly how any conversation of that nature would unfold. What we had was beautiful, miraculous, far out. We found true love in the midst of that tumultuous era.

Neither of us had a job, so reinforcing savings from previous work dealing drugs we earned enough for rent and food. You weren't truly a hippie unless you had at least one dog. No matter how small the apartment, all of our gatherings included several dogs. We'd inherited ours, claiming her after the owner wouldn't reimburse us the seventy dollars to have her leg stitched up. The beautiful, white German shepherd had suffered an accident while we cared for her. I think they were actually relieved being rid of her. We named her Dweezil, after Frank Zappa's son. Relying on her alert shepherd instincts for fiercely loyal protection and defense, Dweezil developed into our early warning system.

With connections to dealers in Arizona, California and Colorado we could buy kilos of pot cheaply enough to have extra for our own needs. Nick had completed his course work at college, with a major in Political Science but needed to write his thesis to earn his degree. His 'rents were sorely disappointed with their 'Sonny Boy', their only child, as weeks, then months rendered that likelihood miniscule. We turned a deaf ear to their frequent complaints, drugs our only priority, as the days revolved around that pursuit. Many of the substances required processing, such as a kilo of pot. It came to us as a two pound brick, about the size of a masonry brick. Compacted so tightly, we would spend hours prying it apart on the kitchen table covered with newspaper carefully weighing nickel and dime bags. A half ounce was a nickel bag (baggie) that sold for five dollars; an ounce was a dime bag for ten. The underground kept us apprised of shipment details. Like a network that extended from our trusted circle and outward, each person discreetly guarded the secrets, being faithful to a code of conduct. If anyone didn't pay up or was short on weight, they were duly noted. Integrity was highly valued in our transactions.

After two months, the MDA having run out, the second drug run to Boulder had a secondary motive, or it could have been the primary objective. Nick's old girlfriend, Cindy, had evolved and was getting into the hippie movement, in a sanitized, Carly Simon version and living in Colorado. I don't know what possessed Nick to disclose that pertinent fact when he got back with our supply of the "love drug" but I was shocked listening to his revelation.

"So you stayed with her?" I ventured hesitantly, so scared to hear the answer, trying to sound cool, all detached, like, "You're a free man, I don't have any claims on your life, we just live together."

Nick probably thought I'd hear about Cindy. I loved his candor and wanted to trust him, even with his ex.

"Did you sleep with her?" God, please say no, my mind screamed. Don't let this be like Jim. I don't think I can handle another betrayal.

"No."

It was the right answer, the one I believed. I didn't know if it was the truth but it was such a relief.

"I didn't know she was going to be there," he offered. "It was kinda weird. She was staying with her friend that lived with the dealer. Bizarre, huh?"

So just one huge coincidence, I thought, but said, "Oh."

I wanted to cry, to run out the door, down the block screaming, "FUCK YOU!"

Didn't he realize how much I adored him with his dark, soft eyes and long wavy brown locks? How could he be so fucking dense? Three years my senior, there was an aura about him; introspection, depth and maturity that I wanted to penetrate. I wanted to know everything going on inside his Greek, philosophical brain, but his very depth insured a lengthy process. That silky, sensual, triangular patch of hair at the base of his spine was so exotically masculine. God, it was exciting sliding my fingers through it while he lay on top of me. But now, here, I had to remain mellow. I had to project the persona that convinced him he'd made the right choice. That I wasn't clingy or desperate, or uncool.

"So you may not have come back?" I asked, my voice deceptively calm.

"I wouldn't have done that to you. It wouldn't have worked out with her. She just doesn't get it."

115

Holy shit, if he could have seen my heart flutter. I won. ME. He came back. It was settled. I wanted to totally eradicate the conversation and the event. Eventually, the ex's shadows didn't bother me, mine or his. We gave each other that security.

Jeff, our best friend and Nick's supposed roommate, fresh from the jungles of Vietnam, was trying to figure out what'd just happened to his life. The three of us spent hours together rapping, playing albums, watching the visuals on T.V. He slowly evolved from the physically and emotionally shattered vet to an anti-war freak like us, hating the government, the establishment, turning on and tuning out. He reinforced, first hand in graphic detail, the immorality and the horror of the war. Quiet, brooding, angry, and broken-hearted, Jeff unfolded his ordeal bit by bit, slowly verbalizing the details as he was able. How any young man in his early twenties could still function normally after what he'd been through was phenomenal. Wounded so severely, Jeff was the only soldier in the amputee ward that lucked out and kept all his limbs.

Jeff related the saga this way:

"After having already set up two positions of a blocking force on the riverside, eight of us were left to complete the final one. There was a sweep going on by the South Vietnamese, the ARVN, (Army of the Republic of Vietnam) supposedly, our ally. We understood the enemy, the Vietcong, to be on the opposite side but in truth, they'd already crossed over. Walking into this clearing, we surprised twelve of them standing there. We gave chase as some dropped their weapons and fled. The radio man with my unit received reconnaissance from the helicopter overhead informing us that the enemy ran unarmed into the wood line.

116

I said, 'Let's go get 'em.'

The troop's response was unanimous. As we stepped into the wood line, my watch broke, falling off my wrist. In the second I bent down to pick it up and put it into my pocket, the machine gun fire ripped past me. Immediately, fifteen feet to my left there was screaming. One of my guys was lying face down in about eighteen inches of water. Stepping into the clearing, I was hit. Blown back, slamming down, my weapon flew into the mango swamp. Frantically searching, I took a grenade and threw it, hitting a Nipa palm fifteen feet away, the shrapnel narrowly missing my head. Dropping down completely under water for cover, I realized how badly I was hit when I heard air sucking through the holes in my body. Every time I tried to get to my man they'd drop the barrel down right at the surface, skipping bullets across to finish me off. I had to back away, leaving my man there, his head partially exposed, brains sticking out. He was dead. I was sure of it. The helicopter, a scout, came within view. They motioned me to go this one direction. I was kinda walking, getting up, stumbling, up, down, stumbling, up, then down. I got about fifty meters. The chopper dropped down but the water was too deep. They motioned me in another direction. Somehow I made it to where they could recover me. The gunner scrambled out to help me and this memory is so vivid: when he jumped out running, he'd forgotten to take his helmet off, all attached with the wires so his head jerks backwards, yanking him down. The humor wasn't lost on me, even under those gruesome circumstances. He got me into the chopper, and as we lifted up, I'm in the back, all by myself, looking up, looking around, observing a few of my guys, and everything goes bright red. Bright red. Blood. I passed out.

In the aide station, the first time I regained consciousness, dozens of people were rushing around. Nurses, doctors, medics. It was seconds, then I passed out again. The next time I came to, there was no one there.

I thought to myself, "I fuckin' died. It ain't that bad. It didn't hurt that much."

But I was in a morphine haze. When I woke up the next time I was lucid enough to comprehend what was going on. The brigade commander, the battalion commander, brigade XO, and the battalion XO were all in the same helicopter, which is a huge no-no. You couldn't have that many command people in one helicopter. On their way into the base, a loaded gun ship was heading out when they collided, killing thirteen people, including all the command staff, the pilots, even people on the ground which accounted for all of the frenetic activity at the aide station. They shipped me by helicopter to the 3rd field hospital at Saigon. Trying to equalize the blood loss, my arm and shoulder had been tightly packed while two blood bags were continually pumped into me. Wheeling me to the x-ray unit, losing his grip amidst all the gore, the gurney aid dropped my arm letting it flop backwards, straight down at a forty-five degree angle four inches above the elbow.

I screamed in agony, "You motherfucker!"

This female nurse, a colonel, pulled up short, remarking, "You can't talk to us that way."

I shot back, "Oh, fuck you. I'll talk to you any goddamn way I please. It's my arm you fuckin' dropped!"

Aside from that particular incident, they actually treated me pretty well. The first surgery at TanSonNhut air base aide station was a stopgap procedure that enabled me to hold enough blood to survive the transport to Japan. I had two more surgeries in thirty days wondering every minute whether I'd keep my limb. It was a mess with bones shattered, the radial nerve severed.

Doctors of one opinion said, "Yank it."

Others, on my side, were saying, "It's not infected. It could just be traumatized. We need to give it more time."

My orthopedic surgeon was adamant, "There's no point in taking it yet."

He won.

A guy lying across from me, after having lost part of one leg, a little below the knee, didn't get his dressing changed for an entire day. In their defense, it was a horrible place for the medics to function, but through their neglect, gangrene set in. They had to keep chopping more and more off. Both legs mid-thigh length by the time he was released. He started out missing part of a leg but because of that one day, both legs were amputated. Another six months at the Kansas military base hospital and I'd gotten to the discharge point."

I couldn't believe the lack of bitterness in Jeff. Deeply, profoundly wounded and shell-shocked, he retained his soft heart. It took him a long time to express the horror of that experience. Instead of talking, for several months he chose to be alone with his thoughts trying to sort through the madness. Solidified in our anti-war stance, Jeff's ordeal reinforced our intention of running to Canada if Nick was drafted. The records were either destroyed or damaged when the draft office was bombed that year in Minneapolis. We were ecstatic. Nick drew a high number when the lottery was instituted meaning it was very unlikely he'd be called. We breathed a sigh of relief but still kept a wary eye convinced of the lying government's corruption.

Nixon's adamant avowal, "I am not a crook!" was ludicrous, a mockery.

God, how we hated him.

Best friends, the three of us hung out, getting loaded, playing albums hour upon hour in the apartment on 28th and Park. The once grand old mansion was sectioned into six units, ours being one of the three lower. Each floor had a community bathroom—very European, but it was really quite disgusting. Monte lived adjacent to our living room in the original formal dining room, separated only by the sliding double doors having been nailed or glued together. We weren't sure and didn't care. No friends, family, nothing, we never heard a peep from Monte's room. Exchanging hellos in the hall one day we dubbed him Monte because of his likeness to the game show host, Monte Hall. Otherwise he was completely nondescript except for one oddity. WDGY, the hip radio station played the uncut version of "In-A-Gadda-Da-Vida" every night at ten. Monte would crank his radio full blast and we'd all groove for the entire seven minutes. And then silence again. We wondered if he got high from all the dope fumes through the cracks in the door. Sometimes we'd compete, ala battle of the bands, drowning him out with our stereo just to be assholes. Couldn't just let him have his one thrill of the day. That huge old house shook from the volume but no one ever complained. Nick and I had the most amazing sound system that my brother gave us from one of his heists. Ricky followed in my

120

footsteps down the path of destruction, his big sister supplying him and all of his high school pals with pot. He was a wildly popular football star.

The 'rents constantly questioned our lifestyle, "How do you pay your rent, if you don't work? Is this what you're going to do with your life? Why are you wasting your life?"

Everything Nick and I told them was a lie including our roommate situation. We decided to play it a bit straight, finding jobs as cover, in an attempt get them off our backs. It was too intense wondering if they'd pop in. That'd be just like mine.

When the City of Minneapolis ran an ad for paving crew openings Nick and Teri's boyfriend, Bill, jumped at the opportunity. For hippies, it was a dream job, paying extremely well while allowing for blue jeans, long hair, and altered consciousness. Both of them got hired after camping out overnight waiting in line to apply. Nick became a raker (highly skilled professional) on the asphalt crew making sound use of his Political Science major. He and his new work buddy, Mike, would fire up a joint on each break while the rest of the crew, older cronies, passed around their brown paper bag. The foreman sat in his truck and slept.

I was hired by an auto insurance firm, doing office work, typing, and answering phones. My straight, high school mini-skirt camouflaged my hippie alter ego, landing my new position with a sashay through the front door. "PollyEsther" by day, "TieDyanna" by night. Bored witless in three months, I moved on to caregiver in a facility called The Guardians. It was a private residence home in Minnetonka for severely disabled children, ranging in age from a few months to about ten years. Straight out of a '60 Minutes' episode, you were introduced to a beautiful, caring façade and then discovered the ghastly nightmare behind closed doors.

Children were bagged up in restraining nets tied to metal cribs from 5:30p.m. until 7:30a.m, many covering themselves with feces. They were force-fed, in the interest of time expediency, cold oatmeal mush. Some of the children were actually treatable but parents had been convinced of the efficacy of this sensible, logical solution. I didn't last long at The Guardians. It broke my heart to see their yearning eyes, the inhumanity of it all. A few years later it was shut down after an investigation exposed its practices. I would forever wonder what happened to those defenseless, abused children.

There's an island in Northern Minnesota, near Brainerd, on Moose Lake. Approximately a half mile wide, in the middle of nowhere surrounded by crystal clear frigid water and virgin pine forest, it seemed like the ideal setting for an acid trip. One of Nick's workmates from the paving crew, Mike, his girlfriend, and another couple we'd never met, comprised our entourage.

"Well, absolutely," I said, when Nick told me the plan. "Groovy, what could be more far out? Sounds great. When we goin?"

Our plan was to drive the four hours, rent canoes, and paddle our way over to the island for a wild night of tripping and partying. I was concerned, though, when I realized that our dogs, Dweezil and her offspring, ten month old Jasper, would have to swim the half mile distance, our supplies leaving no space for them. I probably would have died trying to save them if they'd faltered but they swam easily alongside our canoe. We didn't encounter another person or boat the entire journey to the remote location. It met all my expectations, having an atmosphere so opposite of city neighborhoods, the only sounds being loons, owls, and our own laughter. We set up the tents, built a campfire, and grilled some burgers before embarking on our psychedelic odyssey.

"Here," doling a hit of acid to each person, Mike handed us a bottle of sangria, "Wash it down with this."

We passed the bottle, swilling it down. Sitting around the crackling flames, we came on watching the dance of the golden glow framed against the black backdrop of a million twinkling lights. There were no mosquitoes, no crickets, just serene peace. No one spoke; nothing broke the silence that pervaded dusk except the piercing howls of wolves interrupting from the mainland.

As Nick and I lay next to each other, arms and legs wrapped warmly around, he began breathing heavily.

"You okay?" I whispered.

He didn't answer, but nodded slightly up and down, eyes implying, "so-so."

I got a different sense, though, my perceptions so acute; it was as if I could see right into his body. Abruptly, he sat up, pulling his knees into his chest, doubling over. The wave of nausea made him groan as he shot upright, stumbling away from the others sitting around the firelight. I followed, helping steady his faltering steps. About ten yards away, Nick dropped to his knees retching up the wine-acid-burger concoction. I never heard anyone throw up that way. It sounded like he had to yell it out from the depths of his innards. Instead of expelling it with a few surges, he continued on and on. Silently slinking away to their tents, the retreating shadows gave us privacy. I couldn't do anything except offer Nick water from time to time, hand him a paper towel, rub his back and stay close. Too high to be petrified, I struggled to stay cognizant.

123

"He'll be okay, he'll stop, he will," I kept telling myself. God, he had to.

All the way down to his toes, it was as if Nick was trying to turn inside out in order to expel and expunge the contents of his gut. After a long time (there's no way to gauge on acid, with or without a watch) he lay back against my lap, breathing normally, exhausted. We inched away from the ghastly pile of pink puke but couldn't muster the strength to get to our tent. Eventually, the northern chill forced our limbs to move. In the sleeping bags we thawed with Dweezil and Jasper sprawled across our feet.

When we emerged in daylight, the other two couples had already pulled up stakes, wrapped up their gear and were waiting by their canoes. God, they couldn't get away from us fast enough. None of them asked Nick how he felt the entire uncomfortable, ride home.

"Assholes, thanks for the fucking help!" I thought. Christ, what a fiasco!

At the end of the summer Mike made an appointment to have a mole removed from the back of his neck.

"The doctor numbed it and took off the outer layer. After several more slices, and as many Novocain shots, he gave up," Mike explained to Nick.

"He said he didn't feel comfortable going any deeper in the office."

"Shit," Nick said, "That's heavy. Are you going to be okay?"

"Oh, yeah, it never hurt. They'll biopsy it, yeah, I'll be fine."

When Nick told me about it, I said, "Is he going to have surgery or any more treatment?"

Nick's casual reply was, "I didn't ask him, but I'm sure he'll go back, at least for the results."

Mike was dead, in two months, from melanoma.

9

The Unwedding

Jeff had an old VW Bug convertible that was the envy of all our friends. Gray, funky, but so fucking cool. Bombing around all hours, loaded, the radio cranked, top down, free as the breeze, it felt like a miniature wind-up toy. One evening before dark, Jeff, Nick and I happened to be tooling around downtown Minneapolis when a rain storm hit. Instead of frantically pulling over to yank the top up on the Bug, we just let the rain soak us. With the radio blaring, singing at the top of our lungs, we meandered down Hennepin Avenue. People were in the midst of dashing for cover, ducking under awnings and entryways, when they'd catch the sound of the music. Their looks were priceless. Whether it was incredulous jaw drops or bursts of laughter, the drenching we got was well worth witnessing the surprise and shock! Puddles of water collected on the floor and seats, we were freezing our asses off but high and deliriously happy, the moment was unrivaled. Loose, young and wild. Our only goal.

What happened to our friend, Stan, was probably inevitable. That it didn't befall more of us was pure luck or a miracle. Nick, Jeff, Teri, Bill, and I dropped acid at Jim and Stan's apartment on 22nd and 22nd one temperate fall night. It was billed as the strongest acid ever, black licorice. Completely debilitating us, we came on for about a half hour as it took over. Lying on the living room floor I was consumed by one thought; if I didn't will my heart to beat, it would stop. Thump, thump-thump, thump, thump-thump. Good. Alright. I'm still alive. My tripping brain couldn't determine if it had been an hour or ten minutes but suddenly an argument in the kitchen between Stan and his girlfriend, Paula grabbed my attention. She was explaining why she couldn't live with him anymore and had stopped by to deliver the death blow. Maybe it was entirely the acid, maybe he was a latent schizophrenic that the acid manifested, but their encounter decimated him. The timing couldn't have been worse. I was hard pressed to put two words together in the simplest conversation and there was Paula dumping him, expounding their differences in lurid detail.

"I can't be with you anymore. It's just not working, I'm not happy," she whined.

Stan tried so hard to convince her, "We can make it work; we have to, for the baby."

He was high on acid and she was informing him that although she was carrying his baby, she was going to go live with her eastern mystic guru. I couldn't believe what I was hearing. He snapped. It literally blew his mind. Something broke irrevocably, spiraling him further and further down. Over the next few months the chasm of mental illness consumed him. His parents had him committed, his treatment consisting of electro-convulsive therapy, not unlike *One Flew Over the Cuckoo's Nest*. We agonized over how to get him out and stoned and deprogrammed.

"He just needs to get out of there and have some pot," Jeff explained to me after visiting him, "He's in there somewhere, I know it. When you look into his eyes, it's still him down deep. We have to get him sprung."

The first few shock treatments did zap Stan back into coherence. That's when Jim and Jeff saw him. But his parents didn't want that hippie son so they kept going until he was knocked/shocked into submission. Way too many. He was never the same. We believed "they" The Establishment, turned a brilliant dental school student into a janitor, pushing a broom, relegated to living with his parents the rest of his life. None of us would admit the possibility that it was our fault, our irresponsibility. Acid.

Keith, our obsessive, compulsive, paranoid schizophrenic, post-traumatic stress disordered friend, didn't need a job because his wife, Bon, was the bread winner. Peppermint BonBon, as Nick and I called her, was the straightest of our bunch. She actually taught elementary school. While we'd be hangin' out, smoking dope at their place, she'd be doing lessons, setting her hair, hand-washing her pantyhose and going to bed early. Keith was always rambling on about anti-government conspiracies, imagining phone taps, planning escape routes and his sweet, good-natured wife was making wonderful home cooked meals in nylons and dresses. We didn't really question it. That's just the way it was. Trying to fit in, to be a good sport, she'd attempt a tiny toke of dope but would invariably cough her brains out.

Keith had this fantasy of writing and composing a rock opera and becoming The Who. He and Jim tried learning guitar but no talent, no incentive, and no discipline assured failure. Smoking more pot than anyone I'd ever known, pretty much constantly, his life operated on a very unreal/surreal plain. One of the fantasies Keith entertained was thinking he was the best driver in the Midwest, possibly the U.S., having all the traffic lights timed every place he drove so he never had to stop. It was uncanny. If that meant he had to step it up to forty-five or fifty miles per hour on the side streets, so be it. As intense as the Popeye Doyle getaway chase, and almost as nerve wracking, I hated riding with him!

Due to his prior military training, Keith managed to keep us warm and dry at the Steven's Point Rock Festival in 1970. Hippies and pouring rain at an open-air festival were a given. Hundreds of stoned out freaks littering the hillside, soaked to the bone from the deluge, tripped through the night. Not us. Keith came equipped to hunker down for a month. Replete with tent, tarp, shovel, and Coleman stove; he was prodigiously deft, digging a six inch trench encircling the site where the tent was pitched. We thought he was Looney Tunes but gave him credit when we were some of the only dry fans there. Buffy St. Marie sang her throaty tremolo Saturday night along with an amazing line-up: Taj Mahal, Steve Miller, Nick Berry, Paul Butterfield Blues Band among others. Not that it mattered. The entire weekend was completely over-shadowed by the senseless violence.

Gunshots shattered the pastoral setting as the Chicago chapter of Hell's Angels and freaks clashed at dawn. Bikers disdained our pansy-ass, love-peace mentality and we were scared shitless of them after the '69 Altamont fiasco. At that California rock concert, Hell's Angels, who'd been hired as security, were responsible for killing five people in altercations. Scrambling out of our sleeping bags, we pulled up stakes, piling all our gear onto the tent, dragging it, running from the line of fire, avoiding chains, bottles and rocks hurling through the air as hundreds of love children charged down the hill defying the onslaught. Explosive hostility fueled the confrontation as rampaging freaks backed down the Angels, who narrowly escaped with their lives. From our retreat down the hillside we were shocked to see hippies in blind rage stomp one abandoned motorcycle to smithereens.

I don't know why we even bothered with peyote but the high, totally mellow with profoundly spiritual visions was worth the initial challenge; puking your guts out, retching for an hour or more. They were innocently called buttons, like cute as a button. Not so much. Carlos Castaneda taught an alternative reality through Yaqui shaman don Juan Matus; peyote being one of the avenues to understanding and enlightenment. In our search for truth, for something other than our parent's middle class values, we gladly embraced the fascinating and revolutionary ideas espoused in his books *The Teachings of Don Juan* and *Journey to Ixtlan*. It was an ongoing discovery, a trip into the vast unknown. Gary came up with an experiment for ingesting the plant. His solution was to grind up the buttons into a fine powder with a rolling pin. Filling gelatin capsules with the peyote, we swallowed ten to twelve and then used every ounce of fortitude to keep them down. I always puked with peyote. Every goddamn time. But the trick was to keep the substance ingested long enough to acquire the high. This took about an hour. It was murder for the first part but after the blow out, the singular effects were undeniable. One of the Sioux medicine men described the trip in loving detail:

130

Grandfather Peyote unites us, cuts us off from the outer world to bring us into ourselves, to understand joy. You may see people bend themselves into a ball like they experienced in the womb. Time and space grow; shrink and entire lifetimes are compressed into just seconds of insight.

I had the opportunity to put my new life lessons to the test, endeavoring to see the truth, whether or not justice would prevail, later that summer, when a drug dealer was shot to death during a bust. The story went that the pigs got heavy handed, firing prematurely; of course we totally sympathized with the poor defenseless hippie shot in cold blood. The outrage compounded over the charge that medical help wasn't summoned immediately and the victim bled to death, needlessly. My friends and I marched into the downtown Minneapolis courthouse with about a hundred other protesters to stage a sit-in and confront the law and order authority of Mayor Charles Stenvig. After several hours of peaceful chanting, the mayor emerged from his office agreeing to meet with no more than five representatives. Our friend, Keith, was somehow among those invited into this supposed negotiation. Crazy, stoned-out Keith! The rest of us were ordered to disperse. When we refused, a cop equipped with bull horn explained the ultimatum, one time.

As the tactical (attack) squad was deployed in force, the final civil instruction was delivered, "File out, orderly, and no one will get hurt."

Every member of the hugely menacing battalion was dressed in solid black, armored with helmets, boots, vests, face shields, holding clubs gripped chest length. I was instantly persuaded. The squad came from either end of the corridor

131

occupied by the protestors. Lining shoulder to shoulder, one end to the other they moved ahead a few paces in rank and waited. Holy shit! Well, that was it for us little whiners. I thought, okay, I'll go, just let me out of here.

The ranks, opening a foot wide down the middle, left an aisle for one intense retreat. You could feel the animosity, the hate-filled vibes from those hardcore establishment heavies. They would have loved an excuse to smash our hippie skulls in, but no one gave them the opportunity. Nothing ever did come of it, the mayoral consultation. Keith said it was all a sham. The negotiators simply sat in the office as the mayor informed them that they would also receive an escort to the street, post haste, after we'd been dispersed.

Well into our drug hazed cloud of dope one evening, Nick, Jeff and I were confronted with a bizarre situation. Our apartment on Park Avenue had one long stairway, about twenty steps, leading from the front entrance to the upper units. Following the hallway, past three apartments, the back staircase was so dark and narrow that no one ever used that exit. Every sound was audible from our lower three rooms: the front door slamming, footsteps on the stairway, apartment doors shutting, and essentially, anything that transpired within the thin walls.

This particular night as we zoned out listening to albums, we heard heavy ominous sounding footsteps marching up the stairs. I turned the stereo volume down to listen. Above us, we heard pounding, followed by unintelligible conversation, and then after a few minutes, the boots tromped down the back stairway. The exit being accessible only through our apartment, the clamor quieted at our door. Jeff responded to the rapping, as Nick and I sat, paranoid. Behind his back, we understood Jeff's waving hand; a cautionary signal.

Nick perceptively slid an album cover over the dope on the coffee table. Not a second too soon as five pigs in full riot gear filed through our kitchen, then the living room to the front door. We were speechless, breathless, not wanting to exhale a puff of marijuana smoke!

Nick and I sat in stunned silence. They acted about as freaked out as we were, keeping their heads and eyes straight ahead, bee-lining for the door.

They'd explained to Jeff that they were investigating a domestic disturbance and sort of got turned around upstairs.

"Is there another way out of the building, without going through the upstairs?" the lead guy asked Jeff from the back doorway.

"Well, you can come through here," Jeff offered, nonchalantly, not wanting to create suspicion.

Politely, the cop answered, "You sure it's no trouble?"

"Nah, this way," he said, motioning them through our smoky apartment.

That they didn't take note of anything going on in our place, though, was all very odd. We deduced without a warrant they really didn't have any business pursuing the obvious.

Even though Nick and I shunned convention, disdaining tradition by living together, I convinced him that marriage was a logical progression to our relationship. It was too much hassle trying to keep up the subterfuge, living in sin, avoiding our 'rents. On a bleak February 20th, 1971, we made it official at a justice of the peace located in a greasy smelling office above a pizza parlor in St. Paul. Betraying my bravado, the hemline of my gray minidress shook as Nick and I stood with clasped hands before the officiant.

A few weeks prior Edith had tried to horn in on our plans or lack of plans.

"Can't we have it in the church?" she asked me.

Anticipating the onslaught, I said, "On one condition, that you don't do anything else, tell anyone else, or make it into a big deal."

"Well, I don't see why you don't want your grandparents there. It will break Grandma's heart. And our friends, your friends?" Mom argued.

"Because it's just between us. We don't want the conventional ceremony, the hoopla, and all that bullshit."

"I just don't understand you. How is that bad?" she asked.

Oh God, I thought. Why did I ever tell them? The guilt, the pressure, bummer. Shit. No way was I having my grandpa there. The crime he'd perpetrated against me was not forgotten. I couldn't deal with him. If that meant Grandma couldn't come either, then so be it. The only answer was to keep it to our immediate families. Like a fool I'd let Mom talk me into having a wedding in the small chapel area of Mount Olivet, the Lutheran church where I'd been confirmed. I felt I had to make some sort of concession, which was so strange. Whose wedding was it? But when I got wind of the next ingredient to her plan I knew it had to be squelched.

"You what?" I yelled, questioning Mom.

"Just to our relatives." she answered. "How else will they know?"

"Incredible! Who gave you permission to order announcements? What's wrong with you?"

God, I was so pissed off! I couldn't believe it, but then really, I could. I should have never said yes to the chapel. That gave her the courage to take it to the next level.

"It's just a few," she replied.

"Then that's it. It's off. You are not going to force us into something Nick or I don't want. You had to go too far. You had to take over, step on my toes. You just don't get it!" I screamed.

"What do you mean?"

Emphatically, I stated, "This is how it's going to be. I will let you know of our plans if and when we make them. That's it, so you can just cancel those announcements."

We allowed Jack and Edith to attend the un-ceremony in St. Paul, along with my sister and brother and Nick's folks. Their Greek family tradition meant that the son's wedding was the most extravagant gala imaginable so when ours was the most insignificant affair, it sent his dad into a profound depression. On top of that, he being a floral designer with Minneapolis Floral, not allowed to provide flowers, our un-ceremony was the biggest disappointment in his father's life to date.

Our entire wedding took less than five minutes. The justice of the peace looked at our license, I.D.s, and said some nebulous lines I don't recall.

"That'll be ten dollars," he declared.

When Nick handed the money over, we heard, "I now pronounce you man and wife."

"Weird," we both confessed, as we got into our car for the drive to my 'rents.

The only other people I invited to the house were Meryl and her boyfriend, Harold.

After a strained hour of cake and pictures we lit out for our apartment, firing up a joint as soon as we got to the end of the block.

"It's just a piece of paper," I rationalized. "Nothing's changed. No big deal. We're still the same individuals we've always been, right?"

Nick wasn't so sure, holding his breath with the hit, conveniently prohibiting an answer.

The party, the reception was an all-nighter with our stoner crowd. The keg someone had bought, tapping it up in our bathtub, sat mostly untouched. An opium filled hookah, hash pipes and joints circled the room as we celebrated with our friends. No relatives. Part of me felt like I had to justify our action, our decision to make it official as friends queried me.

A number of times, I explained, "It was to get our 'rents off our backs. Everything's the same. Don't worry, it's cool. "

Albums set the mood, reverberating, weaving the mass of people together in an aura of peace, everyone wishing us well, hugging, congratulating. Many fell asleep, nodding off, catatonic from all the drugs.

Sitting next to Nick on the couch, squished together, the feel of him so deliciously warm and lovely, I kissed him, blissfully happy. Wow, this is so far out, I thought. The last song playing was the Moody Blues, "Knights in White Satin." I fell asleep dreaming those lovely lyrics, cuz I love you, ahhhh, I love you.

Not so convinced about the marriage, I was utterly sure of this man.

* * *

10

The idyllic setting of our Mexican resort

When Nick and I first arrived at the hotel, Oasis Akumal, there was a short, cursory tour giving us the lay of the land. We were sweltering in long sleeves and long pants, having already shed our sweaters, shoes and socks.

"I can't stand this anymore," I whispered to Nick, "Who gives a shit about the grounds. We'll figure it out. Let's bail."

He smiled, nodding agreement.

When he realized that meant there wasn't a valet to carry the bags up three flights of stairs, his smile faded. There weren't elevators. Wanting to appease me or shut me up, Nick lugged our heavy suitcases while I grabbed the two small ones, sweat dripping down his forehead as I unlocked our door.

He plopped down in a chair, grabbing the remote.

Looking at him, incredulously, I asked, "You're kidding, right? We're in paradise and you're going to watch the Tube? Give me a break."

"I'll just see what kind of reception we get."

He lifted the remote over his head as I tried to reach for it. An avid NCAA fan, he was missing some key tournament basketball games, maybe even the finals. I didn't pay much attention to sports. That was his thing.

We'd flown from three feet of snow to eighty-five degrees and sunny blue skies and I wasn't spending any more time indoors than necessary.

Planting myself in front of the T.V., I grinned, saying, "How 'bout a shower?"

With a sly wink, swaying, I started slowly peeling off my shirt, then my pants. The T.V. clicked off, Nick's obvious response making his jeans tight. At fifty years old, him fifty-three, I was damn proud he still reacted like that. After a delightfully languorous shower using sinful amounts of bath gel and water, taking towels, we rubbed each other dry.

"God, what a lover you are," I said, blotting his few thin locks of hair. I'd tease him, saying he had that hard working hair. Hundreds did the work of millions.

"You're not so bad yourself. C'mere, let's go again."

We laid down on the bed, slowly building to our rhythm, feeling the peak, climaxing with shudders. Sighing, I snuggled into his long arms feeling his heart subside to a normal pace and nodded off for a twenty minute siesta. I couldn't wait to get to the beach but the sweetness of the moment was too good to interrupt. After so long, so many years, to still feel this way, to be excited by each other was such a rarity. What a gift!

Abruptly, the airplane engines pierce my subconscious. I groan at the memory. Wrapping my arms around myself I imagine Nick's arms, the pressure, tight, but not too tight. His face, whiskers, almost ever-present bristle, the shadow that he took care not to scratch my delicate Scandinavian skin with. He was so sensitive; the way he knew every curve of my body, his generous technique, the tenderness, his touch now gone. GONE. His freezing body in the darkness below. God, I can't wrap my head around it. I can't imagine you never inside of me again. My love. It's not real.

* * *

"Back to the land" was the mantra Nick and I and all of our fellow hippies embraced in an effort to escape capitalist society's status quo. We'd fed the dream continually over the last two years with rock lyrics espousing and reinforcing that theme. *The Foxfire book* and *Mother Earth catalogue*, our bibles, idealized the country life, nature, and anti-establishment.

Our honeymoon was a road trip to the mountains of New Mexico where we lost both heart and soul to the land of enchantment. Dozens of hippies, fulfilling the dream, cemented our life's goal: move there, build a log cabin and abide happily ever after in utopia. Already having friends, Ed and Dominique, from Minneapolis, living in New Mexico as an inroad, gave indelible credence to our plan. We idolized those brave, convention thwarting pioneers, figuring we had as much chutzpah.

"Let's go back home, work, and save every penny. We can move out to a farm outside of the cities and give it a try," Nick said, forming a strategy on the three day drive back from our honeymoon. "I can commute to my job if we find a place within a sixty mile radius. Work during the week, stay with our friends, be home on weekends. Save and scrimp. Deal on the side. You could find something maybe in a small town."

"How long do you think it will take?" I asked, totally on board, ever the dreamer.

"A year or so ought to do it. We can probably put together enough bread to make it happen."

The 'rents' didn't buy it for a second.

"We'll live off the land," we said, trying to explain the pathway of perfection to Jack. We dumped it on them in separate dinner engagements. One with mine, one with Nick's folks. Figuring if we went to *their* houses, we could bail out when it unraveled.

"Are you crazy?" Edith asked, adding, "That's the dumbest thing I ever heard."

"What're you going to do for money? What about jobs? What do you mean, living off the land?"

Their questions flew at us in rapid fire.

"We haven't got it all figured out yet but we will before we go. Our friends moved out there and it's working for them. They have land, built a cabin, it's really amazing. We're going to save up before we head out there," I answered, calmly laying out my pearls of wisdom.

We vainly argued with the confounded 'rents, getting nowhere.

Wonderful, simple, idealistic stoned out youth!

The next apartment Nick and I rented and still in Minneapolis was a tiny dump on 25th and Columbus owned by a friend of my dad's. The one bedroom was at the back of another old Victorian conversion. We jumped at a way to save as much money as possible, furthering our migration to the Southwest.

For eighty-five dollars a month, we didn't expect much. But the plaster caving in, crumbling behind the claw foot bath tub, paled in comparison to the inhabitants of our kitchen. Opening the cupboard door, dozens of roaches scurried for cover. I slammed it shut, vowing to never cook anything in that place. And I didn't. Fast food joints or the Clark gas station on Lake and Park satisfied our meager diet.

I chose a huge American flag to decorate the living room wall. Demonstrating our rebellion, it was hung upside down, depicting the universal distress signal. Senseless to my dad's feelings, I had no clue how that would affect him when he popped in one day. Visible shock evident as he shuddered, Dad's life was forever altered by his World War II experience. The trauma and scar's imprint painfully imbedded in his core. From conversations with close relatives and one astonishing letter from Dad I was able to glean a portion of the horrific details.

My uncle told me, "Don't ever ask your dad about it. Don't make him ever talk about it."

I needed to understand, though. This was the dad I wanted to know.

Dad was a naval medic assigned to the Marines as they stormed the beaches of Guam in the Mariana Islands, and Okinawa.

This was Dad's account in that letter:

"1944, Guam, on the second day, as night was falling, we tried to dig foxholes, which was impossible, being on the edge of a swamp. So we had to lie above ground in an area aptly named, Crossfire Gulch. Bullets shot past, just above our heads, the entire night. No one moved a muscle as we watched the flares, praying for dawn. 'Beans' right next to me was hit. I rose up, reaching for him, when the tracer bullet creased my neck, above the right clavicle. The pain seared through my back, lower neck and armpit. Leo, a corpsman, said I heaved about four feet off the ground in a prone position. While he dressed my wounds we said the Lord's Prayer together. I was evacuated to the aid station but as soon as humanly possible I was sent back to my unit, the 22nd Marine regiment. I wasn't there long before I succumbed to dysentery and was returned to the aid station. Back at Guadalcanal I was given the proper attention giving me time to heal. There they awarded me the Purple Heart.

1945, Okinawa. We landed eighteen minutes after H hour. Heading north, we secured that end of the island in a matter of days. The army was stuck, not able to advance beyond a certain point, so they sent our Marines into the airport area. This was the fiercest fighting I'd ever seen. Mangled bodies everywhere, strewn about, broken, brains pouring out. I saw legs sliced open exposing bone. Heroes everywhere you looked. Marine Stoddard came limping back to us, bloodied, shredded, yelling, "Put a band-aid on it, I'm going back." I carefully pushed the brains back into my Marine buddy's head as he moaned, knowing he would certainly die. Calling for the stretchers, I started to cry. In my mind I heard, "Here goes another one." Everything went black. I passed out. My memory is completely blanked out until I was aware of someone helping me onto a hospital ship in the harbor. Our destination was Pearl Harbor where patients were supposed to be treated but they were filled to capacity. We sailed on to a base in San Francisco. From there I was transferred to the naval hospital in Memphis, TN. October of '45 I was discharged from the USNR. They sent me home to Mankato, MN. And then on to Windom, MN with one hundred dollars in my pocket. The sadness will never leave me."

He was barely eighteen years old when he was wounded and decorated. Suffering a personal, lonely agony, he received no support, no counseling, and no transition into normal life. His sister, the aunt I stayed with in California after high school, filled in the sketchy details of Dad's complete breakdown upon his return to the States. Her husband and another uncle spent countless hours, into the wee hours listening to sobbing rants, helping him find some coherency.

"This country is in distress," I declared, answering my dad's question concerning the flag placement.

Once, after having been suspended in my senior year of high school for smoking in the can, Dad unloaded a blistering tirade, finishing by declaring to Edith, "She **IS** sick. In the head!" Of course, this just happened to be the only event either of them ever attended and I was glaringly absent.

Their suspicions concerning my mental condition were reinforced with each confrontation. He was undeniably convinced I'd gone off the deep end. Unfazed in my belligerence, I wouldn't back down. Without the slightest compassion for his suffering, I selfishly expressed my know-it-all superiority declaring my independence.

"This is what you're doing with a college education? This is what you're willing to risk?" Nick's parents implored, trying to

143

reason with us. The second of the expository dinners was going no better.

Each encounter, every visit from then on ended with the same heated argument. We endeavored to convince them, explaining how the people we'd met existed in the mountains of New Mexico. It was as if we were speaking a foreign language, which it was. The generation gap could have been better described as a canyon. Their dreams were shattered, their hearts broken over their only son. Nick was it for them. All of their eggs in his basket.

Nick's parents were incredulous over our disdain of the "good life." From their background, their childhoods, they considered themselves fortunate to have overcome the hardship of country life and were proud they had provided their son with the opportunity to succeed further.

Pontelli, 32

I loved the story of Nick's dad's immigration to America from Greece aboard the Themistocles in 1921. Ship records indicate that he was fourteen years old upon arrival but he was lying. Pontelli was born in the olive grove outside a tiny village called Kremasti. The tenth child of eleven, his mother was said to have popped him out, wrapped him up, and continued picking the harvest. There weren't birth records so he figured he was either nine or ten years old when they shipped him to the States. With a pittance hidden in their shoes, he and his brother boarded for their voyage. For some unknown reason, his brother abandoned him, disembarking in Argentina, leaving Pontelli to fend for himself at

Ellis Island. He was so scared that he barely ate, not wanting to reveal that he had any money, surviving on pity from those who shared their meals with him. He spent an entire month being processed before relatives were located in Minnesota that would take him in. If they discovered any defect, like missing fingers, limbs, or illness, you were put on the next ship out. Cigarettes coupled with poor nutrition stunted his growth, everything except his hands, which were the size of a taller, larger man. At six foot, three inches Nick towered over his diminutive five foot seven father. His host family treated him like an indentured servant but he never complained. It was life.

He said once, "I always thought I was a bad boy. That's why they sent me away. For years and years I tried to figure out what I'd done wrong."

He always thought in Greek and spoke with a noticeable accent his entire ninety years. Honoring his mother and father, he sent thousands of dollars home for everything from dowries to sponsoring relatives' immigration. Some shady connections landed one of his brothers in New York City, where he quickly became the proprietor of a restaurant. When the brother was shot and hastily deported, Nick tried to get his dad to fill in the juicy details. We imagined all sorts of underworld connections. Using his native tongue when discussing the episode over the phone, the information was kept under wraps. The specifics remained forever hazy except for the fact that his brother never returned, living like a king off of social security, the remainder of his days in Greece.

Even after he lost his thick black hair, Pontelli was a dashing figure, his smooth olive skin, golden brown year around. Nick inherited the Mediterranean genes turning a lovely, deep brown from one day's sunshine.

When Pontelli's mother died in Greece, many decades later, he had a memorial service for her at St. George Greek Orthodox Church on Summit Avenue in St. Paul. He wept openly, brokenhearted over the loss.

Nick asked him numerous times, "Why don't you go back, visit your relatives, see the village? You and Mom should take a trip over there. Don't you want to?"

The answer was always the same, "It would kill me."

He had a premonition which bore out in anecdotal accounts. Apparently, a significant amount of aged immigrants died on the spot when returning to their homeland after many years' absence. Either directly off the plane or when they arrived at their village they would kneel down to kiss the ground and keel over from heart failure. He instinctively figured that would be his fate, so resigned himself for the next eight decades sustained by those few short years of motherland memories. I tried to imagine what it must have been like for his dear mother, kissing him goodbye, watching her little boy walk away. He held his brother's hand, turned around for one last look at his mama, waving goodbye, walking out of sight. Did she fathom she'd never see him again? And how did they decide which children to send, scrimping and saving the money for their passage?

Nick's mother, Violetta Lou McPherson, was the second of five daughters, born and raised on a farm in North Dakota on the rich Missouri River bottom land. The three room log house was barren and utilitarian. Nick and I were so driven to get back to the land, to work with the earth, and give up modern conveniences, and Violetta, desperate to escape the Depression Era poverty, had done everything in her power to elevate her son

147

from that existence. She knew, firsthand, what the reality of rural life entailed. It was a curse to be saddled with only daughters on a farm. Sons were necessary for the labor. Her older sister, Margaret, and Mother were the designated outdoor chore hands. Violetta was relegated the nanny, chief cook and bottle washer for her three younger sisters, whom she forever referred to, without affection, as beasts. These girls would devise ways to make Violetta's life miserable, causing as much trouble as they could to make her look incompetent. At threshing time, all seven of them camped on the bottom land for days, setting up a huge tent, while the grain was harvested. The girls would gather hundreds of bundles of grain to shock, a process whereby five or six were stacked upright together in order to dry thoroughly. Hot and grueling, it was an austere life. When one of Violetta's relatives near Minneapolis extended an invitation for her or one of her sisters to come live with them and be a part of their household, she jumped at the chance. It was still a farm, but without younger brats to take care of, she hoped it would be an improvement. At fifteen years of age Violetta unwittingly became Cinderella. Her cousin, Nadine, who was the same age, seized the opportunity to exercise her position, commanding obeisance. The very first day, Violetta was saddled with Nadine's chores which included farm work. It was a devastating twist of fate, but she never returned home, courageously choosing to surmount the adversity. Her mother and two younger sisters left her father, fleeing the farm when poverty and alcohol destroyed their livelihood. The youngest sister remained with him, to cook and maintain the house, until he deserted altogether, losing everything to back taxes. After making his way to the Northwest to beg for another chance with his wife, who adamantly refused, he was never heard from again.

Even though Pontelli had to be hospitalized at the VA facility in St. Cloud, undergoing electro-shock therapy for depression, Nick and I, undeterred from our hippie conviction, would not listen to reason. Our hearts, minds and souls had been possessed with a vision. Captive victims of the time, we were swept up in the powerful wave that beset America during the late 60's. Rebellion, fueled by the galvanizing power of Woodstock was unshakable. Crosby, Stills, Nash, and Young's lyrics, "set my soul free... got to get ourselves back to the garden... saw bomber jet planes turning into butterflies" defined the dream we were reaching for. Make love, not war. Give peace a chance. Get out of Vietnam. Completely bewitched beyond our control these strong elements combined to shape our beliefs, validating our goals. The government never even acknowledged the Vietnam War as a war, but stubbornly referred to it as a 'conflict.' If our friends, relatives, and schoolmates were coming home in body bags, it was, indeed, war. Nick and I abhorred the materialistic society we were expected to propagate seeing the lack of humanity that those involved in it needed to embrace. Being the unwilling Pied Piper, Bob Dylan's "Like a Rolling Stone," vocalized my feelings with his poetry demeaning middle class materialists calculating life in a sterile habitation, supporting my minimalist pursuit. Going straight to my heart, indicting the parents who had never understood where I was coming from, being clueless to my sensitive nature, Dylan was my guru. "When you ain't got nothin,' you got nothin' to lose."

Where was the love, the feeling, the care? What was the meaning of it all, the philosophy that engendered the sort of unhappiness I witnessed as a child? Was it the Almighty Dollar that propagated the system we abhorred? Was it ever enough?

It was truly an amazing, once in a lifetime, era. The dates blur when I chronologically attempt to chart every event, experience and metamorphosis and as George Carlin later said, "If you remember the 70's, you weren't there."

After our honeymoon experience to New Mexico, the initial move, the trial run situated us in a Wisconsin farmhouse that we'd found in the rental section of the Star Tribune. Nick commuted the seventy miles to Minneapolis, maintaining his job with the paving crew for a year, driving home for the weekends to endure my bitching. Our 'rents hoped this preview would get the fanatical idea out of our system. I was wavering.

Depressed and bratty, I'd whine to Nick, "I'm lonely, I'm bored, and it freaks the hell out of me being here alone. Christ, I didn't think it would be so hard. Dweezil and Jasper are my only friends. These people are so conservative. I can't go into town without being stared at. And I'm the only one! Shit."

I was paranoid of what he was doing every night in the city partying with friends. I tried to be supportive, tried to mellow out, but not finding any work in the small town made me go sort of batty thinking about Nick's attractively cool mysteriousness in an environment so not conducive to fidelity.

The utilitarian, two-story dwelling was not improved by my decorating sense. Comprised of one lamp, a frayed, threadbare, flattened couch and chair, wooden-box end tables and the stereo, the cheap furnishings embodied minimalism. I hung old sheets over the windows for curtains.

Nick was frustrated by my meager effort toward the endeavor. He was giving ninety percent to my ten.

"Do you want to do this or not?"

Nick's remonstrance surprised me.

150

"I do, but you don't know what it's like here all week."

"Well, this is the deal, Anne," Nick stated, pragmatically trying to reason with me. "We have to figure out if we can do this trip. It's only for a while, a few more months. If you can't hack it here, then what are you going to do in the mountains, without running water or electricity? Keep it together. I'm working my ass off and you're sitting out here playing albums. If we didn't have these dogs, you could work in the city, too."

"Well, what sense would that make for us both to be in the city all week?"

"Then quit bitchin' about everything and support what I'm doing," Nick admonished.

"I will. I really do want to do this."

Self-sufficiency meant we certainly wouldn't be eating at fast food restaurants. Challenged by Nick's resolution, I threw myself into culinary efforts. Following the recipe to the letter, measuring, mixing, beating, kneading the dough until there wasn't a shred of life left in it, I produced two pound rocks in my first attempt at baking bread. When it wouldn't rise properly I continued to let it sit for hours. Hoping for a miracle, I popped it into the oven anyway for an hour. A hatchet might have been able to penetrate the crust but I didn't go that far. Nick was encouraged by my feeble attempt as we laughed at the comic relief.

Green horns from the city, we about froze to death trying to cope with a coal furnace. When we couldn't stand it anymore we'd blast up the oven temperature and hunker down around the open oven door with a blanket wrapped around us like a tent. Coal was tricky, not anything like a barbeque grill or hibachi. There was a knack to feeding, banking, and venting it that we were never able to master.

To my delight, the rich black soil guaranteed gardening success. Vegetables thrived, tomatoes fairly burst with sweetness biting into them like a freshly picked apple. And the pot plants! In full view, fifteen feet tall, virtually trees, I couldn't believe the landlord never said anything about them. We paid the rent on time, didn't give him any trouble so we got a pass; or maybe he really didn't know what they were. After the first frost, Nick yanked them up dragging them inside. To reach their full potential the pot plants needed to dry hanging upside down to increase the active ingredients. The basement being damp, dank and even moldy, the only place long enough to hang the mammoth plants was our stairway to the second floor. After ten days weaving my way through the leafy branches to get to bed, I laid them out on the kitchen floor, broke off the buds, and packed them into plastic baggies. Not the most potent reefer but it got the job done.

Hour after hour I wrote dismal poetry bewailing my plight of solitude. Complaining about society's ills, bemoaning Nick's absence, I reinforced my melancholy filling up page after page. Music was my only true companion. The overdose of my idol, Janis Joplin, didn't help my depression, but did reinforce my stricture against smack.

After three months, I got the sense our landlord's wife, Judie, a few years older than me, was somewhat approachable. I turned her onto dope and did my best to indoctrinate her into the radical liberalism of the times, with limited success. How stupid was it for us to preach to farmers about living off the land? What were we talking about? That's what they'd been doing successfully their whole life.

Each weekend planning the cabin, plotting our strategy Nick and I figured we'd be ready for New Mexico in another month. We bought an International Travelall panel truck, removed the back seat and built in a platform bed using the space underneath to store all of our belongings. With the whopping sum of five thousand dollars socked away in a bank account we headed back to the Twin Cities to say our goodbyes.

"It's the best shit you ever had," Keith promised as he configured the lines on the coffee table.

It was a going away party. A last snort, the high to set sail.

Keith said, "I watched the dealer I bought it from go ahead and shoot it up. I don't know how much he'd had before I got there but he fell back on the couch in a stupor, barely breathing. I didn't want any hassles. I wasn't calling anyone, so I just stayed there and waited. Thank God he woke up."

The coke, straight from Colombia, had to be very cautiously ingested not having been cut with anything. We thought the dealer was an idiot to not have known that or else just got caught up in the powerfully addictive whirlwind of the bounty. That night the apartment floor, with eight passed out or sleeping bodies, four dogs sprawled amongst, littered with dishes, clothes and debris, was a doper's delight.

Walking out from the bathroom the next morning, I slid down next to Nick on the floor, "My period's late."

"You're shittin' me. How late?"

"Five days."

"Son of a bitch."

The disclosure brought us back to reality. I had quit taking the pill because it was too expensive and we'd been relying on various alternative measures, even natural birth control. I remembered the quip I'd heard somewhere: what do they call couples who use natural birth control? Parents!

Digging out my herbal remedy bible I read a section to Nick, "The Natives used pennyroyal as an abortive. I have to find some of that. Fast. "

In complete agreement, he said, "We can check the food coop."

I bought a bag of the tea and drank it constantly for two days. It worked. That shook us up. The thought of a family was not even a remote possibility, not then, or ever. Why would we bring another life into this world, this society that was ultimately going to blow everyone to smithereens with a nuclear holocaust any day?

The one day to bid adieu had turned into a week with the coke shipment, potentially threatening our entire venture. Desperation coupled with the pregnancy scare sent me spiraling into a panic.

"If we don't go now, this moment, it's going to be too late," I told Nick, "Call it premonition, kismet, but I'm going to totally freak out if we don't get out. Today!"

He looked at me, hesitated but seemed convinced, as he helped me cram all of our stuff into a bag. Leaving friends with mouths agape, sprinkling hurried goodbyes I felt as if I was holding my breath until we pulled away from the curb. Rumbling out of Minneapolis at four in the afternoon, amidst a heavy snowfall, I held Nick's hand, both of us feeling that urgency of now or never. One more night of the coke scene and we'd have been hooked, irretrievably lost to its grip, the tenuous dream ripped from our grasp. We had to plow ahead, in the bumper to bumper blizzard, down 35W inching away from the lights and neighborhoods, past the suburbs, into the open rural landscape.

Bread crooned their hit "If" on the radio as I watched the stars fly away. Yellow and orange streaks spread across the horizon, the brown Travelall rolling over Nebraska at dawn. Driving all night, the magnetic pulse of the past week was broken. We felt free: free from drugs; free from perpetual partying; free from aimlessness; free from certain nothingness, sameness, even though we were stamped out of the counter culture mold. Those final days of continual cocaine high, Nick and I, our friends, every hour, someone shooting up, snorting, dealing; it felt like Satan himself was pulling out all the stops to derail us. Breaking the bonds of that life was one thing, actually arriving in Gallina, New Mexico was a miracle.

11

Thatched shelter on Mazatlan beach, Dweezil inside

At 8,000 feet elevation the mountains in the Santa Fe National Forest were buried in two feet of snow. Having no particular date to arrive in that area, Nick and I decided to take a detour to Mexico and avoid some of the winter. The rumor that you could subsist on the beach for pennies a day sounded like a good plan. Warm, sunny and cheap, we'd find some good dope and hang out for a few months. We discovered in Mazatlan that the preponderance of newly constructed resorts was quickly erasing that notion. After a couple of nights being rousted out by local Federales we happened upon a beach full of hippies and ne'er do wells, staking out a flimsy grass hut for the next month.

The strange mix of oddballs included Waylan and David, proclaimed fugitives from up north. They were just weird enough to be believed. Waylan confessed, in not so hushed tones, that he wired his house to explode when his unfaithful wife opened the front door. David was his wife's brother who sided against her: so much for family loyalty. Waylan, a shell-shocked Vietnam vet, had enough edge to make it plausible. Bagging an iguana with a bow and arrow, he invited us to partake of the campfire roasted lizard. It tasted like chicken, seriously.

Waylan gave us survival pointers: most importantly, to bury our pot in a coffee can at night so it wouldn't get ripped off. There was some security in numbers, the hippies sticking together, but the day we witnessed Federales with guns blazing, chasing someone as they disappeared into a wooded hillside, Nick and I decided we'd had enough. It was time to head up to the peaceful mountains. Against Waylan's experienced advice, we traveled at night thinking less traffic, cooler. And like idiots, we also ignored the cardinal rule not to carry any drugs. But it was only five joints. Just enough to get us to the border. Then we would be home free. The road block jarred us out of our stupor. Rolling along in the pitch black night, startled by the mass of tail lights, vehicles idled at a standstill. Our car being fourth in line, gave me just enough time to stick the last three joints under the floor mat. Nauseating panic gripped me as we watched seedy looking men, automatic weapons in hand, those belts of ammo slung over their shoulders like garlands, questioning and searching those ahead. God, this was it! What the fuck were we doing? Our appearance, an immediate red flag, we were commanded to pull over to the search area, a dozen or so men scurrying around the Travellal.

"Papers, I.D.!" they demanded, in Spanish.

With broken Spanish we complied, hoping against hope that somehow we'd be able to smooth talk our way out of there.

"Get out; keep those dogs quiet or we'll shoot 'em."

Dweezil and Jasper were fiercely protective, riled, and ready to attack. They had come in quite useful keeping our campsite secure but now they were a liability. We stood frozen, barely breathing, as they ransacked our vehicle. The aroma was unmistakable, our eyes a dead giveaway. We were warned but in that warped la-la mind set, we didn't consider the consequences. What did two Midwest hicks know about foreign justice? God, why did we ignore Waylan's admonition?

In bashing and ramming everything in the front seat, the Federale knocked one of the joints onto the ground. If I could just inch my foot over to cover it up, slowly, don't let him look. Moving, careful. Shit! He was right on it. Busted! FUCK! They went crazy. Screaming rapid fire Spanish, tearing the seats out, the ceiling, the dash. SHIT! At least we knew that was all there was to our stash.

They shoved Nick, prodding him with the rifle barrel, into a small dilapidated shack (headquarters).

Commanded to stay in the vehicle with the dogs, I thought, "That's the last I'll ever see of him."

Too scared to even cry, I prayed, "Please, God, get us out of here, please help, something, magic, God, do something! If you just get us out of here, I'll never do drugs again, I'll be whatever you say, I'll do whatever you want."

Better known as the tight-place-prayer, forgotten the second reprieve is granted.

Across the front porch where Nick disappeared sat a solid line of thugs (Policia), nasty looking banditos brandishing their weapons, armed to their tarnished teeth exposed by sleazy grins.

All I could think was, there's no way out, we're dead. When I had to pee I debated going right on the seat. But after an excruciating hour I got permission to relieve myself under the humiliating scrutiny of the guards. Back in the truck, the disastrous cloud portending Nick's demise loomed heavily as I tried to will him alive. Was he being tortured, beaten? Guarded by armed brutes, from eleven till about two in the morning, I anxiously employed every means of persuasion, praying for release, settling the dogs, when I heard hollering.

Seeing Nick running for the vehicle I braced myself for the shots, the barrage. Like a wild animal, he stopped, spun half around stepping backward, then hesitating as their hollering intensified, to finally bolt for the truck. We were spewing rocks, spraying gravel, a cloud of dirt billowing behind, screeching onto the highway as Nick floored it. With his door hanging open, I braced against the dashboard, fully expecting bullets to shatter the windows. Eyes straight ahead, incredulous, I didn't make a sound for fear of distracting him. Finally, after several minutes, assured of freedom, Nick, still breathing heavily, related the last hours.

Scooting over to plaster myself against him, letting the tears spill out, I laid my hand on this thigh, "God, Nick, I thought you were escaping. I thought they'd open fire on you and that would be it. Are you alright? Oh, Babe, Oh God."

He placed his hand over mine, squeezing gently, "Man, I thought I was dead. There was one room, totally empty, where they brought me. I was strip-searched in the center with ten soldiers leering, jiving, around the perimeter. One guy bent me over while another spread my cheeks, probing my asshole."

I squeezed his hand tighter.

"With my pants around my ankles, they made me kneel down on the cold concrete. And then they taunted me, badgering,

159

one after the other, continually. I couldn't understand them but I could feel how hostile it was, some even spitting on me. One guy raised his rifle, placing the end of the barrel on the bridge of my nose. Just letting it set there. Trying not to even blink, I figured I was dead at that point."

"Did you say anything?"

"I was shaking, begging them to not kill us. They didn't know what I was saying. But I'm sure they could tell I was desperate, pleading for our lives.

"The only English speaking member heckled, 'No way, gringo, this isn't like America. You're going to jail in the morning and you're never getting out. You don't have any rights here.' "And they'd all laugh, taunting."

Abruptly, remembering himself, Nick asked, "Are you okay, did they hurt you?"

"I'm okay, no one touched me. How did you get away?"

Settling himself for a few moments, still driving, he gathered his thoughts, "I was resigned, pretty much thinking I was either dead or in prison the next day. I knew they might let you go if they believed you were my wife and not just shacking up with me. So I tried to get that through to them. Then the guy in charge took pity on me, I don't know why, like a change of heart."

He had been outside for a while and when he came in, he looked at me. I couldn't get his vibe. And then he just said, "You can go."

"I thought I would start walking away and they'd open fire on me. End of story."

"Rapido, Rapido!" they yelled from the porch.

"That's when I turned around but they got louder."

"RAPIDO, RAPIDO!"

"I bolted for the van, jumped in and figured, to hell with it!"

Looking it up in the Spanish dictionary I read, "Run, it means RUN! Holy shit. Unbelievable!"

Nick and I surmised that the roadblock had been set up on a tip-off about a sizable transport of drugs. The guards, realizing we didn't hold the cache, must have wanted to get us out of the way. We swore we'd never go back. Who knows what it was? Dumb luck, providence, God, whatever, we were thankful to be out of that hell hole near Hermosillo and not in jail. With no more deviation from the original goal, our destination, 'The Mesa', Gallina, New Mexico was the final stop of that near disastrous journey.

* * *

Why didn't we keep our vow? We'd sworn never to go back to Mexico. The turbulence shook me as I snapped into the present. Was I dreaming? Oh, God, please, let it be a dream.

The day before, we celebrated our thirtieth wedding anniversary. I'd compiled a scrap book replete with pictures chronicling our marriage relationship over the years. After breakfast I slipped up to our room leaving him in the courtyard to savor his coffee. He squinted at me as I came into view carrying a wrapped present.

"What did you do? You got me something?"

I shrugged, with a slightly smug smile.

Utterly surprised, Nick's heart melted as he read it and wept, "I was going to say, no gifts, thinking the trip was gift enough."

"Well, you know me better than that." I really rubbed it in, adding, "I'll bet you never forget a gift again."

"I'm so sorry, really, Anne, this is beautiful. How do you write this shit? God, I love you."

Wrapping his big arms around me, he pulled me into his chest, kissing me, tasting me.

Nick loved the way I looked, never neglecting to tell me, giving compliments I thought were undeserved, but the feeling was mutual. We were like newlyweds, affectionate, attentive. As he read, pondering each page, quietly his tears spilled over our life. He couldn't write letters or express himself on paper so he truly marveled, admiring my eloquence.

Afterwards, we walked down the beach hand in hand, past the piers, collecting unusual rocks, brain coral, snapping pictures. Enjoying our connection, we watched waves spray the rocky shore, discussing options for the week. The bus tours didn't interest us in the least. Why would we sit on a bus with a wild driver careening all over the highway when we could lounge on the beach? That bizarre method of driving in Mexico, head on toward another vehicle. Unnerving, at best. On a two lane highway the driver would pull out to pass, whereupon the oncoming vehicle had to swerve onto the shoulder. They all seemed to be aware of the 'rule.'

Our lunch included four beers lending a riotous element to our 'siesta'. The last afternoon delight was especially fine. Always satisfying but still never mechanical. Never.

"I'll have a martini," Nick told Raul, the bartender, later in the courtyard. He didn't make that mistake twice. Adept at margaritas and pina coladas, Raul failed martini 101.

Beginning our five course lobster dinner that evening with avocado, crab salad, "Pace yourself," I told Nick, "You're going to be so stuffed."

Enchanting candlelight danced upon our table as the waiter lit the bananas flambeau.

Beaming, flushed from wine, I told him, "It's our thirtieth anniversary."

He slipped away and brought back a bouquet of pink and white blossoms together with palm leaves that he'd wrapped in tin foil.

Charmingly, he presented it with congratulations, "Feliz Aniversario."

Rising to leave, Nick laced his hand into mine; bending his mouth to my ear, "Let's go down to the beach."

A few feet from the restaurant, we settled into lounge chairs, star gazing, touching finger tips. Sliding up the length of my arm, Nick let his hand rest on my chest, as he stroked my neck. Leaning over for a kiss, slowly licking the aftertaste of our dessert, I marveled at his adeptness knowing how and his wish to satisfy me. A tremor of desire coursed through me.

"I love you forever," I whispered, "Forever."

The fluffiest, billowy clouds floated over us, almost within reach. Extending my arm, I imagined I could touch them. The day had been perfect. Magic.

The next morning, as we sat on the beach, Nick suggested, "We could get the whole family down here next Christmas. It wouldn't be that exorbitant, sharing rooms, we'd skip presents, save until then. I really think we could swing it."

"Sure, why not," I agreed, knowing it would take a miracle.

"Do you want to go snorkeling now?"

He had wanted to sit on the beach and finish his crossword puzzle, but I convinced him to motivate. He was the old pro, swimming away before I could even struggle into my fins. Patiently he helped me adjust the strap, holding my hand as we waded, beginning to float.

"Sorry, I'll get it, how do you breathe?" I asked.

"Relax, float, don't fight it, get the rhythm," Nick said, "Here, take my hand. I'll help you."

He was such a natural. We floated, side by side along the serene, coral reef, becoming part of the aquatic life in all its splendor with every imaginable shape and color, able to see the ocean floor clearly, eight feet below. Squeezing his familiar hand, I glanced over at Nick's form and wondered how we were so lucky to still be this in love after three decades.

In the plane, shaken from my thoughts, the couple sitting next to me excused themselves for the second time, brushing my calf as they stumbled over me. After numerous cocktails, their parade to the bathroom jarred me back to reality. They probably thought I'd gotten a mean case of food poisoning by my demeanor. Shuffling the cards, they dealt another hand of cribbage.

The phone calls back to the states were so shattering, compounding my pain as I delivered the death blow. Holding Nick's lifeless head in my hands was something I had no control over, but now, saying the words, crushing my kids, was a conscious act I took direct responsibility for:

"Zelda, I have some horrible news.

She said nothing.

"Are you sitting down?" I stammered.

164

There was no way to soften it. I had to ravage her heart, over the telephone, from Mexico.

"Dad died."

She implored softly, "Mom. What? What happened?"

I tried to keep my voice coherent, level, giving her the information I had, but I could barely speak.

Realizing Nick's mom had to be told, choking back sobs, I added, "You have to go over and tell Grandma. I can't tell her on the phone, she won't be able to comprehend it. I'm so sorry, honey, I'm so sorry."

There were no words; nothing could make it any better.

"I'll call you in about a half hour, when I think you've had time to get there and tell her. Then I will talk to her," I offered.

"How can I do this?" I thought.

Nick was her 'Sonny Boy', for fifty-three years. Her husband of sixty some years had died less than three years prior. How was this happening?

Nick and I had spent our last night in Minneapolis with Zelda before flying to Mexico. We quietly tiptoed out of her apartment at four-thirty in the morning so as not to disturb her. Weeks later she told me that when she woke and saw that we were gone, she raced to the window to try to catch a glimpse, thinking, "I didn't get to say goodbye."

My sweet, baby girl, now twenty-six years old, was fatherless. I relied on her capability, immensely, to get me through, keep me strong. My paragon of responsibility, not to mention efficiency, I knew she could figure out a way to explain to Grandma that her only son was dead.

I can't live without you, Babe. I can't do it. How will I live?

* * *

New Mexico, with its azure skies, sunny, balmy weather, and richly carved mountains gave Nick and me a sense of peace and sanity after the recent upheaval. Snow frosted peaks amid majestic spruce were set against a backdrop of salmon and rust hued canyons, colored layers of sandstone topped with white hued gypsum dating back some 200 million years where flood plains and rivers along with violent eruptions from volcanoes created the stunningly unusual topography in the aptly nicknamed Land of Enchantment. I saw this sign outside of the grocery store in Espanola; Dios tarda pero no olvida. When I asked the proprietor what it meant she told me, God may be late but he doesn't forget. How apropos, I thought. The grandeur and bewitching atmosphere at 8,000 feet took our breath away. Kept alive by indigenous peoples, the rich spiritual history lent intoxicating mystery to our environment. Surrounded by pristine beauty, this manifestation of love power joined with the philosophy of flower children, materialized in one of the most extraordinary places on earth. Winding our way up US84 past the Abiquiu Dam we stopped at Bode's General Store to discover a time warp. Iron stove plates, with the device to pick them up when burning hot, lamp globes and wicks, kerosene, most everything for our rustic manner of living. I purchased a white enamel coffee pot decorated with colorful violets and fresh ground coffee to begin housekeeping. Nick and I could feel it all coming together as we climbed back into the vehicle for our final 40 miles. To think we almost didn't make it, that we could have been rotting in a Mexican prison!

The Mesa was another world, a new beginning; the year 1972. Like-minded families escaped the Vietnam War madness, political unrest, and unbridled right-wing hatred to find Shangri-

166

La in a sparsely populated area, whose Hispanic residents traced their land titles to the 1600s, some having deeds signed by the King of Spain.

Ed and Dominique, the old friends from Minneapolis we planned to stay with, weren't exactly thrilled to have guests for an indeterminate amount of time in their one room log cabin. Carrying water, using an outhouse, and heating with wood all seemed like one great adventure to us but having lived that lifestyle for a while Ed and Dom had a more realistic view of what it actually involved. They promptly shipped us off to their friends Blake and Sydney, in need of house and dog sitters while they headed to D.C. to break the news to his parents that they were expecting. House-sitting was necessitated because of our resourceful Spanish neighbors who weren't opposed to stewing up whatever meat was available, including puppies. We put two and two together after noticing litters curiously disappear. There just weren't that many dog adoptions going on. Politely, you ate what was put in front of you when invited into their homes. So much for the organic diet we espoused. Natural, wholesome puppy ratatouille.

The road from our campsite

What a shock to be nine miles from the nearest store, post office box and telephone. The main road was maintained by logging companies when they needed their trucks to roll but if timber wasn't moving, we typically needed four-wheel drive and chains to navigate. Aptly described as 'snot on a marble floor,' adobe roads were frustrating. In passable condition when the mammoth log trucks were rolling, an additional hazard presented itself. If your vehicle was in the path of a full load, you had to take the ditch or be mowed down. We learned to hang out of the vehicle window listening for the rumble of the motor. The log truck drivers probably could have stopped if they wanted to but we were dealing with the belligerent redneck attitude; 'one less hippie, one better world.' It kept our ears vigilant. Once you slid off the road, down the four-foot ditch, the only way back up was with another vehicle, preferably a tractor, and a long chain. Or if it was beyond mechanics, the old Spanish men would hitch up their team of horses blowing our minds with their expertise. It was sheer artistry to watch the relationship between man and beast. Our seventy-five year old neighbor, Eduardo, all of ninety pounds, held the reins and made short, soft sounds like hut, hip, ho, hee; the horse knowing exactly what each meant, obeying right, left, reverse, stop, and go. His perfectly matched draft team, Pet and Lily, were artistry to watch. And like magic, the vehicle would slide back onto the road, hopefully with its undercarriage and transmission intact. When our International Travelall suffered such a fate, it took weeks to get the parts and longer to find a mechanic skilled enough to repair it.

Ed helped us locate the plot of land we needed to make our dream a reality. A clear title was so nebulous, so rare on the Mesa that the "hips," we Anglos, submitted to the law of the land. In a method resembling squatter's rights we obtained permission to build our cabin. Two feuding Spanish factions, brothers Rogelio, Nestor and Samwell in contention with their cousin, Tony as to rightful possession, claimed ownership to 'our' piece of property.

"We just want to live here," we innocently proffered, propositioning the opposing family members as we talked to them about our desire to build a log cabin on the plot in question, "What's the hassle?"

I loved the Native belief about land possession; we are one with the earth. Not having a title, simply borrowing the land, was a concept we could embrace.

Securing approval wasn't difficult. The cousins knew Ed, who vouched for us. We were friendly, smooth, harmless looking city folks. Actually, the naiveté was enormous but the drugs still affected our decision making processes. Sensible? Reasonable? Mature? Not so much. Going to each feuding member's house, in turns, with a case of beer in tow, Nick and I nodded in agreement with the cousins, promising allegiance to both sides of the family and swearing loyalty to gain their permission. We had a deal.

Setting up camp with an ancient cook stove that presented no easy task learning its quirks, I burned everything before painstakingly mastering the particular balance of fuel regulation. Our borrowed tent housed belongings and supplies, the International becoming camper as Nick and I snuggled together during the cool nights, Jasper and Dweezil keeping our feet toasty. Daytime temperatures rose to sixty, even seventy degrees but because the air was so thin, plummeted to thirty-five degrees after sunset.

A crystal clear creek running year round provided us with drinking water. We either carried two plastic pails at a time across a quarter mile foot path or drove our truck around the forest road to fill ten of the five gallon containers at once. The tight fitting lids kept mice, bugs and dust out. With the spring thaw we learned the hard way that boiling the fresh water was imperative. For three days we laid in agony, crawling to the woods every time excruciating dysentery cramps gripped our guts.

The multifarious families on the Mesa were our lifeblood; not a commune but a community, joined by camaraderie of intention. We identified with an altruistic dream of working toward the possibility of a socialist ideal. The vision, we believed not attainable in middle class America, was pursued by those bound in a common purpose to live in peace and harmony with nature and mankind, using only what was necessary.

Maggie and Mickey, our closest friends, raised in Brooklyn and the Bronx were open and easy to talk to, making Nick and me feel as if we'd known them for decades. Their candor delivered with heavy New York accents, along with sheer volume, commanded attention. With one hilarious anecdote after another, the four of us sat around the table, drinking coffee and smoking hand-rolled Top tobacco cigarettes, Nick and I listening in rapt admiration to their stories of partying in the Big Apple.

Maggie said, "You won't believe this, it's so fucking bizarre. When we first came here, New Mexico, we explored so many areas before we decided on The Mesa. On the road up to Los Alamos, you know the Labs, the bomb, all that? I won't go into the whole history of the atomic bomb, the nuclear testing, and the lab culture but there's a good book by Frank Waters, a novel, but true, *The Woman at Otowi Crossing*, that is so scary."

I said, "I'm not all that familiar with the specifics but did hear certain aspects. So what happened?"

"What I understand is how the local residents and the environment suffered significant effects. The top secret Manhattan Project that developed the first nuclear weapons during WWII exposed the scientists and surrounding population to dangers not divulged until decades later. Residents of Tularosa, downwind of the testing sites, developed rare cancers having actually hiked and picnicked in the area, sitting on the ground, radioactive dirt, plants. They collected artifacts such as radioactive green glass fallout. So we're driving up this road, winding up and up and I'm looking at the mountain at the top and all of a sudden a huge portion of it slides to one side, the trees, greenery and behind it you can see a building.

"No shit?"

"No shit," Maggie said.

"Mickey chimed in, "It was so far out, like did I really see that. That's not possible. We decided then and there, as soon as we get to the top, we're turning around."

"We don't need to be convinced of this government's complicity in questionable tactics," Nick declared, "I don't put anything past the military."

Mickey, with his blockish physique, soft brown curls, warm penetrating eyes from an Italian Catholic background, was a mason by profession.

"I had somewhat of a Jewish princess upbringing," Maggie told us, "adored and protected by two brothers and my doting mother. My father died when I was very young, 8, but I didn't lack for anything. When I introduced Mickey to them I came up with this whopper; I introduced Mickey as a doctor. You can imagine the hard sell."

She had the typical short stature with lovely voluminous breasts. Wild, dark brown curls framed a beautiful olive complexion complimenting large eyes with lashes that actually curled up giving them such depth.

Mickey said, "The first time Maggie came to meet my family; my mother served 'the other white meat.' Maggie was so nervous and my mom sat watching her to see what her reaction would be."

"I figured I'd take a bite and fall over dead! I'd never had pork. But it was delicious," she added, grinning.

Having lived on the Mesa for over a year, both of them had invaluable lessons to share, from cooking tips to building methods. With strong, seasoned hearts of gold their support was woven into the rhythm of our life. The first party we went to with them included some noted luminaries, no one markedly impressed to see Dennis Hopper, Shel Hershorn and Todd Columbo in the mix. Except me. For real? Are these guys truly hanging out with us?

Blake and Sydney, also from Minnesota, were the couple we house-sat for our first six weeks on the Mesa. The immersion in hands-on experience, including daily wood gathering and splitting, food storage above and underground, and the nuances of kerosene lamps was greatly ameliorated by their smoothly operating systems. The lack of phone, electricity, and plumbing took a huge dose of commitment. They being our nearest neighbors, within a mile hiking distance from our campsite, provided many an evening's recreation together passing joints, decrying the government and planning our futures. With a strong hero worship, I gained courage admiring their accomplishments.

"There's this extremely talented artist I came across today," Blake told us as we sat around the table having had sandwiches of cheese and tortillas grilled on the cast iron stove top, "and he lives near here in Coyote. His house, I'd call it a cave dwelling, sort of hollowed out or into the sidehill, mostly rock. Pretty cool actually."

"I'd be into seeing it," I said.

"Ya," Nick chimed in. "When could we go or is that cool to just drop in?"

No phones, no agenda made us quite Avant Garde, in the sense of winging it. There were so few of us in the entire area we simply assumed we were all of the same mentality.

Blake looking at Sydney, with raised eyebrows waited for a nod in the affirmative.

She said, "We can do it tomorrow. Nothing much going on. Is that good for you?"

"Sure," Nick and I both agreed, rising to carry the cups to the counter. "We'll head out now and come by around 11. How's that sound?"

It was always so interesting to see how folks managed their lives in the wilderness. Our new acquaintance was way out there on that spectrum. Sitting cross legged on the dirt floor we were welcomed to partake of tea with this unusually serene young man. Shirtless, tan and sleek, long blond hair suggesting a surfer element mellifluous conversation ensued. Boyish and unassuming he seemed even younger than me, all of 22. Turns out he was 26 but his aura had such a youthful quality that it was hard to feature he was more than 20. We didn't stay long, maybe about an hour but he impressed upon us that this wouldn't or shouldn't be a regular occurrence in that he was intent, consumed with his work. The vision of this one Douglas Johnson was clearly defined and we respected his request.

Roy and Denise, from California, were straight out of a soap opera. Nick and I thought we were such radical hippies, so far out, but when we got to know the freaks from California, it gave the term new meaning. He, the smack shooting, Haight Ashbury, homeless dude, she the privileged, upscale nurse, doctor's wife and mother of two, were as unlikely a pair as you could feature. Caring for him at a healthcare facility during his withdrawal; they fell in love and ran away to the mountains of New Mexico. With an enormously powerful charisma, he was able to draw her away from her life of privilege even though it meant abandoning her young children. Food stamps were easily procured by all the hips, being the medium of exchange, but most of us had back-up support or savings. Having left everything, Denise and Roy's sole subsistence was the stamps.

Pepe, the ever finagling local store owner, let us barter food stamps for anything in his store, from nails to tires. This helped Roy and Denise in their effort to survive. Edgy, at best, eccentric, and withdrawn, Roy was a stark contrast to Denise's sweetly, gentle demeanor helping him recover from drug addiction. They lived the farthest up the mountain in Jairosa. At approximately 10,000 feet, amongst the clouds, it was over the top on the endurance scale. When the snow fell it buried their living quarters, a twelve by twelve foot log structure. They had to tunnel to the wood pile and the outhouse. With impassable roads we didn't see them for months. It was certainly one way to kick the habit. Nick and I spent two days with them during the summer helping them smoke a deer. Without refrigeration, all of the meat had to be canned or jerked (jerky). As quickly as possible, we hung thinly sliced pieces along a rope line over a slow, smoking fire to dry it. Rife with flies, in a matter of hours there were maggots to compete with. We would just stick to the areas not affected and let them have their space, peacefully coexisting. Roy and Denise only had a one room hut so the butchering was accomplished in a sort of lean to. After that experience I swore off meat for a season.

Canning with wood stoves was quite a feat, as well. Feeding the stove continually, the fire had to be kept hot enough to maintain boiling water for forty minutes. That's where summer kitchens derived from; a tiny playhouse away from the living quarters used for hot weather canning and cooking.

We worried about them so far away from 'civilization,' with their young son who didn't speak until he was four or so. Who was he going to talk to? But Roy and Denise were hiding, escaping, as it were, from their past. We took some small comfort in her background as a nurse.

Nick and I still smoked pot but didn't see the need for heavier substances. That sentiment was held by most of the hips. The simple lifestyle and centering influence of the mountains provided enough stimulation and spirituality. Nick did participate in a few peyote ceremonies in the Native church. Invited by Ed, who was friends with a member, the two or three-day service allowed only the serious adherents to attend, the ritual and events tribal secrets. After two days Nick would return, and much to my chagrin, not talk about it.

"It's sacred. I'm sworn to secrecy," he explained.

"Can I go?" I asked, wanting to wheedle more information.

"No, it's men only."

I had no clue where it was and no way to reach him if there was an emergency, but being that he only attended a few times, I didn't press it.

12

Pontelli & Violetta trying to take it all in

We all took a huge risk living on the Mesa but with youthful idealism it was easy to ignore the 'what ifs.' Our friends had children birthed at home, mostly without incident, except for one unfortunate baby who died from a severe cleft palate. Surviving staph infections, worms, parasites, and general filth, the other children thrived with names like Snake, Sarco, Rainbow, and Sunshine. They wouldn't have if they'd gone to public school.

Our disappointed parents waited, wishing for a conciliatory letter or a white flag of surrender. Through the pay phone at the general store we kept in contact with them about once a week. Faithfully, I wrote, but my timbre was arrogant, boasting pictures of our progress. Nick's folks drove across country to see us before much had been accomplished on our cabin. They were horrified! Their only child had gone to college for this!? After showing them the 'grounds' we drove to Santa Fe for a profoundly strained visit. I thought it wiser not to announce my pregnancy just yet.

Yep, livin' the dream, utopia, perfection! Nick and I kept in touch with friends back in Minnesota, urging them to come out and join us in our ultimate fantasy. It shocked the hell out of us when a few of them actually found our campsite. One friend from up North, Ellie, came walking down our driveway, alone, after having hitched from Albuquerque. We were blown away.

"How in the world did you find us?" we inquired incredulously.

"I just kept asking for The Mesa, described you, and they would know who I meant," she explained.

We weren't aware of our notoriety. There were the core families inhabiting our mountain; the first to arrive, John and Kathy, exceptionally groovy beautiful people from California whom everyone aspired to. Sort of the Homecoming King and Queen of The Mesa. Then came Ed and Dom, Roy and Denise, who no one wanted to be, some middle of the roaders and then Maggie, Sydney, me and our spouses. The three of us women had our own clique managing to carve out time, hanging, drinking coffee and gossiping. Even in that society we couldn't get away from competition, beliefs, politics, all of the plagues we'd run from. Potlucks every week, mostly at John and Kathy's or Ed and Dom's, mainly because their cabins were the biggest, consisted of some particularly unusual fare, the main entrée either bear, elk, wild turkey or rabbit if the larger game eluded us. Someone could be counted on for a chicken weeding out older hens, there was soup, vegetables, tortillas, always beans but generally no dessert. Whole wheat flour and honey didn't make for the most palatable sweets so the understanding was to sneak our treats in town when critical eyes wouldn't judge. At any given time one or two couples or the odd straggler would show up, staying with friends, relatives determined to make a go of this singular locale. They'd make a show of it for a few weeks or even months but invariably the austerity of the lifestyle proved too exacting and they'd float off as quickly as they'd arrived. They contributed to the wife swap-trading partners that was rife providing variety, excitement and unfortunately break-ups. Some of us eschewed all of that, me, for the simple reason Nick was by far the best looking, and most interesting man. Our commitment and bond to each other was unequivocal.

God, we loved our life in the mountains. Exciting, challenging, tough, and exhilarating, everything about it was a learning experience. Whether affected by the elevation or air quality, seemingly at our fingertips, the night sky ceiling shone luminescent with starlight. Drinking in glorious sunsets, the evening often ended settling our spirits before a glowing bed of coals to fend off the chill. Nick and I snuggled around the campfire, the wailing squall of the coyote accompanying our hushed conversation.

"Do you ever wonder or fear we'll end up like our parents?" I asked Nick.

"It doesn't seem likely, we're nothing like them. Why would we?"

"It's just that they had to be in love once, somewhere in their lives, when they first got together."

"Yeah," Nick agreed.

"But something went seriously wrong. They lost it, the magic, the tenderness. I don't want that to happen to us."

"Why would it? It's up to us, right?"

"I don't know, but let's promise to keep trying, to always work at it, so we can avoid the influence of their history. Consciously."

Lighting his cigarette, he took a long drag, "Mmmkay, how do you mean exactly?"

"Just this. Here we are, discussing our relationship, evaluating and addressing specifics. This is it. Talking about it, looking for signs of problems, not letting things fester. It doesn't seem that hard right now when I think about it. I don't think my parents woke up one day and didn't love each other anymore. It was a process that took, who knows how long. I want our connection to be alive, our love growing every year, thriving. I want this."

Nick pulled me closer, assenting with the gesture, his understanding and promise tacit as our lips touched, pressing gently, sealing the conversation.

"Whoa! Did you see that?" I asked Nick, observing the now familiar spectacle.

"I did. Very far out. Who *is* that?" he answered, chuckling. "What is that?"

The phenomenon we'd witnessed on numerous occasions was the sudden appearance of one, bright light, as if someone had just thrown the switch. Thousands of miles up, and yet so powerful, the suspected craft instantly attracted attention. Traveling at tremendous speed, it shot horizontally across the dark sky for two seconds and then disappeared as if you blinked. We weren't far from the Four Corners area where the Air Force could have been responsible for such incidents but we were convinced of something more alien. Jets didn't move like that which we'd witnessed way too closely.

F-111s flew practice runs through our back yard. Developed in the early 1960s, designed to fly extremely fast and low, the jet blew us away the first time we heard the ear drum shattering crack of the sonic boom. The engine noise, still miles away, drew our eyes toward the tall pines, towering a hundred feet above the landscape. As the belly of the jet skimmed the tree tops I instinctively pressed my palms against my ears fearing injury from the deafening volume. So close, we could actually see numbers on the behemoth as I screamed epithets at the military machine. KABOOM! The earth shuddered; branches shook, pine needles shivered to the ground as it exceeded Mach 1 vanishing as suddenly as it appeared. The spectacular sight accompanied by its staggering sound, although stirring, struck me as reckless, endangering the inhabitants of the area.

If we didn't hike down the mountain to Maggie and Mickey's to share dinner, Nick and I would feast alone, on huevos, frijoles, tortillas, and brown rice, staples of our less than balanced diet. A two-foot-deep hole in the ground preserved things like butter, eggs, and meat. Our monthly shopping excursion to Albuquerque replenished the larder providing some variety with various fruits and vegetables but soon it was back to dried, canned and bland. If we were fortunate enough to coordinate the 120-mile jaunt with another couple, we'd stay overnight in a flea bag motel for five dollars, splitting the cost. Pulling the top mattress off the bed, we'd flip for the box spring. With enough cash left over for great Mexican food and tequila, we'd splurge on a rare night out. The monthly showers were another rarity, but you had to make sure you weren't actually in the shower stall when you cranked the water. The cockroaches came flooding out first, then the stream.

Raising of the roof poles

Frikkin' awesome!!

The design for our log cabin was a thirty by fourteen-foot rectangle. With a permit you were allowed to cut standing dead, blue spruce at about 11,000 feet on Santa Fe National Forest land. Perfectly straight with very few limbs, bark mostly fallen off, dense and lightweight, it was the same wood Howard Hughes used to build his Spruce Goose for the war effort in 1944. My job was to peel the rest of the bark with a draw knife; one cross-wise, foot long blade with handles on either side. Straddling the log, I'd pull the knife in with careful, even strokes, skimming off the outer layer. It took about fifty logs for our home. Blake and Mickey, having built the previous year, lent invaluable brain and brawn to the work. We were so fortunate to have the benefit of our good friends' experience.

We poured two-foot square concrete footings and built above ground; our first mistake. Having a Midwest mentality, a house built directly on the earth absorbed ground moisture but one of the benefits in New Mexico was the perfect insulating warmth provided from adobe. Stubbornly, Nick refused advice on that point.

Round after round we notched, fitted, leveled, shimmed up, and spiked at the corner joints watching in amazement as the walls were completed. So lightweight, Nick and I could lift the logs into place ourselves. As progress continued we planned the roof raising day when all of our friends could help to pitch the poles. Instead of a two-foot angle, we ended up with closer to four foot, mainly from miscommunication. We hadn't planned on a loft so it just turned out to be wasted space, taking a ton more boards to finish it. We didn't think of that until after the fifth set was up and with Nick's finger nearly severed;

He and Ned were sitting on the top log, hewing the beam when Nick said, "A little more right here."

"Here?" Ned pointed.

"No, here," Nick answered.

Chop! Ned whacked with the hatchet before he could pull his index finger away spewing blood all over the log. After washing and wrapping it, Nick was useless having to hold his arm in the air for the next few hours while everyone else finished the project.

It would have felt too awkward at that point to say, "Oh. Well, hmm, that doesn't look quite right. Can you take it down and start over?"

My brother, Ricky, arrived that summer, much to the 'rents' chagrin, to follow in our wayward footsteps. Nick and

Ricky, along with whoever else needed building materials, spent two weeks in Albuquerque dismantling a turn of the century church acquiring oak and pine tongue and groove flooring, two by twelve fir boards fourteen-foot-long, all our windows: everything we needed to complete the cabin. For free! They would tie heavy ropes around their middle, attach them to the rafters for a lifeline, and pull off the third story lumber. We used the tongue and groove pine for our roof and the oak for the floor.

With most of the work completed on our cabin, Ricky found a shack in neighboring Youngsville. He hunkered down, hanging out in the lone tavern, playing pool and befriending the locals. His house, missing half a roof, manageable in warm weather, sent him packing to Aspen when the winter snows descended. Not a snowstorm, it was better termed a snow-bomb at 7,000 feet.

On one particular occasion after a week-long deluge, we were only too accepting, causing our prejudice to shift when the military came to our aide. With vehicles buried and the long distance to the highway prohibitive on foot, life slowed to a standstill. After four days holed up in our cabin, Nick and I hiked the two-mile distance to Ed and Dom's.

As we thawed out next to the stove, Ed remarked, "Do you hear that?"

The sound of an engine unmistakable, we grabbed jackets filing out the door to see a helicopter hovering above the clearing.

"What the?" we said in unison, afraid, wondering what or who they were coming for.

"Stay calm. We're fine. They're waving," Ed advised.

The helicopter lowered to within about fifty feet and then dropped two huge cardboard boxes onto the snow. We waved; they waved while saluting and flew away. Government surplus

186

was stamped on the outside. Nick sliced one open revealing canned goods, dried food, and various staples to tide us over until we could get down the mountain. Wherever the helicopter saw smoke from a chimney, the boxes were dropped.

We got a laugh as I wondered, aloud, "Do you think they know we're anti-war freaks?"

In an effort to stem the siphoning of our savings we found a classic flatbed truck to launch a business. Nick and Ed joined together to process logs; cutting, skinning and selling the vigas to contractors for expensive homes in Albuquerque and Santa Fe. It slowed our building progress considerably but it was a much needed boon to our economy.

After seven months Nick and I moved from camping into the cabin. The labor of love had materialized and I was only too eager to build our nest anticipating the new life developing within.

When Dweezil didn't show up for two days I suspected the worst. On either side of our cabin, canyons harbored packs of coyotes. Some nights the denizen's eerie cries wailed interminably. If they could lure the dogs into their territory, they would attack and kill them; conversely, if the dogs remained within their own boundary, the coyotes would innately respect that. For ten days and nights I whistled for Dweezil, to no avail. Nick and I hiked miles, searching up and down the mountain, reluctantly abandoning hope.

It was dark when I heard a soft scratch on our door, then a whimper. Opening it slowly, to peek out, Nick was astounded to see Dweezil hop into the kitchen. The right front paw dangling by two pieces of flesh on either side, her emaciated body, barely skin and bones, bulging eyes appearing otherworldly were still a welcome sight. She'd gotten caught in a coyote trap, the negligent owner, her likely liberator. How she had enough strength to make it home, or more astounding, how she kept all of the coyotes at bay throughout the nights was beyond our comprehension. She chewed the rest of the paw off and licked the stump back to health. Hobbling, three legged Dweezil proved her tenacious will to adapt and impressive ability to survive.

The Spanish inhabitants on the Mesa held a slightly more down to earth opinion of their world, not born into the white, privileged brat class like us city folk. They couldn't call their daddies when the food stamps ran out. Mesa Poleo had a storied reputation for Wild West lawlessness. While we maintained a love/peace philosophy, they adhered to survival of the toughest. Gun carrying, hard drinkin' red necks, most of them were cousin marryin' cousins. For generations feuds festered over property, horses, and cattle, and we hippies had to maintain neutrality learning how to stay out of the way. Just the fact that we were crazy enough to live up there gave us a certain éclat. They didn't quite know what to think of us. As long as we didn't take sides, life flowed along.

Tony, one of the land guardians of the property we were building on, lost the sight in his right eye puncturing it with a hammer claw on the backswing ending a promising career in carpentry. His judgment was permanently skewed, not so much from the injury but from alcoholism. Schlitz beer was his drink of choice, which he pronounced, Ssssccclitch, being pretty continually wasted. In the silence of the midnight hour we'd hear his pickup barreling up our driveway. Parking directly in front of the cabin, brights on, he'd honk until he saw the glow of our kerosene lamp. Nick, would go out, exchange pleasantries, and invite Tony and his entourage in.

His ever sober brother, Armenio, a slight, unpolished shadow of Tony, lent an air of calm to our party. Tony, the Elvis of the Mesa, was a tough act to follow with his slick, lacquered hair upswept and curling onto his forehead, swaggering in tight jeans, shit kickin' cowboy boots, fancy turquoise belt buckle, and pressed pale blue western shirt studded with pearl snaps. Too bad Tony didn't have anywhere else to go but our cabin. He was a smash with the ladies and yearned to run his hands through my waist length golden hair, always an instant hit with the locals.

Hauling in their case of beer, already having put one away, they'd be our best friends for the night. Did I mention their rifles were loaded and in the back window? Drunk and armed. How could we not welcome them?

"No, no, it's a great time, c'mon in!" we'd lie.

Nick and I considered it renter/landlord relations. No money ever changed hands to live on Tony's land but this was certainly a medium of exchange. We didn't have to get up in the morning for a job, so what did it matter? The trouble was, Tony's warring cousins, Rogelio and Nestor, would also drop in at any given time and it was always a possibility they'd pick the same night. The fact was, they actually had rip-roarin' shoot outs. They never targeted the hips but the danger of straining relationships argued the more reasonable option to drink and laugh and be congenial. When all the cans were empty they'd blast off to town to wake up Pepe and buy another case. The highway, after dark, was to be strictly avoided knowing those crazy mother fuckers could be careening towards you.

Days old baby Zelda Rose

The Mesa had been our first experience living around children on a day to day basis. Maybe some of it was peer pressure or simply a natural progression to our relationship but my rationale when beginning a family was, "Shit, we could raise a kid at least as well as those folks," referring to our hippie counterparts, "in some cases, a far sight better!"

My "we'll show you" mentality wasn't the most brilliant motive but suffering no morning sickness, nausea or other side effects made me feel markedly superior. And it was au naturale, no doctors for me. I could handle it all by myself. Women had been having babies without medical assistance for thousands of years, especially the Natives, and that's what I was going to do, by God!

The feeling that morning, the day Zelda was born, though I couldn't categorize it as labor, was definitely unusual, like pressure in my uterus, different. Nick and Mickey had been traveling up the mountain about 2,000 feet higher to get logs for Mickey's addition. Maggie and her baby daughter, Dea, stayed with me so I wouldn't be stranded in the wilderness that close to my due date.

I told Nick about the pressure, the sensation as I scrambled eggs. I'd mashed and fried up the pinto beans, along with onions, a bit of green chile. Standard fare to send him off for the day. Any leftovers were rolled into a tortilla or two for his lunch.

He locked his eyes on mine with that penetrating intensity, "Should I stay? Do you think this is it? It's seven miles up that road, ya know. Maybe I should stick around for another hour."

Putting his hands on my shoulders to square me, he searched for any hesitation, any doubt, really honing in. Gently, he pulled me into him waiting for a response.

"Nah, we'll be fine," Maggie and I looked at each other in agreement, with strong mountain babe bravado.

Watching Nick and Mickey drive away I did conjure an alternate possibility, if this really did ramp up. Sydney was a mile away. Maggie had her VW. We'd figure it out. I couldn't categorize the sensation so assumed we had plenty of time. Was this it? When we were finally able to time the contractions, discerning, okay, this is the real thing, it was 2p.m.

Maggie tried to convince me, "I should go get Sydney. Blake can get Nick and Mickey."

"Nothin' doin,'" forestalling her with my reasoning, "then, what if I'm here all alone when the baby comes?"

By 4:00 I was into hard labor, Maggie coaching, breathing with me, pushing on my back where it hurt the most.

"We'll do this by ourselves, if we need to," she encouraged, "we can do this."

We just had to convince ourselves, at that point. Over my panting, I heard the truck rumble down the driveway at 5:00. Nick instantly took over, supporting me, lending strength and much needed courage dispatching Mickey to Sydney's, our nurse/midwife. Convincing myself with every ounce of stamina, I prayed, "Mind over matter." Nick sat behind me on the bed applying counter pressure to my excruciating back labor. His unwavering love and support made it bearable keeping me focused. The love and encouragement provided by our closest friends had gotten me through the most demanding, most important experience to date. We entered a zone as one, one mind, one heart, a unified spirit coming out on the other side with new life.

They assuaged my fears with faith, cheering me on, always with the, "You're doing great. You're almost there."

Mickey lit the kerosene lamps, as dusk settled on our cabin. The peace and calm from their hearts buoyed me through the next critical hours. Directing everything firmly, Sydney coached us standing a little behind and to the side of Nick as our baby's head emerged. With one powerful, final push she slid right through Nick's hands into Sydney's steady, sure catch. Laughing, gasping, crying, we were astounded by the bold entrance of our daughter.

Cutting the cord with a sterilized Swiss Army knife, we used a fish scale to determine our baby's birth weight of six pounds, six ounces, give or take. According to ancient, native custom, Sydney saved the placenta to make stew. I could only choke down a couple of bites, not because of the taste which wasn't bad, but the thought.

Zelda's lily white complexion was punctuated perfectly by pink, rosebud lips. Marveling at the creation, Nick and I lay on either side of her for three days exclaiming through our tears the wonder, the miracle of life. Initially thinking it too ponderous a handle, we finally agreed that Zelda Rose suited her. She personified her birth experience in every aspect of development with delightful aplomb. This much I learned; babies are resilient despite their parents' ineptitude. Thank God for that. Maggie and Sydney already had a baby so their coaching became invaluable. Initially, nursing was so excruciating before I toughened up, my poor nipples cracked and bled and I either gritted my teeth or cried when Zelda latched on. With beans as a staple of my diet the gas was particularly hard on her little digestive system causing projectile vomiting until her third month. I got so accustomed to it that I'd nurse her, sit her up facing away from me, pat her back and she'd shoot milk out about two feet. Then thinking she was empty, I'd nurse her some more. Somehow she thrived. It stopped almost to the day. Three months. It had been an entire day, going through the routine of feedings, changings, naps, burping, and just like that. She hadn't spewed. Not the entire day. Not once. I was blown away. Incredulous. And that was it. When Zelda was able to sit up I'd prop pillows around her on top of the bed. In a moment of distraction I heard this thud. Off the side, sliding down the wall Zelda had landed face down. Scooping her into my arms I expected to see her face smashed flat. I cried along with her, rocking, swaying trying to calm both of us as I determined there wasn't any serious injury. More scared than anything else I concluded I was the worst mother ever. From then on I tucked her into a cardboard box, on the floor, blankets wedged to keep her secure. Day by day, inch by inch I learned. And she lived!

13

Robin Hood's poly cabin

Cops, law, sheriffs? Not a common sight on the remote Mesa. Robin Hood, that's what we called him, because no one knew his real name, was notorious enough for the authorities to brave the dangerous reputation and bust him at his house. A well-known drug dealer employing planes and Mexican connections, he was apprehended with enormous fanfare. From Albuquerque, 120 miles south, squad car after squad car amassed on the roads leading into the mountain, blocking escape. The locals regaled his saga, embellishing the lurid details each time it was related; how there was a helicopter hovering over his cabin, how he really wasn't even home or had eluded them in swashbuckling drama. Whether prison or flight, we never saw him after that day.

His house was the strangest monstrosity in any environment but particularly in the forest. Instead of using adobe, the typical insulating material, Robin Hood built his log home, sealing the entire structure with polyurethane foam spray. Then he painted the creation brown, so sitting atop the snow covered mountainside, it resembled a huge chocolate sundae. So incongruous with the natural surroundings, it was like happening upon the gingerbread house ala Hansel and Gretel.

The only other occasion the police ventured onto the Mesa was when Siqalito was shot by his drunken, irate cousin, Danielle. Unfortunately, he bled to death on the floor of his kitchen while the petrified cops waited on the highway for back-up.

Eubencio, affectionately called Banjo, was the hippie's inroad onto the Mesa. A sort of Godfather, the elder Spanish settler, ever-ready to capitalize, sold Blake and Sydney an adjoining chunk of his property, against relative's protestations. Banjo was shrewd and conniving in a back-woodsy, lovable manner. He loved to gossip, popping in at Blake and Sydney's daily to shoot the shit. Well known for her nursing experience, Sydney listened to his complaints ranging from lumbago to ingrown toenails offering a myriad of cures. Banjo was the self-appointed authority on land rights, family feuds and most anything else you needed to know about Mesa survival.

His diminutive, eighty pound, hunched-over wife, Esau, with her perpetual, hand rolled Bull Durham cigarette hanging from the corner of her mouth, welcomed us with a toothless grin as she poured coffee from a pot that was never fresh. She'd just keep adding more grounds and water until it was so full she had to

196

dump it out (on the garden) and start all over. She saved all of the empty flax tobacco pouches stitching hundreds of them together to make sheets.

Banjo's was one of the few Spanish households having electricity and telephone. Seconds after he got the call about the shooting, he was tearing up the dirt road in his pickup to get Sydney.

"You have to come help," Banjo implored Sydney, "or he'll die."

"What are you talking about, old man?" Sydney asked.

Her hands were covered with flour, making a batch of tortilla dough. Esau was the one who taught the hips how to make it, showing the rolling technique using a piece of cut off broom handle. Apparently it was just the right circumference for the job. Flour, water and lard. And a pinch of salt. Mixing, kneading, shaping into two inch balls, you'd roll the circles and fry them on the top of the wood burning cook stove. The cast iron was a perfect griddle.

Banjo, totally out of breath, "Danielle shot Siqalito and he's dying on the kitchen floor."

Wisely she answered, "I'll only go and help him if the cops are there."

Wiping her hands off, there was no way out of it. She agreed to drive to the scene but vowed to stay well out of range. Others had the same idea, conferring a half mile down the driveway.

Sydney knew the danger, telling Banjo, "If the cops aren't coming, we're staying put."

Word was a squad car was on the highway at the entrance to the gravel road, seven miles away, but wasn't going any farther until back-up arrived.

The three men, Leo, Danielle, and Siqalito had been drinking for forty-eight hours straight. Danielle was a well-known antagonistic troublemaker, the proof of his reputation, a five inch jagged scar where someone had cut his throat, ear to ear in a bar fight. Mouthy and swaggering, he'd brag about how someone had grabbed his head from behind, yanking it back, slicing through the flesh. Being that it didn't penetrate deep enough to kill him, he brazenly carried on as if invincible.

In an argument over cattle, Danielle pulled out a loaded gun. Unsuspecting and unarmed, Siqalito took a bullet in the stomach. Twelve hours later, three squad cars creeping down the driveway, lights flashing, guns brandished, were glaringly superfluous at that point. Siqalito had bled out in prolonged, excruciating agony.

Leo had escaped down the driveway, dodging Danielle's fire, as his truck careened over the deep adobe ruts at 50 miles an hour. He lived to be the witness but couldn't prevail with the jurors. Danielle didn't go to jail, pleading self-defense. He sold his whole cattle herd to pay for a lawyer that got him off. The cattle were his livelihood, his life, but it was a small price to pay compared to what Siqalito lost.

Everything changed after that. Coming down out of the clouds faced with this fissure in Shangri-La, we hippies lost our innocence. Guns had been for hunting, but now, this senseless, brutal murder, a mile down the road, brought fear upon everyone. Nick and I didn't really think we were in danger being unrelated Anglos, but could have easily been caught in the crossfire, living on disputed land. We had to maintain strict diplomacy between Tony and Arsenio vs. Rogelio, Nestor, and Samwell. We'd been put into a real hot box without the slightest clue as to what calamitous repercussions could befall us. Unwisely vowing loyalty to both sides of the feud put us in an extremely precarious position.

Both families pastured stock on the property. Tony's evil side emerged one afternoon right outside our log cabin. In a drunken rage, he pulled out his gun and fired several rounds at his cousin's grazing horses. Grabbing four month old Zelda off the bed, I made a dive for the floor behind the cast iron cook stove for cover.

"Tony," I screamed, "The baby!"

The shots stopped.

I laid Zelda down and stormed outside, "Goddammit! What the hell is wrong with you? We're right inside, right through those logs! Don't you know the baby's in there?!"

Tony had grown to love Nick and me over the past months. He completely switched gears, breaking down immediately. With a sobbing voice, he apologized, taking my hand, slobbering all over it.

"I didn't know you were home. I'm sorry, Anne, so sorry, I wouldn't hurt you, Anne. You know I wouldn't hurt you. I love you and Nick. I love you guys."

It was disgusting and so pathetic but I couldn't stay angry. We were fine. He was a fucking dip shit alcoholic with a huge soft heart underneath all of the bullshit.

"Yes, yes, I know, Tony. Go home. Go to bed. Sleep it off!" Turning to Armenio, I commanded, "Take him home."

Armenio never spoke. I don't know if he had the capability. He nodded, obediently, leading his weeping brother to the truck.

Zelda slept through the whole barrage.

When Nick got home, hearing the incident, he stormed toward the door, furiously yelling, "I'm gonna find that bastard! What the fuck is he doing? Fucking idiot!"

"Hang on, hang on, if he's passed out, which he must be, he won't even remember it."

"What's happening? This is nuts," he said, grabbing me in his strong arms holding me so tightly I had to tell him to ease up. He was really shook, his heart pumping, breathing heavily. I sensed his doubt taking root. We talked about alternatives that night. What were some options, ideas for our life, where would be someplace else to go? We weren't making any decisions but it was the beginning of the end. It wasn't verbalized but we both knew it.

Working as a nurse, our friend, Dylan's wife, Lillie drove the highway back and forth to work at the Cuba clinic. In those days, picking up hitch-hikers was commonplace and usually safe. She'd given dozens of rides all without incident which is saying a lot. Lillie was sweet, beautiful, and warm in that engaging, comfortable manner that could have easily been misconstrued and taken advantage of.

Driving out of Cuba after work, she slowed seeing two guys with back-packs and thought, "Oh, two young hikers." In the rear view mirror Lillie noticed the rifle sticking out of the back pack as they ran toward the truck. The instant she stopped a message flashed through her brain, warning, "Don't do this." It was one of those weird, eerie feelings, with a gut reaction to floor it, but they already had their hands on the door handle.

The spokesperson, his shaved head sweaty with grime, asked, menacingly, "Where you going? We need to go up toward Regina. Can you drop us there?"

"Yeah, sure," she acceded, feeling unnervingly bad energy.

Lillie's "Night of the Living Dead" vision instinctively told her to keep the dialogue flowing. When she pulled off at the Coon Hollow, they simply got out and thanked her. Relief at being rid of them was overwhelming, but she had that violated feeling all the way up to the Mesa.

The next day she went in to her evening shift. It was abuzz with the sensational details.

"Did you hear about the murder up in Lindrith?"

A wave of nausea went right through her as the words looped, "It was those guys, those guys, those guys."

And it was. They had picked up this guy in the bar, Davis, who invited them to his house so they could continue drinking after last call. Shooting him point blank and burying him in a shallow grave not far from the house, they didn't have the foresight to clean up the pool of blood. A neighbor happening by, figuring to find Davis home seeing the familiar truck parked in the driveway, became the unwitting detective. Climbing the steps, his curiosity piqued seeing the inordinate amount of blood, he innocently figured they'd poached a deer, butchering it on the porch. When he didn't see a carcass, he, naturally wondered where the deer was. The murderers sat in the kitchen like they owned the place.

Where's Davis? He didn't speak it aloud but nonplused, asked them, "What's with all the blood?"

"We were rabbit hunting."

That's too much blood for a couple of rabbits, he thought, realizing something was way off.
"I'll be leaving," he replied, as calmly as he could, gingerly side-stepping the blood.

Scanning the yard as he walked away he noticed two definite lines about two feet apart where something had been dragged. The shallow grave where the lines stopped confirmed his suspicion recognizing a piece of Davis' shirt sticking out. After a cogent phone conversation with the cops, they arrived, acting fairly casual a half hour later.

Their questions answered, it appeared they were going to let it go.

Incredulous, the neighbor was adamant, "Wait, wait, follow this trail," he insisted, leading them to the grave. The evidence irrefutable, the cops finally kicked it into high gear bursting into the kitchen, guns brandished, arresting the murderers without fanfare. Wasted to the point of incoherence, they didn't put up a fight.

Lillie, amazed at her ability to discern the pure evil in them, knew to trust her sixth sense after that. The trauma compelled her to stop giving rides to anyone. Those two hitchhikers, one just released from prison, were intent on killing. The sole motive, a truck. A lousy truck.

Reality was a harsh slap in the face to us anti-war peaceniks. The humanity of the area was severe and suffered no foolishness. We learned to keep our wits about us, knowing life could be unpredictably cruel.

We didn't mention any of these incidents to our 'rents. They longed to pounce on the slightest suggestion of capitulation. Jack and Edith, along with my grandparents had driven out to see Zelda when she was a month old. It was a strained, perfunctory visit, me attempting to pacify their arguments. To the contrary, more questions surfaced. How would we raise a daughter in the wild? Nick was blamed for not having the sense to get me to the hospital even though Zelda was perfect and I suffered no ill effects. They stayed two days, spending nights in a motel.

I did muster the grace to hug and kiss them when they left, saying, "I love you."

They returned the sentiment, but added that dose of guilt, "You'll be sorry someday."

Nick and I clung tenaciously to Thoreau's admonition, "Go confidently in the direction of your dreams. Live the life you have imagined."

Ebulliently, Nick and I had expected all of our problems to disappear when we disentangled ourselves from city existence. Many of the hippies, after abandoning dreams of a perfect society in neighboring communes, had sought a new beginning on the Mesa. Now, faced with glaring discrepancies between theory and practice, sensing the dawn of dissolution, our search for peace took a dramatic right turn.

Jesus came to town! The Jesus People movement from California hit New Mexico and the hips got saved. Jesus Freaks. Our friends, Eli, with his crusty, matted cave man hair, along with Matthew, surrendered in Santa Fe, shocking the hell out of us when they showed up at a pot-luck dinner sporting white side-wall haircuts and Salvation Army suits. Yessirree! We were in for a real live revival! With tracts and preaching tapes, they tromped to our cabins, proselytizing, telling us how spectacular we could be if we repented. And what do you know? One by one, the families gave it up. Along with Maggie and Mickey, Nick and I fought, resisting the onslaught. We were the autonomous hold outs, going to their weekly Bible studies to get the free meal, then sitting in the back to light up a joint or Satan stick, the condemning epithet for our cigarettes. When they started speaking in "tongues" we were incredulous, thinking they'd lost their minds! Yeeee Gods, I'd never heard of that at Mount Olivet Lutheran Church! Matthew got a guest slot at the local Pentecostal church in Gallina and at his behest we witnessed his preaching debut. The rest of the service was entirely in Spanish but he delivered his message in English, most probably for our benefit. I had to admit, I was moved, so much so that I couldn't wait to get outside in the dark so my tears could escape. His topic was, "You are the temple of God and the Spirit of God dwells in you." His amazing sermon delivered in love, on his knees, pleading, with tears streaming down his cheeks, emphasized our importance to God and our value on this planet. He was so sincere I thought my heart would break. Hearkening way back to confirmation and Cathedral of the Pines summer camp in northern Minnesota, I couldn't recall any other experience like that in my pedestrian religious experience, not one iota of the truth Matthew expounded. There was an undeniable depth, a tangible presence of God or spirit that left me confused, challenged, and curious. Riding home, we talked about it, the four of us, Maggie and Mickey, Nick and I, trying to discount it, explain it away, but the powerful effect couldn't be denied. Still wanting to mock, not ready or willing to adapt and capitulate, we ridiculed their fanaticism.

"We've been speaking in tongues all morning!" Mickey declared, as we came through the door of his house the next day.

We laughed and laughed, me looking over my shoulder, expecting lightning to strike from my residual Lutheran guilt. Speaking in tongues was just too out there. In 1973, without televangelists, no one knew what that was. So we parodied the nut cases who used to be our hippie friends and kept sullying their Bible studies with our damnable presence.

Call it peer pressure or a genuine need within, but after several weeks we caved to the wave that washed us into fundamentalism. A definite ethereal presence flooded the cabin that day in November, when Matthew led us in the sinner's prayer. We asked Jesus to come into our lives. Peace blanketed me. Peace, so tangible, peace, so calming, it was uncanny, incomprehensible, but profoundly moving. Nick and I basked in the soothing light. I'd never known such loving warmth, such all-encompassing acceptance.

For weeks, my thoughts had been tormented by Tillie's illness. Dying of cancer, inch by inch, cell by cell, the life was sucked out of her scourged body. Tillie was the beautiful, loving mom of my old, best friend, Meryl, and our constant, sympathetic advocate. She had continually bailed us out, writing excuse notes for us when we ditched class, making my 'rents listen to reason when they were at their wits end with my delinquency and now there seemed to be no hope as the disease vanquished her. What precipitated our conversion that day was supplication for a miracle. As I asked God to intervene on Tillie's behalf, I found genuine faith.

"Please, God, heal her ravaged body, give her more years, she doesn't deserve this," I pleaded, begging from my heart for mercy, for the impossible.

Edith, being Tillie's close friend, helped with her end-life care informing me, in a gut-wrenching letter, about Tillie's horrible death.

Sad and guilty that I hadn't seen Meryl in two years, I determined to look her up when we got back to Minnesota. Winter was closing in on the Mesa and I needed a break from the

205

relentless routine. Washing clothes in a tub on an open fire was losing its appeal. Once bolstered by the achievement, the two-day ordeal tackling one load of laundry was becoming a wearisome chore. The conveniences of civilization beckoned, and I found myself softening to grandparent's offers to lighten our situation. The moment Nick and I mentioned a visit, plane tickets were in the mail. Our vehicle was on its last legs so we planned to fly up North, find a truck and drive back to New Mexico. Nick's dad generously agreed to foot the bill.

"Baptized?" I questioned. "Is that really necessary?"

Maggie and I were discussing the topic, sitting around her kitchen table.

"That's what Matthew and Eli want us to do," she answered, adding, "The pond will fill up from run-off and there's only a short window before it dries up."

"Are you and Mickey going to do it?"

Maggie answered, "We're thinking about it."

At the last Bible study, Matthew had given Mickey a bunch of verses pertaining to the subject.

"I'm reading something else right now," Mickey told him. Matthew asked, "Oh what's that?"

"*Portnoy's Complaint*," Mickey declared, unabashedly.

I cracked up at Roth's preeminence over the Bible.

After more sessions with Matthew and Eli we agreed to meet at the pond for the prescribed dunking, but when the day arrived, I freaked out.

"I have to wash clothes. I have the fire roaring, the water on. I really can't do it now. You guys go ahead."

Loaded into their crew cab, Maggie, Mickey, and Matthew had come to pick us up.

Matthew mustered all his powers of persuasion, "But if we don't do it now, the pond will be too low. Everyone's meeting us there, you know. Satan is trying to re-ensnare you. This will break his hold from the past."

The truck idling in the driveway was waiting to whisk us away. I wanted Nick to back me up but he wasn't voicing any objections, apparently acquiescent, which disconcerted me. If anyone, he was the voice of reason, reluctant to dive into anything haphazardly. I was the one who'd act, asking questions later.

"Maggie and Mickey are ready," Matthew said, applying peer pressure, "You won't be sorry. You'll see."

"Oh, alright, let's do it," I conceded.

What could it hurt? Is it really such a big deal? Ten minutes later, we arrived at the pond surrounded by all of our Jesus freak friends awaiting the transformation of us hold-outs: the victory of finally seeing the deviants in submission. That was my attitude. Still cynical, defying this to have any effect on me, the weirdest thing occurred. Eli and Matthew plunged me back into the fresh, pure white snow-melt, pronouncing their spiel. When I came up out of the icy water, an astonishingly powerful force seemed to lift me into nirvana. It was a remarkable experience, tangible, undeniably outside of my control as my arms floated heavenward, akin to surrender. The water was freezing cold but I was in no rush to get out, glowing warmly from this wonderfully illuminating energy. I couldn't deny the divinely unusual phenomenon. The feeling was uniquely, inexplicably peace filled. Was it Native American spirit, God, some innate need to connect with a higher power or understanding? I only knew what I felt. Love.

That night curled next to Nick, I dreamed of a kitchen with a red and white checked linoleum floor. I was on my hands and knees scrubbing it with a sponge and a bucket.

"There I was on this ugly, filthy floor," I laughingly related to Nick the next morning.

I loved our languid early hours, before Zelda woke up, drinking coffee. Strong, boiled on the cook stove in my flowered enamel pot, doctored with sugar and Carnation evaporated milk. It took some getting used to, the milk, but it kept well without refrigeration.

He poured our second cup, "Thanks honey. As if we'd be in a place like that," wincing as I said it, "God, it was so ugly and so vivid. Linoleum. Can you feature it?"

"Do you know where it was, or anything else about it? Any other elements about the house?" he asked.

"No, just that checkered floor, like an imprint."

That's all we said about it, a fleeting conversation that immediately faded into the recess like a file folder.

I tried to convince Meryl of the love of God, my newfound enthusiasm bubbling over during our visit. She steadfastly rejected any entity that would allow her dear mother to suffer such a horrendous demise.

"No, really," I explained, "There is a God that truly cares for you. God is love. It's beautiful."

She was so deeply wounded, bereft of both parents, her dad having died when she was only eight, that she wasn't buying one word of this religious bullshit. Insensitive to her true need, totally missing the opportunity to show God's love, I plowed over her with my dogma, feeling like a failure when I couldn't convince and win her to Christ. I really should have shut up about it and been responsive to her pain, but zealots were typically obnoxious. I was no exception. We had a strained and limited relationship for years afterward. That particular brand of religion, fundamentalism, dictated a set ideology along with a cloned adherence to Biblical tenets prohibiting individuality and free thinking.

It wasn't such a stretch from hippie to religious fanatic. It was our search for the truth that caused us to reject our parents' values in the late 60s and now Matthew told us this was "the way, the truth, and the light." We took our self-righteous, hypocritical, my- way-or-the-highway philosophy and fit it right in with God. No middle of the road, just black and white, good and evil, heaven or hell. My search, my quest for the meaning and purpose of life now included the Word of God, a sanitized language, and no more dope.

We even informed our old city friends during our Midwest trip that we had all of the answers. They completely freaked out, thinking we'd been brainwashed into a cult. No wonder! We actually told them they were going to hell if they didn't accept Jesus, then and there. Some "good news" alright!

After a month in Minnesota, with old friends, grandparents and other relatives, Nick and I were ready to embark across country with our used Ford pickup. The journey carrying us back to the Southwest provided hours of discussion concerning our mounting doubts. We both felt the vibe, which we now called the Holy Spirit, shaking things up with a myriad of questions about our present situation. A shift had occurred. Something was gelling.

The road up to the Mesa, snow covered and treacherous, required chains to conquer the last miles. With freezing hands, Nick's back wet from hunkering down to get under the wheel well, the price we paid to live in the mountains was exacting. We sat in silence, the truck idling as Zelda dreamed on my lap. Cupping Nick's icy fingers in mine I blew warmth into them until the feeling returned. Something in me wanted to stay there, not moving, just sitting.

"What's wrong?" Nick asked, seeing the tear drop onto his hand.

"I don't know."

He kissed my cheek, saying, "Here goes. Hang on."

Flooring it, the chains ground through the drifts down to the gravel. It took a skillful driver to balance enough speed to keep our momentum while maintaining control. The final nail biting, nerve wracking miles culminated as the pick up ground to a halt at our gate.

A dusky purple haze sky, gossamer gray wisps outlining the last vestige of pink contrails, illuminated our solitary cabin as it came into view. Cerro Pedernal, the familiar peak ahead in the distance of the Jemez Mountains, sat atop the pine horizon. My heart warmed as the incomparable beauty of our home spread its tapestry across the landscape.

Almost home, it took a full ten minutes to plow through the driveway, inching forward, backing up, rocking the truck, getting close enough to carry our essentials the last twenty yards.

Nick carried Zelda; I loaded my arms with everything I could manage and walked in the door of our log cabin. It was exactly the way we left it. No break-ins, no signs of infestations. That vibe now stronger, I heard distinct words in my mind. Turning to Nick, "It's over," we both said in unison.

Our eyes bugged out, "You heard that too?" Nick asked.

I took his hand and nodded, mouth agape, shaking my head in disbelief.

We both understood the feeling, at that instant, as if the chapter ended. Was it a voice, a premonition, a spiritual insight? We'd never be able to explain it, but totally blown away, we were convinced.

"We can live here, alone," Nick reasoned, explaining his thoughts, "but how can we raise Zelda here? How will I make a living? How can we provide what she needs? This isn't fair to her, or to you."

Our conversation went well into the night, as we stoked the fire, hashing over the particulars of now what? Neither of us wanted to bail out but didn't see any way to sustain our life in the mountains. Mickey was able to work as a mason while Maggie maintained the land; Sydney and Lillie were both nurses supporting their lifestyle while Blake and Dylan raised the children. Nick and I couldn't come up with any options to meet our financial needs. Reluctantly, we decided to go back to Minnesota.

I took his hands across the table, as my tears spilled out, "It's you and me, Babe. Whatever we do, wherever we go, we'll figure it out. Together, that's all that really matters."

Raising his hands to my face, I kissed his fingers one by one.

"I love you," Nick whispered.

Anne and Nick

*   *   *

14

"Goddammit, if you two don't stop climbing over me, I'm going to lose it, I swear to God. I'm gonna start screaming and not be able to stop. I can't breathe. Help me! Somebody help me! Please, you have to leave me alone. You have to stop making me move," I thought to myself, my brain ready to snap, being roused every twenty minutes from the dark shelter of my thoughts.

"We're sorry, do you want to change seats?" they offered, perceiving my distress.

I could only shake my head, almost imperceptibly, but they got it. The flight attendants kept their vigil, anticipating a meltdown.

"Close your eyes, keep it together, this is the last few hours until you collapse," I would tell myself, willing my breath to flow steadily.

In. Out. In. Out. Breathe. I had to keep my wits, to get to the airport in Minneapolis where Zelda, Aaron, Chloe, and David were waiting. Four kids in six years. God, we'd been prolific! David, the youngest, had just turned twenty-one.

"Do your lungs hurt?"

Nick's last words to me. We were astonished by the myriad of wonders next to us as we snorkeled, buoyed by the ocean. Floating in the serenity, the beauty of sea life left us incredulous. We stopped at a point shallow enough to stand, and remarked on the sights, conversing about what we'd seen.

It was the most calming scene: the stunning coral, the sea so gentle. Angel fish, rays, anemones, yellow striped, aqua luminescent, multi-colored, flecked varieties along the reef accompanied our progress across the 100-yard expanse.

He spoke in normal tones and then abruptly, Nick said, "Do your lungs hurt?"

"No," somewhat taken aback.

He looked strange, troubled.

"Let's head in to shore," I said, alarmed.

At chest deep, I could see across his back, it was gray up through his neck. His legs were struggling like slow motion, as he tried to take the next step. Thinking the snorkeling mask, still at the top of his head, was too tight, impeding circulation, I yanked it off. With all my strength, I pulled, locking my arm in his. At knee deep, suddenly, he was gagging, vomiting foam, yellowish foam, tinged with blood, oozing from his mouth and nose.

"HELP!" I screamed.

He couldn't get his breath, wasn't cognizant, his eyes glazed over, unaware of what was happening. I knew he didn't hear me, but his legs kept on in a forward motion. Instantly responding, a man who had just pulled his boat onto the shore and a couple walking nearby plunged into the water. Three more feet to the water's edge, keep moving, one, two; Nick collapsed in a heap, hitting the sand as if he'd been dropped from ten feet up. The tremor, the sound resonating as his body hit the ground, reverberated in my ears, shaking my very soul.

His color was ashen, terrible, the yellow foam. The boater, a surgeon from the States, began clearing it away. He used the scuba tank from his boat to initiate CPR in less than a minute. I was petrified, uncomprehending, but steady. I needed to help, not freak out, not be a hindrance. My health class training, God, when was it, eighth grade, blowing into that molded, rubber dummy, named RescusiAnne, reminded me to tilt Nick's head back, slightly, to open the airway. His lifeless head, so inert, his eyes, so dark, portending doom. I tried to wipe the sand out of his eyes but made it worse. Another man, stepping forward out of the gathering crowd, spelled the surgeon, taking over chest compressions.

"You're not doing it right," someone barked, from the powerfully charged scene, "it needs to be much faster, I just took a class in CPR."

"Move him up higher on the beach, water is splashing on him," another called out.

Their eyes were burning into me along with the noonday sun that fried my back. Nick was so hard to move, so heavy as we shoved our hands under sliding him up the sand.

With my lips just touching his ear, I implored, "Breathe, breathe, c'mon, Babe, breathe. C'mon, c'mon, Babe, BREATHE."

Garnering every fiber of my being, calling, beseeching him back to me, I waited for the gasp. I knew it had to happen quickly, fully expecting it. Any second he would choke, gasp, sputter, cough out the foam, come to, and be revived. This wouldn't be the end. He wasn't dying on the beach during our dream vacation!

I kept it up, in his ear, getting louder, "Please, God, Oh Jesus, please, give him breath, spirit, life, air, heartbeat, PLEASE, don't leave me, Babe, don't leave me, GOD, I need you, come back, don't go. Babe, babe, come back… Babe, COME BACK TO ME!"

The surgeon had run to his room, returning with his stethoscope, inquiring about a defibrillator. An ambulance, even though a half hour away, was summoned, while heroics continued. That kept me hopeful, unable to process, unwilling to fathom the already evident conclusion.

"He'll just be very ill, very weak," I surmised, rationalizing, "We'll have to go home."

Bending over Nick, I couldn't look up into the horrified faces who were only too relieved that it wasn't them. I kept my eyes fixed on Nick, his chest, his eyes, and ears, now also with the foam seeping from them, the tinge of blood. His skin was discolored, the texture unreal; the impressions, the smells, and sounds fixed in my brain, forever.

When the ambulance arrived it was like a surreal Keystone Cops comedy of errors. The diminutive Mexican rescue workers, tremendously outweighed by Nick, could barely move the stretcher across the sand lending more drama to the catastrophe.

"God, oh God, please, will you come with us?" I beseeched the doctor.

He didn't hesitate. The EMTs almost let Nick roll off the gurney as they tried to lift him into the ambulance. For twenty-five minutes we screamed down the highway: me in the front seat, eyes closed tightly, afraid to watch. The shock paddles blasting him, pounding his body, arcing, slamming down again and again, I heard the competent surgeon calling the shots.

Silence jerked my eyes open, "Why are you stopping; we're not there yet?"

They were removing the equipment, setting down the paddles, quietly giving up.

"We're not there yet," I reiterated, begging, "Please, don't stop, they can do something if you keep on. Please, please don't stop, you can't stop!!"

"It's too late," the doctor said calmly, softly, as he shook his head, "It's been too long."

"Ohhhh no," I moaned, "Ohhhh no," as I climbed over the seat folding Nick's head in my arms, pressing my face to his, still burning from the sun.

I kept saying, "Ohhhh please, God, this can't be, please, can't he come back?"

As the ambulance came to a stop at the ER entrance, completely numb with shock, someone took my hand and led me to a chair near the entryway. I asked the surgeon every question I could think of. He explained the signs of the massive trauma, understanding the finality and the futility of reviving Nick. Everything was done, every effort made and it had been out of our hands.

I signed some papers and thought, "I have to go to Nick, he's all alone in the ambulance. People are gawking; they can see him through the open door."

His head was hanging down backwards; it struck me as so uncomfortable. I wrapped my arm around the underside, pulling him next to my face, still wanting to feel his skin, his whiskers. I wanted to put my mouth on his but the hard plastic tube still in place was covering his lips. Laying my hand on his chest, I began to push my palm into his heart with all of my strength trying to feel anything, even imagining a thump. It was only my own pulse, my own heart beating violently.

I still said, "God, isn't there a miracle? Can't this be different? Is this true?"

My thoughts bombarded me as I slipped in and out of reality, feeling semi-conscious. My body was trying to cope with the shocking truth. My heart, my soul, my spirit shattered, my mind unable to conceive or comprehend the unthinkable.

"How could it be? How could it be?"

The same horrendous question pummeled me over and over and over.

"Answer me, someone. Answer me. How?!"

He talked to me. In a normal voice. He looked at me, neck deep, in the water. And in less than five minutes, he was dead. He slammed to the ground. DEAD! Peering from the second floor balcony, strangers witnessed my most personal horror, me, still in bathing suit, in public, a Mexican societal taboo. They watched as the police pulled Nick's wedding ring off of his finger. I had to tell them he also had a signet ring on his right hand. They forced that off, too, and handed it to me. I put them both on my middle finger, making a fist to keep them on. Can't someone please make sense of this to me?! It's not happening. Not real. Can't be real!!

* * *

The next morning, I basked in the comfort of Nick's embrace as Zelda snuggled next to me, wanting to pretend the night before was a dream when Nick said, "We better go down to Maggie and Mickey's and tell them we're splittin'."

Reality.

"Uh-huh," I agreed, dreading that visit as I forced my legs over the edge of the bed onto the icy oak floor boards.

We bundled Zelda into the snuggly, piled into the pickup and rumbled down the road to break the news to our best friends. Maggie thought we'd been brainwashed by our folks who made us feel guilty about having their grandchild so far away in such an untenable situation.

"Every time I go back to New York, I get the same pressure. You really have to have a strong conviction and commitment to stick it out here. They're pulling you back in," Maggie argued.

It was a difficult conversation. We couldn't explain our unequivocal decision other than we felt there wasn't a viable method of raising our daughter there. They could hear the finality so we didn't debate it overmuch. The atmosphere was sad, almost of desertion, abandonment. We'd spent more time with them, with their daughter, Medea, than anyone. Our hearts were so entwined but now we were ripping that apart.

"When are you going?" Mickey asked.

"As soon as we can pack up our stuff and get rid of what won't fit in the pickup," Nick said.

"Just like that, that's it?" Maggie asked, her voice breaking.

I looked down at the floor, not able to hold the tears at bay any longer.

"Yeah, there's no work for me out here, unless I want to spend a week at a time in Espanola or Santa Fe, but we don't want to live like that. We want our daughter to have a relationship with her grandparents and that can't happen out here," Nick answered, his eyes welling.

He sat there holding Dea on his lap, for the last time. That was all the explanation we could give for our hasty decision. We hugged for a long time, knowing that when we passed through their door, it would be conclusive. With a promise to have dinner soon, a farewell meal, I felt a slight reprieve.

Nobody agreed with our abrupt departure. Blake and Sydney were some of the only ones that hadn't succumbed to the religious wave like many of us, so trying to explain that God was leading and dictating our path was even more disturbing to them.

Maggie and Mickey understood the Holy Spirit argument. Blake and Sydney thought we were certifiable with all of this fanaticism.

Every day another friend dropped by attempting to dissuade us. With certain doom, the Jesus freaks tried to convince us that Satan was ensnaring us.

"You're going to regret it. You're being deceived. It's too soon to leave. You'll fall away from Jesus if you don't stay with all of us," they admonished.

Within a week we'd emptied our cabin, fitting all of our worldly possessions, enclosed in a topper, into the back of the pickup, leaving enough space for Dweezil and Jasper to barely curl up. On December 23, 1974, with final goodbyes, we headed north.

Driving straight through, frazzled on caffeine, jammed together in the cab of the Ford, I lost it.

Kicking and smashing the half dozen Pepsi cans strewn at my feet, freaking out, I yelled, "What the fuck are we doing? I can't sit in this truck another second."

With wide eyes, shaking his head, Nick calmly pulled into the next gas station and got out. Not a word was offered.

He gassed up while I sat there in defiant silence, thinking, "What the hell is going to happen? What am I going to do with this baby? Where are we going to live? It's so goddamn cold up here! Shit. We made a huge mistake. NOW WHAT?"

Nick got back into the driver's seat, reached for my hand and said, "We'll find a place for the night, just settle down Anne, okay? Anne?" Squeezing firmly, he brought my hand to his lips.

I was pouting, stalling. He smiled, looking into my eyes and I forced myself to smile back. He took my other hand, lacing his fingers through mine. I always trusted his self-assurance. It centered me. I flashed on Chief Joseph's words, "It doesn't require many words to speak the truth." The simple feel of his steady hands, holding mine was enough. My knight.

The three of us spent Christmas Eve in a motel in southwestern Iowa where a raging snowstorm had closed the freeway.

"Everything is upside down," I said, trying to sound reasonable.

We laid on the bed, Zelda asleep between us, listening to the howling gale, feeling a constant draft through the single worn window of our room. The decrepit heating unit just below the window barely kept up.

Nick pulled himself up leaning over to kiss me, "It'll work out, we'll be fine," he reassured, "Sleep now, relax, I love you."

What a rock. His confidence was so secure. I needed to believe that, nursing nine month old Zelda. She had been an excellent traveler, unlike her mom, over the 1,400-mile trip. As long as I could sense that beacon of courage in Nick, it was manageable. Our commitment to each other was undivided, unwavering. Together it was possible, his Aries complimenting my Gemini.

Nick had the map spread out on the table the next morning.

Looking up at me, he proposed the plan, "Colfax, Minnesota is only a hundred miles north. Keith and Bon live there, remember? Let's call them and see if we can leave the dogs with them so we can head up to St. Paul, to my parents."

"For how long?"

"As long as it takes. For me to find work. I can still get reinstated with the City paving crew, they'd pay the best. But we can't take Dweezil and Jasper to my folk's house."

I couldn't even respond.

"Oh God," I argued, "this is the plan, living with your parents, your mom, the clean freak, spraying Lysol until your eyes burned, 'kill those germs' she'd chirp, your dad retreating to the basement, glued to the T.V., where he could smoke in peace, till he fell asleep at night? This is the plan?! Well, shit, it just gets better and better! God, you've gotta find someplace else for us, you gotta!"

Keith and Bon were happy enough to see us, to have someone to relate to in the miniscule redneck town of Colfax, Minnesota. Their back to the land journey had taken them to the Southwestern corner of the state where hippies were in short supply.

It was so cold in their house, Keith crazy about rationing the oil that I had to hold Zelda constantly to keep her warm. They kept wood stoves fired up but the place was too drafty to ever reach a comfortable temperature. Supplementing their income or maybe this was the sole subsistence; Bon kept chickens and sold the eggs to neighbors for a whopping forty cents a dozen. Keith never really did have a job, to my knowledge, well, except for drug dealing, and manipulating everyone, trying to control all aspects of life, but that wasn't a steady income.

That day as Bon left to peddle her wares, Nick offhandedly said, "Ask your neighbors if they know of any place to rent around here."

"Okay," she replied, with her sweet Peppermint BonBon smile.

Hoping, praying, wishing, I thought, "Could it actually happen? God, it has to happen. Help!" We hadn't even discussed it, but I would have done anything to avoid our other alternative. Nick must have come to his senses, the feasibility of an extended visit with his parents virtually impossible, recalling the scream fests with his mom throughout his teen and college years.

"There's a farm house five miles from here, in Walnut Valley, that you can inquire about," Bon told us when she returned.

"Really, do you know how much it is?" I asked, knowing our funds were near zero.

"No, but cheap, and you can do chores in trade. It only has an outhouse and wood heat," she added, "but does have running water, really tiny."

We didn't even have an outhouse in New Mexico, so this was an upgrade. We just took a shovel and tramped out to the woods, or crapped in a bucket, if nature called in the middle of the night, to haul out and bury in the morning.

Tucking his ponytail into his turtleneck, Nick donned a hat to camouflage his freak flag and we drove over to talk to the Lutsons about their rental. Earl, his wife, Fran, and children lived in the original house. His mother and dad, Florence and Edwin, were across the driveway in a little pre-fab, where they could be close enough to hold the purse strings and call all the shots. Earl was thirty-five but still the 'boy,' essentially making Edwin our landlord. We waited in the living room, making small talk with Florence until Edwin came in from milking.

Disheveled, smelly, in walked Edwin, forgetting to remove his 'shit boots' when he saw us, clomping across the carpet, right hand extended in a welcoming shake.

"Edwin Lutson," he declared to Nick, then with a perfunctory nod to me, grinned at Zelda.

"Nick, glad to meet ya," Nick said, rising to shake hands, towering over the pint-sized Edwin.

"Get off the rug, git yer boots off!" Florence gasped as she hurriedly shooed him backwards.

In his haste he caught the ornaments dangling from the Christmas tree, knocking it over, he atop, flailing to untangle himself. We about choked trying not to crack up pulling Edwin to his feet, Nick righting the tree, as Edwin bent to tighten the stand.

Florence took care of the spilled water, Edwin commanding, "Get these folks some ice cream," while turning to us, "You like ice cream, dontcha?"

Wrestling with his rubber shit boots, now joining us for ice cream Edwin consented to the rental, shaking hands again to seal the deal.

When we'd driven down off the mountain our youthful ideology evaporated along with the utopian dream. The Land of Enchantment now a memory we were supplanted back into reality. Down, down, down, into boring Heartland, USA, but at the same time growing up in time to parent our baby girl. January, February, and March in rural Minnesota were the hardest months to date of our married life, Keith and Nick braving sub-zero temperatures trudging through knee deep snow to scavenge wood. Our round oak wood burner in the living room needed continual feeding to keep Zelda from freezing in the uninsulated, clapboard house. Prohibitively cold on the floor, she was very late to crawl and went quickly to walking while she grasped each chair for support.

15

Zelda, crawling on the kitchen floor

"Nick!" I hollered, when it struck me, "This is the floor I dreamed about! It's exactly how it looked in my dream."

He looked at me, questioningly, "Are you sure?"

"Positive, I'm having déjà vu; really, it's uncanny, except that I was scrubbing it, on my hands and knees."

It hadn't registered until I looked at the picture I'd taken of Zelda in the kitchen, on the checked background, and Bam! That's when the lightning bolt struck.

"So this is where we're supposed to be?" Nick quizzed.

"Exactly," I responded, assuredly. "It's a sign from God. We were led here!"

It was the first in a myriad of experiences that seemed to signify God's direction.

Attempting every conceivable means to warm our house; closing off the entire upstairs and using the living room for the bedroom, we were able to achieve a comfort zone. Under the kitchen sink if I didn't leave the cupboard doors open the water pipes froze several times before spring came to the rescue.

"Hot!!" we'd warn, as Zelda neared the heat stove.

"Hot," she'd mimic, wide eyed, as we held her hands near enough to feel the sensation.

It was her third word, after momma and dada. She'd mimic our smoking picking up the cigarette butts we carelessly left in the yard.

"Acky!" I'd reprove, "put that down, pewwww!"

She'd look at me with furrowed brows, her critical eyes accusing, "You do it," cutting like a knife.

"Acky, throw it down," I repeated, feeling totally hypocritical.

Bold, self-assured, no nonsense, one of her favorite expressions at ten months old was, "Do it myself!" pushing my hands away, forbidding me to assist with eating or dressing, making for some unusual outfits, such as white fur lined winter boots and a striped T-shirt. Nothing more.

Nick and I'd tried to quit cigarettes so damn many times. Quitting pot had been much easier. We continued to buy the yellow tin can of Top tobacco and rolled our own, probably worse for our health but frugal.

"How can we tell Zelda it's bad, if we keep doing it?" I queried Nick one evening referring to the previous episode with our toddler, "She won't let us get away with anything."

"I know, it's confusing, definitely, we have to quit."

"Alright, then, let's do it."

"Just like that?" Nick asked.

"Well, I guess. Yeah, let's do it."

We resolved, we promised, and like the dozen or so other times we'd attempted it, we failed. I'd scrounge enough butts, scavenging the yard, filling a fresh paper with the most disgusting smoke I'd ever tasted. The outhouse was a perfect cover to sneak a few puffs and then stash it atop one of the two by fours that framed the structure. No telltale odor in there! Of course, he was sneaking just as many on his way to work and on breaks. He'd found employment that spring in the coating department of the local car parts factory spraying toxic lacquer on dashboard components and even though safety masks were standard equipment he exuded fumes all night long as he slept next to me. Nick's new acquaintances invited him into the established joint-smoking-break-huddle at a picnic table adjacent to the parking lot enabling him to endure his six-month stint at the factory.

From there he stepped up to the lumber yard one mile outside the tiny community of Emerson, Minnesota. The money was better, summer, July able to benefit from the fresh air, not exactly on course with his career path goals but, hmmm, I don't recall having had any established. He majored in political science at the University of Minnesota but the detour into the counter culture subversion became a derailment that littered his history with a useless degree. Nick got along with everyone at the lumber yard except for the psychotic sawyer.

"If I hadn't moved at that split second, that asshole would have taken my head off," Nick explained one night over supper, "the guy's a maniac."

"What's his fucking problem?" I asked, hating this man for endangering my husband.

"He has an amount of board feet that he drives himself, along with everyone else, to cut per day and God help the poor schmuck that can't keep up."

"Did you tell your boss?" I asked, belying my ignorance.

"Yeah, like that will help. Benny will get more pissed off if we have to slow down at all. He's the best sawyer they've ever had and production is at its peak."

"I don't get how he can risk your life."

"He just gets in that box with the controls and goes sort of crazy. He sends the log through the blade and as each outer layer is trimmed off," Nick said, explaining the process, "I trip the lever that flips it to the next side taking it back to the blade, continuing until the boards are sawn one by one, which I channel onto another conveyor. He controls the speed and doesn't care if they're flying at me before I can get the last one off. We're kind of playing against each other, sort of in a competition to see if I can keep up."

"That sounds ridiculous," I exclaimed, "like, it's not really a game, you know, if he takes your head off."

"I can't give the bastard the satisfaction."

"God, you're stubborn."

Nick didn't respond to my obvious conclusion. He got up from dinner, pulled on his gloves and went out to haul in arm loads of wood for the next day's cooking. We left the conversation like that but I despised Benny with a passion for putting Nick in such danger, for not considering what a few seconds either way would do to my marital status. What a prick.

That night in our homemade, platform bed I took my husband into my arms, holding him with such strength as if to say, "I won't let anything take you from me."

Knowing my thoughts, he said, "Don't worry, nothing's going to happen to me."

Our tender love making seemed to seal the promise.

"You know how much I need you," I said, nuzzling his neck, "You know how much I love you. Always."

"Always," Nick whispered, so as not to wake Zelda, sleeping inches away.

There was no greater security than being wrapped in his loving embrace all night. The ferocious thunder clap all but knocked us out of bed. Looking at the clock, it was 3a.m. The sultry humid day had foreshadowed a violent release.

"Are we okay?" I asked Nick, wondering if he could see any damage.

He'd jumped bolt upright and was peering out of the window.

"I can't see anything down, no trees, nothing burning."

"That had to be so close," I said, somewhat shaken, "I can't believe it didn't hit our house or barn. God, my ears are still ringing."

Zelda slept right through it. We fell back asleep listening to the steady downpour as it pummeled the shingles, thankful for the lightning rods that could possibly have saved our lives.

"I've got to run into town for groceries this morning, can you think of anything?" I asked Nick, jotting down my list.

We survived on pennies a day: eggs from our own chickens, milk and cream from the neighbor, vegetables from our garden, either fresh or canned and meat that our landlord had butchered.

When we'd first moved in, 6 months prior, we came back from town to see Dweezil running full speed down the road towards our truck, amazingly brisk on her three good legs. Just rounding the last curve bringing our house into view we saw three men standing in the road, one holding a rifle. Nick hit the brakes as I opened the door for Dweezil. Shaking wildly, her eyes bulging in terror, she jumped right onto my lap. There, in front of our house, was the landlord, Edwin, and his son, Earl, along with our new neighbor standing over the fresh kill lying at their feet.

Bursting into tears, I screamed, "What the fuck?! They killed Jasper!"

Slowly coming to a stop, their expressions fell as the realization struck full force.

"Oh shit, these are your dogs?" Earl asked, "We thought they were strays. We have a lot of trouble with strays and coyotes and you never mentioned you had dogs so we couldn't take a chance with our young stock up here, ya know, by God, they kill 'em, ya know, and we can't have strays killin' the young stock," he stammered.

One shot to the head. Jasper, most probably, had run right out to greet them, wagging his tail, ready to play. Goddamn motherfuckers! I was so stunned, speechless, trying to calm Dweezil.

"We are so sorry," their lame-ass condolence offering not a shred of comfort.

Nick tried to be gracious, "You didn't know, you couldn't have known."

I was thinking, "Well shit, couldn't you have put two and two together? We just moved in, now there were two new dogs, and you might have asked us if we had pets!"

Damn, what kind of assholes were they? I didn't say a word, just shook my head carrying Zelda as I climbed out of the truck, Dweezil on my heels. Nick stayed outside with them, even helping load Jasper into their pickup. Later that afternoon, Earl and Edwin showed up with bags of groceries, including pork and beef from their freezer. A peace offering. This continued for some months, helping stretch our budget. We couldn't realistically afford to be feeding two dogs; it was guaranteed rent control and also gave us the bonus of their humble obeisance. The rent remained twenty five dollars a month for three years at which point they finally had to jack it all the way up to a whopping forty dollars, to cover utility increases.

Following the morning of the stormy Friday night, setting out for town, I slowly rounded the gravel curve watching for downed limbs or a washed out section of road, when I slammed on the brakes. Up against the barbed wire fence was one of the most outrageous scenes I'd ever encountered. In one grotesque conglomerate of hooves and bodies, legs and heads, eight or nine Black Angus cows were dead. Huddling together against the fence, they'd been struck by lightning. The multiplied force as it traveled through each cow appeared tantamount to a bomb blast. None of them were dismembered, but the spectacle with limbs sticking out every which way in the six-foot-high pile was mesmerizing. It was hard enough to make it as a farmer without suffering this sort of financial injury. Mother Nature could be a merciless bitch, I thought, driving to the next farm to deliver the blow!

Rap, rap, rap, the door opened, "I was driving by your pasture and saw that your cows got struck by lightning last night."

"My cows, how many?" Marvin inquired.

"Umm, you better go see, I couldn't quite tell," I lied, not wanting to be that harbinger.

I drove back home to tell Nick, "You've got to come see the farthest out thing ever!"

He was sitting at the kitchen table, crayon in hand, entertaining Zelda.

"What's the deal?" Nick asked.

"I won't even tell you. You just have to see it. It'll blow your mind! Totally!"

We climbed into the truck. As the extraordinary catastrophe came into view, Nick began, "What the?" and was left speechless.

"I know, it's like they were blown off the ground and then crumbled into this gruesome monstrosity."

"Yeah, it's like they've been set in concrete. They're so stiff."

Finally, our morbid fascination sated, I drove Zelda and Nick back home and continued on to my original destination. Two hours later, passing the scene of devastation, the dead cows had all been hauled away, leaving a black scorched section of land. God, I wish I'd taken a picture! That memorable night turned out to be our son, Aaron's, auspicious beginning.

* * *

Back in my hotel room, I dialed the number Zelda had given me for Aaron's office. The receptionist in his office at DePaul University, in Chicago, informed me that he was in a staff meeting and would I like to leave a message?

232

I had to stay coherent, I had to make her understand without screaming, "This is the most dire emergency and I need to talk to him immediately!"

"Well, please hold the line."

I said, "I'm calling from Mexico, don't, <u>do not</u> disconnect me."

"Okay."

Another person came on the line explaining, "We're going across the street to the staff meeting to get Aaron. It will take a few minutes."

I thought, "What will he think when they tell him there's an urgent message from Mexico?"

I waited an interminable five minutes.

The receptionist came back on the line, "I'm transferring the call to Aaron's office."

Again, I reiterated, "Don't lose me."

Incredulously, she said, "Aaron's line is busy."

On the next try I heard his voice.

"Mom?"

"Aaron, it's me, Oh Aaron, your dad died."

He yelled from the depths of his soul, deep in his gut, a wrenching cry.

"No, no, Dad?! He died?"

"I won't know what happened till the autopsy report is done but there was some major trauma; it was instantaneous when he hit the beach."

We were sobbing. I was trying to explain the incomprehensible.

"I'll leave and get Jillian and head home. We'll figure out what to do."

"I love you, Aaron, we'll talk soon."

"I love you, Mom."

There was nothing else to be said. Aaron and Jillian, newlyweds, had been married the summer before. I was so thankful he had someone.

My head hurt so horribly I thought I would burst a blood vessel or have a stroke. Hunching over Nick for that half hour, my knees ached from the ground-in sand leaving hundreds of tiny pin pricks.

In my mind I repeated, "I have to keep it together. I have to get out of here, get Nick's body out of here."

Hearing Aaron's cries, knowing his pain, his agony over my dire words from Mexico, made me feel like **I** was inflicting the wound on this strong young man. That I couldn't wrap my arms around my children, couldn't deliver the words in person, couldn't do anything to soften the blow pierced my soul.

On the plane, digging my fingernails into the armrests one lone tear escaped from my tightly squeezed eyelid. I couldn't start. I brushed it away. Stay sane. You have to. Just breathe. Listen to the engines carrying you north. Think of Zelda, Aaron, Chloe, David, holding them, having their arms wrapped around you. Another hour. Breathe.

* * *

When Nick and I left New Mexico, our fellow Jesus freaks delivered this dire warning; "If you don't seek out a church or Bible study, you will fall away from the Lord."

We searched in Minnesota, but ultimately named the area Deserton, describing the dry and dead spiritual community. Invited by Nick's workmate, we attended a Seventh Day

234

Adventist revival, but then learned we were pawns in a contest for a giant sized, gleaming white Bible awarded to whoever racked up the most guests. I never saw anything like it. Instead of setting it on the coffee table, this one could actually become the coffee table, the ultimate proof of one's faith in gilt edged genuine leather displayed for all to see. After attending a couple of church services, evangelical, trying to avoid the mainstream denominations, and having nothing measure up to the moving Mesa gatherings where we felt such a peace-filled aura, Nick and I devised our own method of worship with Bible reading and televangelism, namely Oral Roberts, donating a few dollars to build his college and tower of Babel.

"Doesn't anyone else get it?" I implored, as we sat at our kitchen table, Bibles open, "Doesn't anyone want anything besides that canned, normal, boring religion? I mean, there has to be someone, some people that need more than one innocuous hour of bullshit on Sunday morning. I did that Lutheran trip, you, your Greek Orthodox."

"Maybe not in conservative rural Minnesota," Nick replied, adding a reference to Matthew 7:1, "judge not, that ye be not judged".

I assumed he was admonishing me for my pejorative description of the locals. Judging me, ha!

"Well, I can't believe God brought us here to dry up," I sighed, "and no other hippie types, either, no spiritual connection on any level. It's depressing."

Nearing the third trimester of my pregnancy, I wanted a home birth but there was no support in Deserton. Keith and Bon had bailed out on the country life and retreated to Minneapolis. He was just too freaky for the locals. As much as Bon made inroads and friends with her personality, Keith scared them away.

235

One day he charged out of his house, wrapped only in a sheet, to deter the landlord from popping in unannounced. In those parts if a farm was rented out, the owner felt like he had every right to just walk into his 'own' home.

Edwin did that to us as well, opening the back door and at least having the forethought to announce, "Don't mind me, don't have no manners, just walk right in."

And there he'd stand in the kitchen. Unnerving! Especially incredible, given the fact that we bathed by the cook stove in a galvanized tub.

"What if I'm making love to my wife?" Keith argued with his landlord, trying to make the case for privacy. He really was more concerned about his drug habits being discovered than his sex life.

His landlord replied, "Well, who, in their right mind, would be doing *that* in the middle of the day?"

Earl had a similar attitude about sex as Nick learned in conversation.

"God didn't intend that fer fun, ya know," Earl said, expressing his backward belief.

"Bummer," thought Nick.

Reaching down the inside of his pants, as Nick told me about it, I copped a feel,

"If they only knew what they were missin'!" I said, feeling Nick's discernibly turgid response.

16

One day old, Aaron Pontelli

Successfully having run off our entire former Minneapolis crowd by preaching the "Good News" to them, namely impending doom and imminent damnation if they didn't accept Jesus, a few brave diehards remained our friends. Bon was one of the only ones that hung in there, driving three hours from the Cities to visit, not threatened by our fanaticism and would have helped me with a home birth, if she still lived nearby. Keith never came with

237

her to visit, though, ("Turn or burn" wasn't actually that endearing!) attributing our behavior to lunacy.

Seven miles from medical facilities in February, with no one to care for Zelda, and continual pressure from Jack and Edith, we opted for a hospital birth. Somewhat restored in relationship to the 'rents, they offered to babysit Zelda when I went into labor if we promised to abandon a home birth. Labor began just as it had with my first experience; uncomfortable pressure, indeterminate contractions, but instead of 3 hours of hard labor, this time it ended with one continuous half hour push. The on-call doctor, in a snit about the dinner interruption, convinced me to let him rupture the membranes. From that moment I could barely catch my breath. Slamming against my pelvis with such incredible force, the baby distinctly blue from the intensity of birth was whisked away with a promised return from the nurse after a few minutes in the incubator.

Aaron's birth experience personified the bull-dozer attitude he displayed throughout most of his years, especially the formative ones. From the moment he could accomplish it, my hard-headed little toughie pushed the envelope. Walking at eight months, running and climbing soon afterwards, Aaron was a disaster waiting to happen.

Nick made the twelve-mile distance from Emerson in less than ten minutes the day I called him to rush us to the hospital. Aaron, at nine months, had taken a dive down the staircase, landing on his face, biting through his lower lip. Screaming, bleeding, I held him with one hand, dialing with the other. By the time Nick barreled into the driveway Aaron had settled down, his bleeding stopped, already attacking the stairs. Virtually invincible through dozens of tumbles, we were reasonably certain if he landed on his head, there would be no serious damage.

When he didn't make a peep, falling and smashing his head, one concerned friend asked, "Is he knocked out?"

"Nope, he's fine," I reassured, as Aaron pulled himself up toddling off to his next challenge.

Carrying Aaron on my back, pushing Zelda in the stroller, doing grocery shopping for the week, I stopped into a jewelry store to see about getting my favorite earring fixed.

"Hi, how are you doing today?" the jeweler asked, in a soft, laid back manner.

"Ah, fine. I was wondering if you could fix this earring?" fishing it out of my pocket, I picked the lint off of it before handing it to him.

Pulling the loupe down to cover his right glasses lens, he held it up to the light, peering at the mangled mess that had been crunched in the truck door.

His eyes searched my face, as if to say, "You're kidding, right?!"

Aloud, he offered, "Let me show you some earrings that are similar and you can start fresh."

"Oh, well, no, I can't afford anything like that right now. Thanks anyway," I countered.

"Yeah, you don't really need any of these things, anyway."

His curious unorthodox reply took me up short drawing my attention to a three inch, hand carved wooden cross hanging from his neck.

"Hmmm, that's quaint," I thought.

Here's a guy surrounded by gems, gold, silver, and he sports a wooden ornament large enough to heat the house with. I bit.

"That's an unusual cross."

Not missing a beat, he declared, "Jesus Christ is my personal Lord and Savior. Do you know Him?"

I looked from side to side, not as candid or free with my confession. No one was within earshot.

"Yeah, we moved here a while back and haven't met anyone who believes the same way. What church do you go to?" I asked.

"We meet in a home a few blocks from here on Sunday afternoon with about twenty-five people. It's at 1:00 o'clock. We'd love to have you come."

"What do you do?" I queried, cautiously optimistic.

It was the first ray of hope, the first lead suggesting a semblance of spirituality. A far cry from the hippie conglomerate we'd come from but maybe. I mean, this guy was straighter than straight, with his polyester leisure suit, imagining the other twenty-five faithful all decked out in their finery.

"We sing some praise songs, people play guitars; we share scriptures, give testimonies, and pray for each other. It's a loose format. You can stay as long as you like, one hour, two hours, all afternoon. We just let the Spirit lead us," he explained.

With his promise to make an attempt at the earring and my profuse thank yous, we said goodbye. My inner hope reflected in a permanently plastered smile, I drove home anticipating Nick's reaction.

"Wow, Nick, it was so far out!" I related excitedly.

He came through the door with an armload of wood, letting it crash into the box next to the stove.
"I couldn't believe it, he had this really far out way about him, like he could have cared less about selling jewelry, like his sole purpose there was to tell you about Jesus."

Nick listened politely, never one to show enthusiasm or jump into anything.

"I really want to check it out. What do you think?"

"Yeah, sure, when is it?"

I gave him all of the particulars as I finished getting supper together.

If there were forces working against us, if there was an actual good and evil competing for our future, those factors hindered our attendance for more than a month. Weather, mainly, dictated that we tend our home fire every three hours or come home to frozen pipes; or our truck wouldn't start, or the roads weren't plowed, or someone had a sore throat. I couldn't believe week after week our intentions were thwarted. At long last, we were sitting cross-legged on the floor in the living room of a monstrous old house, picking up simple kumbaya choruses, feeling loved, sensing the spirit, and knowing tears sliding down my cheeks were accepted practice. It had the same vibe as our New Mexico meetings; beautiful, real, striking a chord in my soul. That earring changed our lives for the next twenty years.

Over the next two decades a rag tag populace of strange members paraded through the doors of the church we built with our donated labor. Not wanting to condemn anyone, embracing Christ-like ideology, we associated with ersatz prostitutes, lepers, and murderers. If Nick and I could have been objective, able to see the subversion of the truth, we probably wouldn't have submitted to it for so long, but as in any radical belief system, the lack of balance caused reason to suffer. In the thick of it, we definitely couldn't see clearly but in hind sight recognizing it as brain-washing.

Let me recount: there were the demon possessed psychotics; at least two, no, three pedophiles (those that we were aware of, believing we could rehabilitate them), untold philanderers, and drug addicts, all rubbing shoulders with conservative Midwestern families. The decisions were handed down by five elders who submitted to a hierarchy of self-appointed apostles based in Ohio that derived incomes from our tithes and once a month, brought their leadership and teaching to us on the wings of a small airplane, also paid for with our sacrificial offerings. When the BMOGs (Big Men of God) arrived, church became a carnival. We hauled our children to 'meeting' marathons, making them endure Friday night, Saturday and Sunday all day services. The inhumanity and oppression included corporal punishment, a dress code, with tacit rewards for long-haired women, according to the Biblical crowning glory, and if pants had to be worn by women, then side zippers were the accepted standard. There was an obscure verse in the Old Testament forbidding women to wear anything that pertained to a man inducing me to sew some ridiculous slacks acting all holier than thou. When our religion dictated the refusal of medical services, we slid further into dangerous blind faith believing if we were good enough, we'd be healed by Jesus. Judged for not measuring up, condemnation was heaped upon those seeking a physician's treatment. Our family was lucky enough to avoid any major medical necessities and fortunately, the babies born by fellowship members without medical aid, all lived, but when immunizations for children were frowned upon because God would protect them, we drew the line opting for the standard course of shots, unwilling to jeopardize them.

Not hard to miss was the unholy competition running rampant throughout the congregation. At times the Sunday service took on an air of dueling oracles. To demonstrate one's spiritual giftedness, any number of congregants would prophesy or speak a

242

message in tongues. Not to be outdone, another person would embellish, prophesying something more glorious or outrageous until the undisputed oracle of God glowed with recognition. It was a tremendous amount of hooey, but at that time we really did believe our words came directly from God. Bandying about colloquialisms at our gatherings God had that much to say to us and nothing better to do. We couldn't call it church, because *we* were the church. It was 'Fellowship Hall' to enlightened followers. When we had buffet style dinners after the service we couldn't call them Pot-Luck because luck was 'of the devil', (the oft used taboo phrase) in our enlightened thinking. They were Pot-Bless dinners. That made it holy. And spit that food right out if you started eating before it was prayed over. None of this 'Come Lord Jesus, be our guest' BS either. You made up your own ad lib prayer on the spot. Vain repetition was for those luke-warm Lutherans or Catholics. We lumped everyone into two categories: us charismatics, the chosen, elite class of believers, and everyone else, who were as good as heathens. Hard core heavy metal rock music was Satanic. There was secular music and Christian music, which of course, was what Jesus listened to.

When one family moved to the area from Minneapolis, our conservative community was blown to kingdom come. Normal enough, to our distorted perception, home schooling their four children to limit exposure to worldly influences, like many Fellowship families, the malevolence turned out to reside within their own four walls. Jake, the father, had a 12-year-old son from his first marriage, Ryan, who had grown up in Chicago with his mother until he was out of control, precipitating the hasty heave-ho to his dad. Minneapolis wasn't too much of a culture shock, but when they moved to our little town of 1,000, we would have never guessed the seismic tremor that would ensue. Knowing

Ryan couldn't have adjusted to home school, they sent him to the small-town high school where he stole, dealt drugs, cut class, set up other kids to get busted, creating a virtual hell on earth for the podunk staff that had never encountered an all-out delinquent. His overwrought father and stepmother, Corrine, brought the matter to the church elders for counsel. Figuring Ryan was too old to spank they advised grounding and withdrawing privileges. The decision by his parents and church sanctioned, to discontinue the ADHD medication he'd been on for ten years may well have contributed to the disaster.

Whether it was the restrictions or circumstances combined, pent up in that farm house so many miles from town, Ryan went berserk. After everyone had gone to bed, he took a shotgun into his parents' bedroom, firing point blank at his dad. Corrine jumped from the bed, bounding to the doorway, as Ryan ran down the hallway.

"Ryan, come out," she said, fearlessly, turning on the light. He had gone into the children's room, ages one to six.

"Come out and give me the gun. Everything will be okay. Your dad's okay," she lied. "Just come out. We can fix it."

She kept on, eerily calm and composed, using all of her powers of persuasion to entice him away from the children.

Ryan stepped through the doorway, raising the gun, the deafening blast ripping through Corrine. As her chest exploded, splattering everywhere, death was instantaneous. Catching sight of his dad's bloodied hand as it grabbed the doorway, Ryan fled, bolting down the stairs.

"Wait, Ryan, Ryan!" Jake begged, with choking gasps.

The four little children hovered over their mother, wailing, "Daddy, Momma."

Jake told them, "You stay with your momma till Daddy gets back."

He had to have known Corrine was dead but maybe couldn't absorb it. How could he be thinking straight, blood draining out of him? Ryan had pumped one shot into Jake's shoulder while he lay in bed. Who knows? Divine intervention holding him together?

As he dragged himself to the phone in the kitchen, "Oh God!" he moaned, seeing the cord ripped out of the wall. "Neighbors, I've got to make it to the neighbors."

Jake inched his way across the kitchen, holding onto the counter, out the back door, and across the driveway to the barn, feeling Ryan's eyes, expecting gunshots.

"If I can pull myself onto the tractor, I can get help. I have to make it, have to save the kids, have to."

A shot whizzed past his head as he maneuvered out of the driveway. Miraculously, he made it.

Nick and I heard the details from him in his hospital room. Ryan hid in the machine shed until the cops arrived. Then he surrendered without a fight. They hauled him away, took Corrine's body, and removed the traumatized children from under the bed where they had huddled together. Social services provided them with care for the next weeks while their father recovered.

"Oh my God," I exclaimed to Nick as we drove home from the hospital.

"What a bizarre scene!" he said. "I can hardly believe it. How could he be capable of such cold blooded murder?"

"I have no idea. How could that happen?"

"No clue. I never saw that one coming. Who could have?"

"I wonder what made him snap."

"Unbelievable!"

"How is this going to affect our body of believers?"

There it was. It was all about saving face. They referred to us as the cult or the hippie church already. Our reputation was always suspect to the community, anyway, being so radical but this would remove any last doubts.

To compound the matter, during the ensuing investigation, a friend of Jake's family, Monica, accused our pastor and Nick, now an elder, of manipulating and brain washing Ryan with counseling sessions. Her testimony came off as not credible due to her whacky persona sitting in the witness chair wearing a see-through tapestry print get up. The defense attorney just let her ramble on about the church's practices and beliefs. Amusing if it hadn't been for the tragedy.

"It was ludicrous, a regular sideshow," Nick told me, relating the account of Ryan's hearing.

"She said we used mind control on Ryan. I wouldn't be surprised if she was the one who suggested the whole plot to him!"

"There's no way to prove that. But I do wonder what they were doing alone, spending all of that time together. What's a thirty-five-year-old woman doing hanging out with a 12-year-old? Listening to records, my ass. Duh!"

"When Jake put a stop to it, that's when Ryan snapped," Nick surmised.

"What will they do to Ryan?"

"He'll go to a juvenile facility until he's eighteen and then be scot free."

"Isn't that crazy? For murder. Bizarre," I said, with a shudder, remembering all the times our children had been in Ryan's company.

The Fellowship barely survived, evolving in some aspects, moving away from fear mongering over the anti-Christ, hell, Revelations and the mark of the beast into trying to adopt some semblance of normalcy. So many members came and went over the years but we hung in there. Truly, it was beyond comprehension.

* * *

Watching the uniformed man peer through the rear door of the ambulance and snap a picture of Nick enraged me.

"What the hell are you doing? Who is that? What is he doing?" I snapped at one official.

"Politzia, official record, police," he responded.

It hadn't hit yet— Nick was completely and utterly gone from me. I looked at his rings shining on my middle finger. Raising my eyes to the sunlight glinting off them, I saw my privacy invaded by curious second floor gawkers voicing unintelligible questions. That was the beginning; an ignominious nightmare, glutted with corruption, mistreatment and inhumanity. I felt naked, my feet burned from the pavement, sounds swirled in and out of my consciousness as I stood frozen, leaning on the ambulance door. Shock.

Our trip, booked through a specific package, employed an American travel agent in the Mexican office. Well versed in protocol, like an angel, she appeared at the entrance to the ER, briefcase in tow, immediately taking charge, fluently directing the dozen assembled authorities. Shelli and her assistant walked up to me and introduced themselves. She proceeded to gather information, her expertise well able to surmount the obstacles presented by the reprehensible system.

Arguing in my defense, running themselves ragged, they attempted to move heaven and hell getting clearance to leave the country. I never imagined a law abiding citizen would have to endure what transpired. But I soon learned that outside of the tourist milieu, Mexicans abhorred Americans. Met with disdain, humiliation, and prejudice, the officials appeared to take pleasure in having me at their mercy. Rendering me powerless with virtually no recourse, my situation procured no sympathy adding torturous pain to my circumstance. I could sense, even felt hatred in their tone of voice hearing the vitriol directed towards me. Undoubtedly, it helped that the language barrier stymied my response.

Summoned by the police, the coroner's van waited to transport Nick. Climbing into the front seat with Shelli and me, I was so grateful the surgeon hadn't abandoned us. Nick's body, his hands tucked into his swim trunks, was lying on the black, rubber floor rolling from side to side with each turn, nothing around him, nothing over him. Listening to him flop around, my instinct was to climb over the seat and hold him, help him. I watched the buildings, dilapidated shacks on poverty ridden streets, the squalid dwellings, abandoned vehicles, garbage everywhere, getting more wretched the farther we drove from the tourist venue. I couldn't fathom a medical facility in this neighborhood! The van stopped, backing into a driveway next to a gray sheet metal sided, garage type building. Around the yard was an eight-foot, rusted-out, tin fence, a carpet of rubble and garbage everywhere. The smell was unbelievable. Medical procedures were being performed here?! Barefoot, I tried to avoid the broken glass, inching along the narrow space between the wall and the van. My legs trembling so hard, I grabbed Shelli for support.

Stepping through the door, my eyes took in the primitive surroundings: a concrete slab, like a meat counter you'd see behind the butcher case, stood in the middle of the concrete floor, a green garden-type hose dangled from the ceiling. Everything swirled and went black, my legs crumbling under me as I collapsed to the floor.

As if in a haze, echoing, I heard the surgeon who had accompanied us in the ambulance ask, "Would this autopsy be performed by a licensed, certified doctor?"

The response, "Indeed, it will, si signor."

Shelli crouched next to me on the floor, wrapping her arms around, my stomach contracting as I groaned, oh God, oh God, moaning, trying to get air, until the wave finally passed. Incredulous that this was where my dearest love, my husband's body would be examined, I tried to comprehend it. So many thoughts raced through my head, my tortured state ameliorated by vacuous shock; now what, what do I do, what were they going to do to him, and most acutely, why did he die, this robust man, in the prime of his life?? Shelli held me, trying to soothe, comfort, helping me to my unsteady feet. Walking me to the doorway, very professionally, she delineated precisely the next steps. Mountains of red tape.

Desperate to see Nick one more time, walking toward the van, I opened the double door, forcing my eyes to focus. His body, his shell, lay there empty, and I knew at that instant he was gone. Gone. An employee at the facility standing about ten yards away watched me.

Noticing him, I flatly stated, "He's gone."

Familiar with the neighborhood, knowing Mexico, he apparently thought someone had stolen Nick, "No aqui?!" he said, his eyes bugging out.

I shook my head pointing upward toward the sky to communicate the spiritual departure.

"Si," he nodded, comprehending the inference.

Shelli's attaché, Ramon, arrived with a car to drive me back to the hotel. Following their instructions, zombie-like, I seated myself in the back staring out the window until the garage slipped from view.

At the hotel, I was met by the concierge holding our beach paraphernalia, along with our newly found friends we'd sat next to that morning with the most dour expressions as they conveyed their shock and sympathy, "We're so sorry, Anne, please let us know if we can help. Anything."

We'd sat next to them on lounge chairs acquainting each other with where from, what we did, kids, all the typical inquiries. Just a few hours earlier we laughed and basked in the splendor of a sun adorned beach. Their compassion, the pained countenance, and genuine concern were the beginning of a pattern I would witness over the next two days that kept me from literally jumping off my balcony. I wanted to explain, needed to have arms enfold me, but the next calls were weighing so heavily on my heart that I collected my belongings and put off answering anything else, leaving questions to hang in the air.

My beautiful children, up north, youthful optimists with successful lives, were oblivious to the lightning bolt racing to shatter their existence mangling their hearts. Two down, two to go. I called them in birth order trying to have some method to the madness.

In the room, rifling through my purse, digging out my address book, I almost passed out sinking back on the bed as I tried to focus on the blur of numbers. My hands shook so violently pushing the phone buttons I had to cradle the receiver against my shoulder using my other hand to steady my wrist.

"Come on," I told myself, "you've got to do this."

A million miles away, I rehearsed what I would say to four wonderful kids who loved their dad immeasurably, while imploring, "God, help me, you've got to help me. Oh God, how am I going to tell them, how can I say this to them, how can I hurt them like this? God, help me. Goddammit, is this really happening?"

"Hello", I said, "who's this?" I didn't recognize the voice at Chloe's apartment.

"This is Bill."

This is Chloe's mom, "Is she there?"

"No, she's at class. Can I take a message?"

I had to tell her. I had to say the shattering words.

"No, Bill, I have horrible news that I have to talk to her about, immediately. Is there any way I can locate her?"

"No, I don't know her schedule. No one else is here that might know."

"Do you know when she usually gets home?"

"I think around 3:00."

"Bill, I can't have her be alone when I talk to her. Someone needs to be with her."

"How 'bout if I leave a note for her to call you?"

I was so distraught I had to use all of my faculties to devise a cohesive strategy.

"Just alert your other roommates, [there were three] about the circumstances so someone will be with her. Please, whatever you do, don't let her be alone."

"Okay, I have to go to class but Annie will be back and I'll tell her."

I could tell that he was freaked by then. It did add to the drama, my insistence to have someone else with her, but I had to protect her fragility, however meager my attempt. She was my shrinking flower, always the most sensitive, tender, and fearful.

Unable to stop shaking, my stomach in cramps, back hurting, every muscle aching, and aware of how Bill's note would affect her, I determined to keep calling Chloe at fifteen minute intervals.

Shelli had said, "Take all the time you need, shower, change, and we'll be waiting down here for you."

But I knew the clock was ticking. It was prudent that I get back to Shelli to begin wading through the Mexican legal system.

I dialed David's dorm room number at the University of Minnesota-Morris. No answer.

"Shit, how can I do this?" I yelled to no one.

* * *

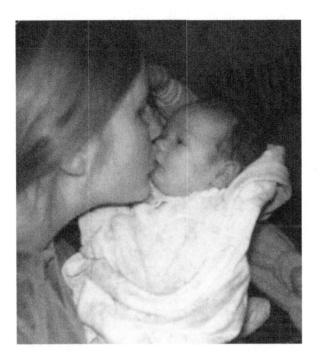

17

Day-old, Chloe Anne

It was December 31st, 1978. At seventeen degrees below zero, one of the coldest days of the year, Nick stoked our cast iron, pot-bellied wood burner with the driest and smallest hunks of pine and oak in a valiant effort to keep me comfortably warm. A brutal Minnesota wind howled through the cracks of the poorly insulated farmhouse. We would have been wise to move the birthing area to the living room next to the stove but I was already too far into labor, into my zone, to rearrange everything. My contractions from midnight to 6:00a.m. felt like strong downward pressure but were mild enough to sleep through. From 6:00 until noon, labor gradually intensified, culminating with only three pushes to bring Chloe into the world. Yes, it did hurt; yes there was intensity, but nothing like other women's experience. I marveled at my good fortune. Back in New Mexico I remembered seeing a back woodsy gynecologist, just once, for obvious reasons. Pregnant with my first I needed reassurance that all was kosher in my lady parts. His confidence building advice; "Yeah, you'll have no problem. You could drive a truck through there!" Well, Nick never complained and neither did I when these babies emerged. Like the first two labors, Nick was my stalwart coach, spiritually in tune, breathing with me, holding, supporting my back, legs, attentive to my every direction. My girlfriend from church, Gayle, was our midwife, lending strength and expertise. The aura of the home birth, so wonderfully peaceful, seemed to infuse the room with happiness as our second daughter was born.

Pouring over baby names Nick and I'd decided on the name, Chloe.

After experiencing the peaceful presence of our home birth, cuddling her in my arms, gazing at the face, I gushed, "She's my Chloe Anne. It's perfect. So fresh, like a delicate blooming flower which is what Chloe meant."

I could count on this remark whenever she was around others, "Is she always this pleasant, always this cheerful?"

She had her moments, but was indeed, Chloe personified, kind, considerate. So sweet. Zelda and Aaron were in awe of their tiny baby-doll sister. With solicitous attention, protected and doted upon, they helped to create her dependency as they competed to hold her.

Her favorite place was to doze snuggled in Daddy's arms. Nick and I managed the first two quite handily, but when the third

254

was added, life went into overdrive playing a constant catch up game trying to juggle all the duties. The entire system broke down; laundry, baths, and wood stoves overwhelming us in our rented farmhouse sans bathroom.

One morning I opened the oven door of the wood stove to discover Aaron's toy tractor, its rubber tires melted to the bottom.

His innocent answer to my inquiry, "I wanted to warm it up."

I never heard him open the oven door. I'd completely missed his dangerous proximity to the fire. At two and a half, Aaron kept, at least, two steps ahead of me. He would straddle the motor of Nick's chain saw, holding the bar handle, riding it like a bronco. The blade did have a cover on it but that didn't exactly make it a safe game. His cute little rosy cheeks resembled a chipmunk because of the two dog food morsels he constantly pilfered from Dweezil's bowl.

I'd squeeze the sides of his mouth inserting a finger to flip the offending matter out, admonishing, "Acky, that's Dweezil's food. We don't eat it."

But ten minutes later, the puffed out cheeks would tattle on him once more. Maybe it felt good on those molars breaking through.

With help from our parents for a down payment we were able to purchase a four bedroom farmhouse when Chloe was nine months old. The only furniture worth taking with us was our oak kitchen set and a couple of living room chairs. We hauled the remainder to the dump and moved into the 20th century. Replete with modern conveniences our outhouse days were over. Hallelujah!! For seven years I'd cooked every meal with wood and frozen my ass off taking a shit. Twenty miles from the old place our new house situated off a gravel road atop a hill, above surrounding fields of corn and hay, had an acre of tree filled lawn, the perfect playground for kids.

Nick and I had our "other life," our secret existence, which is probably what kept us hanging in there so long with the draconian Fellowship. Every six weeks or so we'd head up to St. Paul for the weekend to party, imposing on Grandma and Grandpa to babysit. About twice a year, we'd meet our friends, Hal and Julia, who'd been members of our Fellowship but moved to Canada, Julia's homeland. Away from the church influence they no longer subscribed to its rigid tenets. Hal's parents also lived in St. Paul, where their children were, likewise, shuffled off. It was a perfect set-up. Morphing into reality, out from under the oppressive cult our normal alter-egos were unleashed. Best friends when they lived near us, we kept up an almost yearly trek to spend a week with them in Canada unleashing the children, eleven in all! Eight unsupervised boys, feral imaginations liberated, somehow kept their shenanigans under the radar. Hal and Julia's home was seventeen miles from town, in the bush, home to bears and possibly more deadly, mosquitoes. Mammoth. Hordes. Folklore claimed if a person was somehow unconscious in the woods and had any significant amount of flesh exposed, mosquitoes would suck out the unfortunate soul in a matter of hours. It seemed plausible.

Julia and I spent the better part of our time in the kitchen, either preparing meals or handling the mess that ensued. It was our girl time carved out, valued in that kindred spirit mien. We epitomized Emerson's understanding of relationship, "A friend may well be reckoned the masterpiece of nature." Ever the gourmet chef, Julia managed to add elements of panache to every meal, whereas I was the definition of utility able to eke out meals with one pound of hamburger stretched into a casserole that fed six hungry mouths. Julia's rich cream and butter recipes delighted the taste buds. After dinner with everyone off to some other pursuit, she embarked on a chocolate walnut caramel upside down cake. Well into the evening the creation baked, thrilling our senses with delicious bouquet. Finally cooled, dolloped with whip cream we devoured our dessert with no regard for the eleven o'clock hour. Absolutely, sinfully luscious. One more glass of wine and we bid goodnights sated and content. Two hours into deep sleep I was roused instantly when Nick shot bolt upright with a groan.

"Yaah, aah, yow, ooh, mmm,"

"What is it, what can I do?"

Concerned but also amused, I tried to offer support, thinking, "Oh shit, is he going to throw up? That fabulous cake?"

I got him a glass of water watching to see what that would produce. He settled a bit and I tiptoed out to the kitchen to look for antacid or baking soda. That seemed to recover him as he tried to get comfortable in a mostly vertical position. Relating the episode that morning embellished by my wit, I knew I'd get mileage out of that one for years to come.

Impervious to that Holy Roller, charismatic conservatism, that haunting weekend in the Twin Cities we were lucky to have survived. Hal was wise enough to be our designated driver. Nick and I left the kids at home that time, opting for a downtown hotel. When Hal and Julia were an hour late to pick us up, we drank a bottle of wine, figuring we'd spend the night by ourselves.

So irate they hadn't even called, I sneered, "How rude. That's it for them!"

"Yeah, fuck 'em, we'll have our own party. They couldn't even call?"

"Even if they do show up now, I'm not going anywhere," I declared, "How could they just forget about us like that? We come all this way, set this all up, I don't get it. "

"Maybe something happened. No one would know how to get a hold of us, you know."

"Oh, yeah, I wonder if I could find her cousin's number where they're staying. Now I'm worried," I said, opening the second bottle of wine refilling our glasses.

Pushing the remote button to catch the 10:00 o'clock news, reporters were swarming a garish heap of vehicles and people. During the winter carnival parade, a cop had lost control of his vehicle and plowed into the crowd lining the sidewalk. The gruesome wreckage fueled the suggestion that Hal and Julia's tardiness wasn't their choice. My ruminations interrupted by a knock on the door, through the peephole, Nick saw Hal holding a large box.

"Great," I said, "Now he wants us to go out, hammered, at this time of night? I'm so pissed, I don't even want to go."

Nick had his hand on the door, ignoring my bitchy remark, "Hey, where've you been?"

"Why, is it late?" Hal answered, nonchalantly.

Handing me the box like the gift bearing magi, I was instantly appeased. All was forgiven as Nick and I tore the paper off.

"What did you do this for?" Nick asked Hal.

"It's just something I've been working on."

One of the most creative people we knew, Hal was a wood carver, photographer, painter, ever learning, always challenging us with a different theory, or unique philosophy. His genius amazed us.

"It's beautiful," I exclaimed, lifting the hand carved white cedar bowl from the box.

Approximately 14 inches across the top, Hal had labored, painstakingly, on the fabulous, one of a kind creation, not stopping until he had fashioned a matching ladle. I regretted my petty impatience, sensing the love that obviously went into Hal's gift.

"Julia's waiting in the car. I'm double parked. You ready to go?" he asked.

"Really, at 10:00?"

So smashed already, judgment skewed, I abandoned caution, as we grabbed our coats.

After a sumptuous Italian dinner, guzzling more wine, whooping it up annoying nearby diners, we set out for a bar. Appropriately named 'Still Standing', Hal, an ex-Minneapolis cabbie was at home with the North side's sketchy night life.

In a half-assed attempt to clear my head, I wandered out to the back parking lot where I was accosted by a humongous dude wearing full length fur coat couture along with funky side-cocked Fedora.

"Hey, you want rock or powder?"

"Ahhhh, where did you get that idea?"

My polluted brain, a swirling cesspool of questions, I thought, "What the hell am I doing out here? How did I get here? Where's Nick?"

"No, thanks," I said, backing away, shaking my head.

Stumbling through the door to the bar, I thought, "I've gotta find Nick. Where the fuck is he? This time we've gone too far. This is nuts. We've gotta get the hell outa here! What the fuck?"

Nick was still standing at a table with some woman, three scotch and waters lined up in front of him.

I said, "Are you ready to go?"

He gave me a glazed nod.

The woman said, "I'm having people over to my apartment. Why don't you come?"

"Sure, why not?" Nick said, as I looked at him, daggers shooting out of my sockets.

"You really want to do this thing?" was my implied question.

But he was already informing Hal and Julia that we were following this stranger to her apartment.

Julia and I proceeded through the apartment following a guy up to the rooftop to see the cityscape, a spectacular sight, for sure, but at 2:00a.m. we were becoming one with the icicles. Raucously laughing, we walked back into the living room where one glance from Nick quelled my mood. The green eyed monster conveyed jealous fury as scotch fueled his fantastic imagination. I had no idea how long we'd been up there but the sizzling fuse was ready to explode. Nick took my arm, shuffling me down the stairs and into the car before I even had a chance to dispute his implicit accusation.

"Wait, my purse is in there," I yelled, as Hal started the engine.

"Leave it!" Nick hissed at me.

"Are you crazy? I've got my I.D., credit cards, everything in it. It'll just take a minute. Wait, Hal, let me run back in."

"I'll get it," Nick snapped, as he staggered out the door.

"God, what the hell is with him?" I thought.

I'd never given him any cause to doubt me in all of our twenty-some years of marriage. Back in minutes, the purse under his arm, he hunched against the door as far away from me as he could. I slumped in silence, in and out of coherence.

Past the knowing eyes of the desk clerk, I focused, keeping my balance, as I leaned on Nick who had to all but carry me through the lobby to the elevator. Consciousness escaped as I hit the bed, the whirlies hurling me down, down, down the funnel.

"Did you fuck him?" Nick asked, grabbing my arm to pull me upright, jarring me back into lucidity.

"ARE YOU CRAZY?! I groaned, "Where in the hell did you get that? No, I did not. What the fuck are you talking about?!"

That was all I remembered.

Beginning sometime in the wee hours, I crawled to the toilet. Holding the waste bucket under my mouth, the expurgated contents from both ends were horrifying enough to garner Nick's compassion. Sufficiently, sympathetically assuaged, the supposed indiscretion was never mentioned again. For the record, though, I had told the absolute truth. Did he think Julia and I were up on the roof having a three way? Twenty degrees, open air ménage a trois? After Hal dropped us off, Julia had to hang her head out their Volvo station wagon's window, letting fly down 35W, hurling most of the way to her cousin's.

In the morning, her kids, bringing their backpacks out to load up for the ride home stopped in their tracks, "Eeeewwww, what's on the car?"

Julia, feigning innocence, lied, "Someone must have thrown something at us. Disgusting. Why do people do such things?"

"Gross," the kids responded.

"Well, just get a soap bucket and a rag," Julia said, "It'll come right off."

"GROSS!" the kids reiterated, screwing up their noses.

Julia kept a straight face.

It was a horrible three hour ride home after the regretful night. Having wretched for hours, I slept the entire 150 miles back to the straight and narrow with a puke bucket on my stomach and a coat over my head. In some ways it was like being let out of a straight jacket, escaping the asylum for immersion therapy. We didn't let on to our church family, ever.

Our pastor's wife, in the mother of all mid-life crises, decided to abandon her husband and five children causing a monumental shift in the Fellowship. At an emergency meeting, called to figure out what damage control was needed along with what direction to follow after the shocking separation, the solution was prophesied.

"If you don't take the reins of this Fellowship, it will die."

Those cumbersome words were spoken by the divine apostle with the upmost gravity to Nick, now the most senior Elder.

"Put the whole side-show on our shoulders?" I asked, incredulously, when Nick told me about the edict. "If this church can't live without one person, then maybe it needs to die."

"I have to give it a shot. I feel a responsibility," Nick said.

"But how will you handle all of that with your job, your children, us?"

"I'll just do what I can do. I'm only human; I'm one man," he said resignedly.

He never wanted or vied for any position, wasn't a front man. The acceptance of "pastorship" was out of character for my serious husband. He was about as charismatic as a log. What he did possess, though, was down to earth work ethics, loyalty, and decency that would, hopefully, lend credibility to our bizarre church.

262

* * *

Still no call from Chloe. I tried David again.

"Hello," David said.

"David, hi," I answered in my softest, lowest tone.

"I have some bad news. Are you sitting down?"

"Yeah."

"Dad died in Mexico," I said, point blank.

It was so brutal. David didn't say anything. It was complete silence on his end.

I began to explain, "We were snorkeling, his lungs hurt."

Abruptly, David said, "Mom, stop talking. You don't have to tell me!"

I stopped and waited, not knowing what to do.

I said, "Are you okay, honey?"

"No," his definitive response, loudly avowed, was so out of character.

Silence. The empty void reverberating.

"Oh, David, I wish there was something else I could say. I don't know what's going on now. I've tried Chloe but can't get through to her."

Still no words, I waited a few seconds.

"So we'll talk again honey, when I get more information. Is there anyone you can talk to right now? I hate for you to be alone."

"I'm okay," David said, gently.

"I love you."

"Love you, Mom."

I couldn't stand hanging up the phone each time, leaving our children with that awful, horrible news, not able to take them into my arms and cry with them. It broke my heart. I tried Chloe again. Machine. Zelda was almost at Grandma's. I took a quick shower, dressed, and sat down on the bed dialing her number. Zelda had to say it three times for the words to register.

"Dad died in Mexico, Grandma," Zelda repeated, trying to get Violetta to comprehend.

After it finally registered, Zelda handed the phone to her.

Distraught, barely able to speak, Violetta said, "Oh, Anne, what are we going to do, how could this happen to us? I'm all alone now, how could he take them both from me??"

She was referring to her husband's death three years prior. It was wrenching. It was unfair. I couldn't stand hearing her despair. It sent me down, deeper into my own miasma. After a few perfunctory remarks, not able to deal with her, I turned her over to Zelda.

I fell back onto the bed, hugging my knees, sobbing until I thought my breath would stop.

Closing my eyes, I could see Nick's lifeless ones. Steely black, dead, nonresponsive, empty. He was gone.

"Okay, keep going," I told myself.

I sat up and dialed again. Still no answer at Chloe's apartment, so I gathered my papers, Nick's I.D., water, Kleenex, whatever I could think of and went down to the hotel lobby. Various personnel were waiting; Liesse, the concierge, Shelli, and her assistant, Ramon, the beach friends, with hugs, and tears. Theirs was the same look I'd see over and over and over, for days. No words, just pain.

"I got ahold of everyone except my daughter, Chloe," I explained. "It was awful. Horrible."

In her businesslike manner, Shelli ushered me into the car, "We better get into town and see about getting papers in order. It's going to take a lot of time and effort. We need to move quickly to get the autopsy completed before they'll release the body. Hopefully, with a little luck, that will be tomorrow."

* * *

18

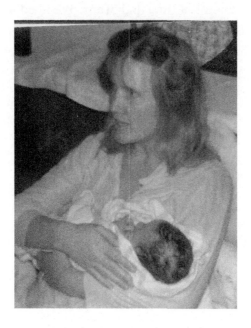

David, minutes old

David's reaction to my phone call was certainly the oddest but remained consistent with his personality and demeanor. Pregnant, yet again, when Chloe was only fourteen months old, it finally occurred to Nick and me, kind of slow on the uptake, if we didn't do something permanent, we'd have eighteen children!

"All you have to do is look at me sideways, and I'm pregnant," I joked to Nick.

We were practicing birth control but our lack of diligence combined with various failures, and my erroneous belief that nursing mothers weren't as fertile resulted in my fourth pregnancy in 6 years. David was conceived using the diaphragm minus spermicide.

"Oh, it'll be fine. C'mon," Nick argued, enticingly, stroking my neck, planting kisses on my shoulder, brushing my breasts.

"Yeah, you're probably right," I resigned.

He never had much difficulty persuading me. I melted into his chest as he pulled my body on top of him. Right there on the living room floor, kids asleep upstairs, we rolled the dice with fertility yet again. Desire trumped logic and number four was hatched.

Beginning with Zelda, we'd devised a unique system of selecting names. From name books we compiled a list of five, both genders. By the time we agreed on one name, it worked out all four times that it matched the sex of the baby. When we both chose a male name, we had a boy. We figured it was some sort of divine providence. Nick and I were stumped when we couldn't pick between David and Joshua. Growing larger and larger, beyond the size of my three previous pregnancies, we entertained the idea of twins, one being David and the other Joshua. I never went for pre-natal check-ups so when only one baby arrived we settled on David Joshua.

Eight months into the pregnancy, on one of those balmy Indian summer days, Nick and two of his buddies were putting up cords of wood for the winter's demanding supply. They'd rented a hydraulic splitter and were pleasantly surprised at how quickly their pickups were being filled when the unit malfunctioned. Nick prodded the various gears, locating the jammed cog. With his finger inside the shaft one of the other guys pried loose a chunk of bark freeing the ram. In a split second, Nick's right pointer was all but severed. His finger was soaking in a disinfectant solution while x-rays were studied when I arrived at the clinic. He lifted it out so I could see the mangled mess. I grabbed the doorway, literally feeling the baby drop about an inch.

I thought I shit my pants, excusing myself, "I'll be right back," and ran for the bathroom.

Nick's deathly looking finger was dangling by a thread of flesh. Sitting on the toilet I gasped for breath. He was a self-employed timber buyer with no insurance. How was this going to play out?! I drove him to the hospital, thirty miles away, where he underwent an eight hour surgery reattaching all the nerves, tissue, and muscle. Nick's painstaking recovery sent us deeper in the hole every week, and if it hadn't been for his dad, we would have lost the house.

With every cost cutting initiative Nick and I had managed to keep afloat by the most inventive budgeting. My garden augmented our meals with hundreds of hours spent harvesting and canning, freezing and preserving. When tomatoes were ripe or the sweet corn was at its peak I pulled all-nighters processing the provisions. Corn was picked and shucked, par-boiled, cut off the cob and no matter how slowly I did this I always ended up slathered in kernels with dozens more sticking to every surrounding surface. When it was cooled I spooned it into bags and sent a kid down the basement to the twenty cubic foot chest freezer which burst with a year's worth of bounty. Tomatoes required a few more steps involving either par-boiling, peeling, stewing or cooking up sauce. Then after sterilizing jars and lids, they were filled and processed and sealed in a boiling water bath. I'd haul the kids out to a nearby strawberry patch to help pick fourteen pound lugs of fruit for jam making. Black caps and raspberries, apples and pears, beans, beets, and cucumbers; pint jars by the dozens lined the fruit cellar shelves. Carrots and potatoes were packed in sand in bins staying if not fresh, at least edible for months. When I happened upon pickling string beans I never had to coax the children to eat them. The 'Dilly Beans' recipe included a measure of chili pepper adding zing to their new favorite vegie. We bought beef and pork in quantity from local farmers having it processed by the butcher who also rented lockers to store the hundred or so pounds. It was demanding to keep all the plates spinning but nothing on the grocer's shelf came close to the delectable fare fresh from my garden.

When my labor began that November, the brace on his hand relegated him to a back seat position. Two of my friends assisted but were almost unnecessary. David was born at home, after a mellow, effortless few hours. His head, positioned sideways, slid out with a gentle push. My body knew instinctively to ease up or I could have broken his nose. Up on my haunches, gravity basically brought him out. It was uncanny how I was able to flow with it. We figured in a hospital they probably would have used forceps to turn him face down, exactly the intervention we rebelled against in support of our home birth philosophy, but in truth, we were lucky to escape without life-threatening complications. Lucky to have four healthy children.

Each of the children's personalities, in the first year of their life, evidenced an uncanny similarity to their birth. The theory remained consistent as David's demeanor developed. He was calm, quiet, and continually pleasant, except for a bad habit of biting, perpetrated against many an unsuspecting victim. David wasn't malicious, just teething.

Zelda and Aaron used the vice on a one-time babysitter convincing him to stick a finger into David's mouth, saying, "He just likes to suck on your finger."

They watched, gleefully, the babysitter's expression contorting, as he tried not to swear in front of the children. The razor sharp baby teeth left a distinct indentation but didn't draw blood.

David, the spongy cuddler, would curve his entire body around whomever was holding him to fit as snuggly as possible. He had plenty of arms vying for their turn with baby brother. He also had the distinction of being the only baby to sleep through the night, which frightened me enough to get up anyway to determine if he was dead or alive! Requiring far less sleep than his siblings, at three years old, I'd hear the muffled sound of tiny plastic arms clicking together as his G.I.Joes battled it out under the covers well past 11p.m. Quietly and stealthily, as soon as he could crawl, David would entertain himself exploring the household. If I lost track of him for more than five minutes, I'd know he'd made a discovery. In some type of experiment, he'd be sitting on the kitchen floor with a dozen eggs, breaking them one at a time, or pouring a jar of honey or a bag of flour down the front of his shirt. One time, he coated a piece of furniture with Vaseline, smearing it through his hair and in his ears, relishing the mess.

The innocence of childhood whizzed past me without perceiving, without imagining how quickly the years would evaporate. Everyone told me that would happen, but the day to day pace of our busy household didn't allow much time for reflection.

Chloe was our quintessential little darling, playing dollies, dressing up in a chiffon gown, flowing through the house, pirouetting in her ballet slippers, and as soon as she could manage, clomping in high heels, dramatically acting, performing Disney adaptations or her own made-up plays.

Disarmingly precocious, at three years old, Chloe cracked me up with her definitive anatomy explanations.

Pointing to her behind, she'd say, matter of fact, "This is my butt," then bringing her hand around, "and this is my front butt."

"Well, it's actually called a vagina," I corrected.

With furrowed brows, I watched her formulate a thought, sounding out the pronunciation.

"Furgina?" Chloe asked.

"That's right," I answered, giving her leeway, not wanting to be overly didactic or technical. Later, I came to the realization that she was incorporating her knowledge of my pubic hair into the word. Logically, phonetically, it was a fur-gina.

When Chloe was 7, we sat on my bed as I gave her a cursory lesson about sex. With an age appropriate book, I led her through the pages.

"The man inserts his penis into the woman's vagina," I read, pausing to see Chloe's reaction to the words, watching her eyes grow as she envisioned such an actuality.

First, the slightest chuckle escaped, then giggles gushed out, disarming her so completely that she fell back on the bed in hysterics. All serious discussion over, the hilarity so contagious, I burst out laughing, knowing it was an extremely healthy note to end on.

Aaron, at five years old, was David's hero and mentor. Mr. Rough and Tumble had only picked up momentous velocity with each year. Still averse to crying, I ran for the front door one summer afternoon hearing howls of pain. At full speed, down the gravel hill road, Aaron steered his bike into the ditch, then blasting up, jumping over most of the driveway, he'd wiped out against a tree. Wailing and screaming, the cries were spine tingling. Imbedded the length of his arms and legs, gravel protruded. Bruised but miraculously, requiring no stitches, ice packs, hydrogen peroxide and bandages patched the dynamo, as he rallied a half hour later, bounding out the door, primed to tweak his dirt bike trajectory.

Policing the four kids was so exhausting that for sanity's sake, I creatively cut corners, in an attempt to keep up. Vacuuming the crib was probably one of the most disgusting time savers but spitting on the floor to loosen noticeable grunge ran a close second. With spray cleaner in hand, a wash rag under each foot, I'd skate over the kitchen floor deftly erasing the first layer. Five minutes, and my floors were done. Granted, eating off them wasn't recommended. Also, skate-dusting in socks commandeered the dust bunnies. Always cost conscious, I reused paper towels after they'd cleaned the counter, the second time for the floor, even a third on the back porch floor. Before laundering, I'd whip the damp shower towels back and forth under beds to catch hairballs. Dirty clothes came down the stairs one step at a time also doubling as the Swiffer. Economizing never sunk to the level of my neighbor, who'd 'wash' her paper plates and hang them out on the line to dry for reuse. When David was finally in kindergarten I was able to embark on a varied part-time career in mostly retail from Ben Franklin five and dime to a jewelry store and a few years later into full time floral design. Stretched to the max, Nick and I somehow managed to stay afloat.

If I didn't hear fighting or horrendous crying, I didn't intervene. So they all learned to surreptitiously battle it out. They'd be dangling from the top of the garage roof, sending toy trucks off the edge, rolling balls down, balancing on the ridge line, covertly under my radar. In our attempt to have a semblance of safety, Nick and I filled an old water bed mattress, positioning it so they would ostensibly land on it. Another landing platform was a dilapidated orange vinyl futon, already broken beyond repair. The back yard resembled a circus. When old enough to be responsible, relatively defined, each child relished taking the trash out to burn it in the barrel, a 55 gallon metal drum. In preparation for said use, the barrel had to have ventilation around the bottom to allow air to pass through and rain water to drain out. With a dozen or so shots from the .22 rifle, we'd make the necessary modifications, ripping through it like butter. When too many ashes piled up in the bottom, sometimes an added incendiary was necessary to consume the trash. Aaron was a bit older, all of eight, when he was allowed, after Nick's instruction, to pour a little gasoline onto the mucked refuse. Living seven miles from town was probably just the right distance. Far enough so neighbors couldn't witness what was happening but close enough for the fire department to get there expeditiously.

Aaron and David were also instructed in the use of gasoline eradication of the ant hills in our yard. Pouring a half cup of petrol on the foot wide mound of industry, throwing on the stick match, ants met their fiery demise.

"Now this is not something you can decide to do on your own," Nick admonished the boys while methodically demonstrating the process, adding, "Gasoline is very dangerous. You never add it to anything that's already flaming. First the gas, then light it. Got it? And Mom or I need to be home."

"Yep," the boys assented in a swaggering tone, confident they were ready for the responsibility.

Zelda, at the ripe old age of 13, was babysitting, when that edict was tested. David, a neighbor boy, and one of our church member's boys were having an afternoon at our house, playing outside away from watchful eyes. In a display of prowess regarding pest control, David poured gas from a pop bottle onto an ant hill, firing it up with a stick match, according to Nick's instruction. Jeremy, the neighbor kid, unimpressed with the progress, grabbed the bottle, tipping it right over the fire. The flame leapt straight up the stream as Jeremy flung the bottle away from the boys. Everywhere the gas flew, grass ignited, the trajectory ending in the woods with an explosion of shattering glass.

"Get the hose!" David yelled.

Providence was on their side as they doused the yard, extinguishing the fire.

That evening I answered the phone, "Hello. Oh, Hi, Ron. How you doin'?"

Ron was the father of the boy at our house that afternoon. The church member.

"Fine," Ron answered. "That was something today with the boys, wasn't it?"

"Ahh, yeah," I answered, slowly, not having a clue what he was referring to. While his son was quite a tattle-tale blabbermouth, David was extremely tight-lipped, especially where calamity was involved. But I wasn't letting on my ignorance to Ron, the church member who, annoyingly, always appeared to have all of his ducks in a tidy little home school row.

"They could have been seriously injured," Ron continued.

Jeez, I was thinking, "Wait till I get off this phone!" But I played along concernedly declaring, "All's well that ends well."

"Just so that never happens again," Ron admonished.

274

"Oh, you can count on it."

I hung up the phone, immediately hollering, "David!"

"Yeah," he answered from his room upstairs.

"Get down here, NOW!"

As he casually walked into the kitchen, I said, "That was Danny's dad, Ron, on the phone."

"Oh."

"What happened here today?"

The jig was up. I could see it in his expression as I fixed his eyes with my anger.

In his most intellectual manner, he innocently queried me, "Did you say we *couldn't* burn ant hills when you were gone?" Shortly after that incident Ron and his family left the Fellowship. Citing many other glaring failures, they didn't want to be associated with people who didn't have their houses in order. It's no wonder the kids had their own wild alter-egos with all of the prohibitions heaped on them from our religion.

Halloween was outlawed explained away as the Devil's holiday. They weren't allowed to attend school on that day so as not to participate in the party celebrating paganism. Christmas was sanctioned but Christ was the theme, not Xmas. Ever. We taught them it was Jesus' birthday so they could make a present for Jesus and put it under the tree! They did receive presents but mostly because their grandparents coughed up enough money to fund them.

Having proven to be mechanically challenged, Zelda surprised me when her driving abilities earned a license. A couple of years prior, in utter panic, she had driven the riding lawn mower into the front quarter panel of our Buick LaSabre.

Catching the scene from the kitchen window, I hollered to Nick, "Hey, quick, you gotta see this."

Zelda, with a frozen look of horror, eyes bugged out, was heading straight for the car. Crash! Not able to maneuver the steering wheel or step on the brake, she put a sizable dent in the car but a larger one in her ego as we gathered around. Needless to say, she was relieved to see her dad and me laughing.

The meager amount we were able to provide in the clothes venue was spelled out, exactingly, to each teenager. If they wanted designer brands, it was up to them to earn whatever extra dollars were required for the upgrade. Zelda became a nursing assistant at the local hospital caring for elderly occupants. What began as a means to keep up with her peers evolved into a character building opportunity. Handing us the permission slip, our pride in Zelda swelled as we read the particulars. A patient was dying of AIDS which in '89 was an appallingly misunderstood disease. Most of her co-workers flat out refused to enter the room.

"Is there any risk to you?" Nick asked.

"The staff manager said we'd employ precautions. We have to wear a mask and double gloves. I won't be giving any shots or anything, just helping with meals."

"Are you able to talk with the patient, or rather, is the patient still able to talk?" I asked.

"The oxygen mask is on most of the time, so not really. I don't see what the big deal is. I want to do this."

"I'll sign it," Nick said, adding, "You're an amazing kid. I'm so proud of you."

"Thanks."

Those were the moments that made the trials fade reminding us what a precious gift our children were. Piano and dance lessons, sports activities and practice, extra-curricular interests and a myriad of friends required hundreds of trips to town. An added driver was a Godsend, albeit we had our share of teenage incidents. Speeding, crashes, lies and manipulation lent indelible drama to those years, thankfully without serious or permanent injury.

Chloe's involvement with an alternative lifestyle taught me numerous karmic lessons. Beginning with rebellion against our beliefs, she followed a path of destruction, shunning convention and embracing the counter culture with all of its abusive practices.

"I guess I had it coming, after what I did to Jack and Edith," I told Nick, as we agonized over our concern with her dangerous choices.

"Now we know how they felt," he said, "We were such assholes—what we put them through. You can't understand until you have your own kids, I guess."

I was in total agreement. In an apologetic phone call to Jack and Edith I told them I didn't know how they put up with everything I put them through. Incredulously, they told me I wasn't so bad, me thinking, "Who are you and what have you done with my parents!?"

We'd ground Chloe to no avail, making her go to church with us hoping God would change her. When we forced her to go to summer Bible camp she and another boy were kicked out for smoking dope. At our wits end we allowed her to move in with her best girlfriend whose mother was much more reasonable than us.

The other three kids took a more conventional route to adulthood, heading off to college in close succession.

The day Nick and I dropped Zelda off in Pella, Iowa she was only 17. Fed up with high school, stymied by small town life, Zelda had applied and been accepted at Central College, choosing to forego her senior year and get a jump start on the next phase of her life. Nick and I had our reservations but agreed to let her go for it.

We moved her belongings into the dorm room, got the initiation tour along with campus protocol and prepared to leave. My heart was so heavy, wondering how we'd gotten to this juncture, seemingly, in the blink of an eye. Determined not to let her see my anxiety or sadness, I toughed it out, smiling, as she walked us down to the van for goodbyes.

"Get in so we can pray with you," I said, needing to have those last few moments.

So confident, so nonchalant, she shrugged, answering, "Mmmmkay."

The three of us held hands, Nick and I both saying a blessing, asking for protection and guidance for our daughter. We kissed and hugged, my plastered smile cracking.

I said, "You're gonna do great."

She smiled as she walked away. Nick started pulling away from the curb as Zelda turned around. She raised her hand with a breezy wave, mouthing goodbye.

My heart felt like it ripped in half.

"Go," I commanded Nick. "Don't let her see me cry."

The dam burst. I couldn't stop the entire four hours home. Nick didn't cry but was completely tuned into me knowing I needed his calm to settle my emotions.

"She'll be fine," he soothed.
"I know, I do, it's just that I can't believe it's over. I can't believe she's gone. No one ever told me that's what it feels like when your child leaves home. How did I miss that? I had no idea. Why didn't someone tell me?"

None of the kids held onto our faith once they got out from under the authority of home. Along with each child's departure came a soul searching shift in our thinking as we re-evaluated our life. After Nick became leader of the church, (pastor) we determined a new course reflecting that change. By the time David was a junior in high school our beliefs had evolved tremendously from the original Pentecostal doctrine. We determined to move the system into a more progressive philosophy, even naming ourselves a Church! Oh my God, how radical, how utterly innovative. We fought, struggled, pushed and prodded to move the congregation into the current culture and depart from the previous hard core wackiness, but the stubborn die-hards wouldn't or couldn't get on board.

"This is the direction the bus is going," Nick explained in his discussion of advancement, "If you don't like where it's going, then I encourage you to get on another bus."

We wished, we prayed they would, but instead, the disgruntled mutineers hung on, making life very difficult for us with back stabbing and outright revolt.

"I'm exhausted," Nick confessed to me, shaking his head.

Late into the night we sat talking about our blind faith, the unshakable commitment to the Fellowship for two decades. I gingerly slid my arm through his as we sat on the couch sipping an after dinner glass of wine. We were so on the same page having our eyes opened to the untenable situation. Finally. Finally it was apparent there was no more light, not even a glimmer, nothing to hold us. What we believed, where it had begun on the Mesa was utterly corrupted.

"I am done, finished, used up. It's like I've been trying to build this church into a welcoming place where change isn't feared, where we can relax, embracing the differences in everyone

279

who comes here, and all I get is resistance. Obviously, it isn't working."

"So what are you saying?"

He sounded so decided, like he'd been mulling these things over for some time, which he was wont to do.

"I want out; it's as simple as that."

"Out of the pastor position?" I asked.

"No, out of the whole thing, church, what we've been doing for the past twenty years. I've given it everything I had and more, and for those hardcore assholes it's not enough, it's never right. I'm so sick of it, sick of the fight. It has nothing to do with Christ, you know. At least in my understanding. There's no justifying it."

"Yeah, I know, but it's not everyone," I said, "There are some really decent, pure hearts that will hate to see you go. They agree with what you're doing. What about them?"

"Yeah well, I know that. That's what's kept me going this long. We'll still keep those relationships with our true friends, no matter where we go. But the rest, they can have it, along with all the never-ending bullshit. I mean it, Anne, I'm burned out. I'm too tired to do it anymore."

"I know, Babe," moving my arm around his shoulder, pressing closer. "They are some of the meanest, nastiest, hateful people, supposed Christians, smiling to your face, professing love and forgiveness, and well, I don't have to tell you!"

Nick concluded, "That's always the way it's going to be. I don't believe they can change. That's the reality."

We held each other, sort of hanging on for support, knowing everything we'd known for most of our married life was drastically changing. Everything we'd ever done, every direction, every decision we made, it was ours, together.

The most recent and ultimately decisive sore point precipitating the late night discussion was our support of and membership in a gay rights organization. Nick and I adamantly opposed the gay bashing, hate-filled mentality of the religious right and decided we would take a stand, joining RAAN, Rural AIDS Action Network. The true message of Christ extended grace, embracing the underdog, the down and out, the prostitute, those that suffered persecution, and we endeavored to demonstrate our conviction. We rejected the conservative belief that homosexuals were aberrant, that you could "pray the gay away"; our compassion and outspoken support of AIDS victims distancing us further from the church. We were ashamed that we couldn't offer our place of worship as a safe haven, knowing that the prejudiced judgment would be obvious to our gay friends.

"I'd rather not be a part of that either, then," I explained to Nick, "If they can't accept everyone on their own merit, then screw them!"

Nick agreed, coining a new term, "Assholier than thou."

We cracked up at the moniker. God, when he was funny, he really nailed it.

On a roll, he added, "We put the 'fun' in fundamentalism."

Whatever happens, Babe, I'm with you," I said, suddenly serious, "I love you, forever, you know that."

"I love you, too, Anne."

And he kissed me, his moustache tickling my upper lip. The kinship in our hearts was tacit, an understanding that confirmed our solidarity.

Nick asked, "If I died, do you think you'd remarry?"

I had to ponder that one, answering after a moment, "Probably not. I can't imagine ever finding anyone that would come close to you."

"I was thinking the same thing. This is the real deal. I don't think it comes around again."

For twenty years, we'd cruised along at breakneck pace, raising four children, not cognizant of fundamentalism's heavy-handed influence snatching precious few 'dates', up on logging trails, taking our long anticipated overnight honeymoons, not able and seldom wanting to trade one moment.

How could we know for days, months, and years our love would wait and take a back seat, while time, energy, and resources were channeled away? Brainwashing had to play a part in our obfuscation but we also had to take responsibility for skirting so many issues, for glazing over all of the lies and hate filled attitudes. Through necessity we coasted, we rationalized but given our previous life-style of sex, drugs, and rock and roll, maybe Christianity had kept us together for decades. Maybe Bible teaching had kept us faithful all those years. Possibly. Once our decision was final, the scales fell from our eyes in liberating embodiment.

A year later we were able to look back with some distance and objectivity, Nick quipping, "We were mentally ill."

"Fundamentally ill," I smirked.

Sitting at the kitchen table savoring strong, dark roast coffee, I relished our relaxed mornings. We both had a particular fetish about that first cup of the day. A quarter cup of half and half plus sugar, but because so much cream cooled the coffee, I would begin by heating the empty cup with hot water. Dumping that out, I'd pour in cream and nuke that for twenty seconds, finally filling it with coffee. It was impossible to get it anywhere else to our liking. I called it a "coffee malted". With all of our children out of the house, Nick and I loved our private chats in the empty nest.

His job afforded him so much autonomy that we could savor an hour together while we sipped our favorite quaff.

"We have to get out of this fish bowl," I said to Nick.

"Yeah, this small town is so played. We need to get to a larger area, where there's more going on, like life."

"I hate running into the old church crowd at the grocery store or on the street, anywhere I go. I always have one eye cocked trying to spy them out. It's always the same uncomfortable pleasantries, phoniness, where I just want to run in the opposite direction."

The censure of condemnation, judgment, and guilt were unmistakable. I tried my best to avoid any contact.

"Let's get outa Dodge," Nick suggested.

"As in, run away? Or a trip?"

"A trip, a vacation, to some place really fun, like New Mexico."

Not even giving it a second thought, I replied, "When?"

"How about my birthday, early April? We'll have a reunion with Maggie and Mickey and Blake and Sydney, Lillie and Dylan, the old gang."

19

Maggie, me, Blake, & Nick sitting in front of what remains of
Ed's log cabin

I couldn't imagine anything better or more fun. It had been
so many, many years, more than fifteen since we'd seen our old
best friends. Church life had virtually severed all of the past
connections, not really by design but our paths were so divergent
that separation just evolved. My Christmas cards and letters, full
of God this and Jesus that, had been sickening enough to give
them ample reason to steer clear of us.

"It's about time. I'm going to call Maggie and Sydney and
see what their schedules are like. This will be our coming out," I
declared.

Both Maggie and Sydney were more than ready to have us come and stay with them. They'd organize everything, even planning a few days up on the Mesa. Excitedly, we booked the tickets.

Sex had always been great between the two of us but our recent awakening jettisoned us into new territory, experimenting, stretching, discovering yet new avenues of expression. Our old hippie attitude helped us keep things smoking as my wild man husband pushed the envelope. It wasn't that I was averse, even encouraging the unorthodox developments, but the flare-up of a urinary tract infection, the second in three months, tempered my complicit attitude as we drove the seventy-five miles from Albuquerque to Santa Fe. Mounting pain coupled with an increasing urgency to pee made it apparent this wasn't going to abate without medical attention.

As I reevaluated our newfound freedom, I blurted, "I'm setting some boundaries."

Looking over, Nick was shocked, "It's that bad?"

"I can't stand it anymore. This is way beyond the last two!"

I winced, doubling over, breaking down, sobbing, "I can't take it, it's killing my lower back, like it's in my kidneys."

One mile from Santa Fe Nick saw the hospital icon on a highway sign.

Speeding, running every light, he encouraged, "Hang in there, Anne, there's the ER entrance."

After signing in, Nick called Sydney, our old midwife, who it turned out, had worked at that same hospital. She and Blake were there in minutes. The test confirmed another infection. Going home to Blake and Sydney's, loaded with antibiotics, I encamped in their guest bedroom for two days. Having my very own private nurse, who brought me chicken soup, juice, and TLC, hastened my recovery. Within two days we were able to play catch up, reminiscing about our hippie/Mesa days. It was as if we picked up where we'd left off fifteen years earlier. The ties that bound us were as strong as ever; the camaraderie as if we'd never left. What had begun that April evening in '74, the connection when the six of us had labored together witnessing the miracle of Zelda's birth, had knit our souls together like family.

Blake, Mickey, Nick, Sydney, me, & Maggie out for dinner

Spending two nights at Blake and Sydney's home on the Mesa, we hiked into the old cabin site having some difficulty locating it. The only things left to bear witness of our place were the concrete foundation footings. It had burned down, or so the story went. Blake had heard that one of the inhabitants, more likely, moved the entire structure, reporting a fire to claim insurance money.

"This is the most beautiful place I've ever seen," Nick remarked to me, "Someday we're coming back here. To retire, probably."

"I totally agree, there's nothing like it, the skies, the mountains, the atmosphere, the friends. We will. I know it."

Just like that it was settled in our hearts. We smiled, knowing this latest desire felt exactly right. I couldn't ever remember a time that we didn't go in the same direction. It was such a gift to have that kind of a relationship, the ability to sense each other's innermost needs. After almost thirty years we had only grown closer and more in tune with each other's psyche. How could I, could we, be so lucky? Most of our friends and relatives had divorced at least once, or if they were together, they experienced something akin to indifference or tolerance, being united out of habit. It was so very rare to be attracted and truly in love for all of our years as a couple.

Nick and I came home from that reunion determined to figure out our next move agreeing we'd been marking time long enough. There were no guarantees in life. There was no way to get back any of the years. If we didn't like where we were living, then we had to change it. The next phase of our life calling us, we set our minds solely on finding where that next chapter would unfold.

After looking in various localities for a year, and finding nothing suitable, we set our sights on a small town twenty-five miles south of where we'd lived those last twenty-five years. It was uncanny, synchronistic, how everything fell into place. The 110-year-old Victorian home embraced us as we walked through the front door. With its parquet floors, original woodwork, and enchanting character, we were convinced. Within two weeks, our offer was accepted and our farmhouse sold. After going through three realtors, we'd listed our place personally, as a last ditch effort. There was no rush but we'd been frustrated with the lack of success deciding we didn't need to pay an agent seven percent.

"It's a sign," I told Nick when our offer to buy the house was accepted. "I know we're supposed to be there. It's just too smooth. Things don't happen like that. Can you believe it?"

It was July 2000. When life moved along so perfectly, I typically wondered when the boom was going to lower. Not actually a foreboding, but I just couldn't be free enough to fully enjoy the good fortune, as if I had to look over my shoulder. It was a carryover from the church teaching along with childhood Lutheran guilt trips.

We had raised four children in a smaller house with only one bathroom and now we were sprawling out into a four bedroom home with two bathrooms, living and dining rooms, foyer, kitchen, sun room, music room and a full attic with three more rooms. I had a secret goal to make love with Nick in each and every room, including the attic and back yard!

"God, I love this place," Nick declared, as he walked from room to room, "Look at this. Anne, did you see this?" he asked, pointing out yet another spectacular feature of our new home.

It wasn't really cold enough but he so wanted to feel the hot water heat from the old cast iron radiators, "Co'mere, sit on this," he invited, perched on the warm fixture. "This is the best heat," explaining, "even after it's off the warmth stays for over an hour. Check this out. I love these floors," as he launched into a description of the workmanship that went into assembling every facet of the design in the foyer. Being a timber professional, he understood how valuable and impossible it was to come across original details like that. Every 12x12 inch section in the parquet floored foyer contained twenty different cuts of wood. The entire house had been meticulously maintained for over a hundred years.

In the dining room I displayed my collection of Fiestaware and knick knacks in the glassed in side board and cupboard decorating along my English literature bent, every room decorously arrayed with flowers, either in prints, doilies, arrangements, or pictures. And the yard; a veritable surfeit to the senses. The entire south side of the house was lined with vibrant pink peonies, orange poppies, and pungent lilacs bringing to mind Jane Kenyon's essay in *A Hundred White Daffodils*, '*The Moment of Peonies.*' The north and east contained an oasis of lush ferns, day lilies, beds of perennials, and an eight foot privacy fence topped with grape vines. The double lot was home to no less than eighteen trees, a bucolic sanctuary in the heart of town.

Nick and I would finish supper, take our coffee or wine out to the back yard, and snuggle as we watched the stars peek out. Birds serenaded us while the neighborhood retired. Even in the midst of nearby street traffic and next door neighbors we felt such peace and solitude, as if everything in the world was right.

With Nick's arms around me, my happiness idyllic, looking into his eyes, I asked, "How are we so fortunate?"

It was early October but the warm Indian summer allowed us to encamp in the yard well past dark.

"What?" Nick answered.

"Just the way things have worked out. Who gets this? You know, the contentment, the fulfillment, it is almost too good to be true."

"But it is true. We've worked damn hard all our lives. Do you think it hasn't been rough? That church shit? Raising four kids? My job? God, we deserve some R & R."

"I know, yeah, we do, but there are so many people working just as hard, that struggle all their lives and still don't get any reward. I can't help feeling that we are very lucky individuals!"

"Just enjoy it."

His lips pressed against mine (one way to shut me up) leaning me down on the chaise, where we 'christened' the yard, under the blanket of stars.

Running from the living room, across the foyer and dining room into the kitchen, I grabbed the phone on the third ring, "Hello."

"Hi, Anne, it's Julia. How are you doing?"

"Great! How are you and Hal?"

"We're good. We're thinking of driving down and seeing your new place. Are you busy this weekend?"

It was Monday, our old Canadian drinking buddies never did anything on the spur of the moment, at least, not like this, and we did, indeed, have plans. We hadn't seen Hal and Julia for a year so I hated to put them off.

"We do have something going on that we can't change," I answered, thinking, damn, why is the timing like this?

"So, what about next weekend?" Julia offered.

"Really? You can come then? Fabulous, do it. I love it!"

"Hannah wants to come too. Can Zelda come?"

Our two oldest children, graduated from college, working and living on their own, were eager to catch up.

"I'll call her and see, but I know she won't want to miss it. How often do we get this sort of opportunity?"

I thought of keeping it a secret from Nick, doing the surprise thing, but too excited to keep my mouth shut, as soon as he got home, I challenged, "You'll never guess who's coming next weekend?"

"Who?"

"You have to guess," playing the game.

"Hal and Julia," he said.

Just like that, disappointed it didn't take him longer, "How did you know that?" incredulously asking, "Did you have a sense?"

Mr. Down-to-Earth said, "Just a guess."

"Well, you're no fun!"

The over- indulgent weekend was non-stop raucous, hilarity; the six of us eating, drinking, laughing. Julia made her famous sausage, pasta dish filling Hal's carved white cedar bowl to overflowing. It was easily a gallon or more bursting with fresh mushrooms, spinach, and basil, velvety white sauce and piled high with grated parmesan. She couldn't cook for less than ten but this meal would have sated twenty. Just as we'd let loose in the Twin Cities all those years prior we were now able to let our true character blossom. Best friends. No religious hang-ups, no second guessing or guilt looking over our shoulders. The true heart, the hippie heart came through in a deep soul connection. Hal and Nick stayed up late into the night, after the rest of us had gone to bed.

When I asked him about it the next morning, wanting to know their conversation, all I got was, "It was a guy thing."

I loved that he had that kind of relationship. To my knowledge, Nick never had that with anyone else. Guys didn't develop friendships like women. Not in my experience. And I felt slightly sorry for them. My girlfriends were life long, Meryl dating back to junior high.

291

Gleaning a bit more with my query to Hal, he said, "We didn't say much. St. Paul guys don't talk that much. It's just a brain wave. We just sat there. Comfortable silences with Nick adding, " Glad you came out."

There was one question Hal asked that seemed fairly important, "Do you think it's possible for people to be open and honest?"

Nick replied, "Not in this world."

It was very simple. Nothing more.

That was October. With November snows threatening, I bundled up for a short walk to the store. Heading down Main Street, enticed by sandy beach posters lining the travel office windows, I detoured in. The agent sent me home with answered questions and a dozen brochures. Nick and I poured over the maps, agreeing on Oasis Akumal, the last resort near Tulum on the eastern coast of Mexico.

* * *

I had no clue regarding the involved complications to get Nick's body out of Mexico. As we left Ramon's office Shelli's cell phone rang.

Finally, the connection with Chloe, "Mom, what's going on? Mom, what is it, what happened, are you okay?"

Chloe's voice was strained, scared. She was ready to freak out. I could feel my legs buckle under me, so I sat down, right on the sidewalk outside the building we'd been heading into. The connection was poor, but I pushed through my paralyzing fear.

"Chloe, sit down."

"What?" she yelled, beginning to wail.

"Oh, Chloe, Dad died, Dad's dead."

She screamed the words, yelling, sobbing in the throes of agony, "NO, NO, NO, Noooo!" on and on, "NO, NO!"

The anguish absolutely destroyed me.

"Oh Mom, oh no, Dad, my dad."

I could hear other crying alongside her, someone comforting her. I was so extremely grateful to know her friends were there. She just let it out while I explained as best I could.

"Oh Mom, you're all alone, I can't stand you being alone."

God, please, God, help her, I thought. Oh God, how could this be happening? How could you let this happen?!"

Chloe, 20, sporting the vintage glasses I gave her one Christmas

1 year prior to his death

That chosen name, Chloe, the name that I had picked out for her my entire pregnancy, gelled the first time I wrapped her in my arms and looked at her tiny porcelain face. A name depicting inner and outer beauty, the definition had explained that one would want to keep her safe and always make her smile. Finding herself, finding direction took a few years after high school enabling her to tackle college much more seriously than her siblings had, but the singular sense of humor remained uniquely Chloe. Her smile exuded warmth inviting an extraordinary number of friends.

Acutely cognizant of my death blow, I could almost hear her core shake as the tremor penetrated to the quick.

"Oh, Mom," Chloe cried into the phone.

Her heart was rent. Her words shattered me, knowing I couldn't do anything. I was helpless, the void, the miles between us, huge. I wanted so badly to hold my Chloe. At least, that would

294

be some minute comfort. I explained, as coherently as I could, the details of what was happening. I needed to get back on track with the process, the paperwork, the asshole officials giving me such a hard time.

I said, "Call Zelda, get Steve, (her boyfriend) and head up to Grandma's in St. Paul. I'll be there as soon as I can get Dad's body released."

I tried to convince her that I would make it, a hard sell, not believing it myself. She called Zelda nearly every hour that night, sleepless, distraught, and beside herself with grief.

Shelli and Ramon shuttled me to the police station at approximately 5:00p.m, five hours after Nick had died. We'd been guaranteed about an hour's wait in the queue, Americans automatically being bumped to the end of the line while petty theft, minor crime issues, and traffic violations were processed. Everything Mexican was given priority. My concept of time was sketchy, at best, until 6:30 when my interminable wait was punctuated by an intense shouting match. Ramon reluctantly explained to me that the uproar was over who was going to do the autopsy on Nick. An alternate facility in Cancun was bargaining for his body.

"What sense would that make? I don't get it. Why doesn't he just stay here until we're ready to transport him home?"

I couldn't follow the rapid-fire screaming and hollering in Spanish but knew the tension and animosity were aimed at me.

"Just be patient, try to stay calm," Shelli counseled.

As I sat alone in the waiting area, trying to find a comfortable position in the faded aqua, molded plastic chair, Federales filed offenders past me. So confused, shock obstructing my reason, the foreign language analogous to a dream, I fixed the vision of my kids waiting for me. We just needed to be together, I told myself, then I would survive. Closing my eyes their faces appeared.

Finally, an officer motioned me over to the desk, introducing me to the official interpreter, pulling a chair up next to me. They had this slick, oily presence, greased back hair, mustachioed, the resemblance to banditos so unnerving. Making no attempt to mask their disdain for me, a few terse words expressed in Spanish, I assume were, "sorry for your loss." With hours dragging on, my anxiety multiplied as the possibility of securing the death certificate dwindled. No death certificate, no autopsy. No autopsy, no escape. Leaning over on the desk with my whirling head on my arm, I sat weeping, completely exhausted. My grip on reality, hanging by a thin thread, depended on getting out of Mexico before it snapped. Even one more day and I'd unravel beyond rescue.

As the tragic news spread back in the states, every half hour or so someone would call me on Shelli's cell phone, "I just needed to hear your voice. I needed to hear you say, you are okay."

I lied without even thinking about it, "Yeah, I'm alright."

What could I say? "I've lost my mind? I can't think? I can't grasp what's happened? I am ready to start screaming and never stop? If someone doesn't come and get me, I'll never make it?"

No, I told everyone, "I need to be about the business of signing papers, filling out forms, keeping this whole process on track."

It was mechanically rote, but I had to hoard every ounce of energy to stay focused on the task at hand. If I let go, that would be it. I wouldn't come back. I could see the dangerous precipice. And I was so freaked. People came and went, things happened around me, not *to* me. Waiting, waiting, waiting, hour after hour. I drank water but couldn't tolerate food. Shelli gave me some crackers to nibble on but they sat in a lump in my gut.

At around 8:00p.m, right there, about a foot away from me, the scene ratcheted up with heated yelling, now among a judge, police officials, my people, the interpreter, and coroner.

"Shelli, what is going on?" I asked, acutely aware that this was about Nick.

Haltingly, carefully, Shelli tried to explain as gently as possible, "Well, the coroner in Cancun has an agreement with the coastal police to process any American deaths."

"So he's out X amount of dollars if Nick doesn't go through him? You're telling me it's the fucking money? Oh, that's just perfect! These guys here get a cut of that?" my voice rising with the impact of the insidious practice, "Fucking assholes!"

I had been aware of the corruption, recalling our drug days and bust in '74, remembering friends of ours who'd spent time in Mexican prison, but I was astonished to see how pervasively the venal system permeated society. That I was a pawn in their under-the-table collusion was utterly debasing, like a back-hand to the face.

Wanting to attack every one of the arguing, money-grubbing bastards, I blasted Shelli, "What do they get for the deal? Find out how much. I'll write them out the fucking check right now!!"

Shelli took me by the shoulders, firmly, trying to gain back some calm, "I know how this system operates. You can't push or hurry. And they especially resent an American that thinks all she has to do is throw money at them and solve the problem. Yes, it takes money, but they call the shots. Patience is the only remedy. You have to dial it down, play it their way. They're in charge."

Mercifully, they did take the harangue behind closed doors, flimsy enough to still hear, but the separation afforded me a semblance of dignity. I wondered how much more lunacy I could take.

In regular communication with Zelda or Aaron, they, in turn, kept everyone else informed.

Suddenly, at 8:30, all was quiet. Capitulation. The door opened and with documents in hand, the officials emerged. My signature completed the transaction to enable Nick's autopsy.

Each hurdle produced a noticeable effect on my emotions, my frame of mind, somewhat like a relief, but also a letdown as the tremor quaked through my system. Shock, grief, and fear were crippling me. Mentally, nothing registered, but as precious minutes ticked by, I hardened my thoughts, step by step toward the border.

During the drive back to the hotel, Shelli and Ramon detailed the agencies and offices we had to tackle the following day.

"We'll be lucky to tie everything up in one day. I'll do my best," she said, offering, "I'll stay with you tonight if you want me to."

Thinking about it, coming to a stop in the hotel driveway, I could barely utter, "Thanks, but no. I need to be alone."

"Call me any time throughout the night. Any time and I will come," Shelli assured.

She blew me away. She was my salvation, my sanity.

"We'll pick you up at 6:00a.m, O.K.?"

"I'll be ready," I answered, knowing I'd be awake all night.

We hugged.

In my room, rocking on the edge of the bed, I stared at our belongings, wondering how to cope with packing. As the umbrella of sadness closed upon me, agonizing pain like contractions erupted from the depths of my soul. With visceral groans I felt like I cried from the insides of my toes, scaring myself as my nose started to bleed.

Shelli had wisely said, "Write down everything Nick liked about the trip, make a record of it."

Pulling myself up, pacing, I determined to begin the journal. Nick loved everything—it was perfect—small, tasteful, only 126 rooms, secluded, intimate.

He loved the beach, the views, restaurants, the European flavor, the strong, dark roast coffee, the sound of tumbling waves, sun, warmth, slight cooling breeze. It was ideal. We couldn't have asked for a better spot to spend our last two days together, his last two on earth. That's as far as I got before the next breaker crashed down on me, pummeling, forcing me to the bottom as I gasped for breath between sobs.

I dozed maybe a little that night. My thoughts were relentless, quieting for a precious few minutes, resuming with countless details. I'd write lists and notes for Shelli or my kids or folks or anyone else that could possibly be of assistance. Or I'd pen a few more lines about Nick. Digging out our checkbook, I read back over the ledger to see when things were due, but it made no sense, so far beyond my conceptual logic. At about 4:30a.m. I showered and dressed, put everything in my beach bag: water, crackers, a banana, tissues, Advil, Tums, and started to organize Nick's suitcase looking for clothes to give the funeral director. Numb with yearning, overcome touching his shirts, inhaling his scent, I abandoned the task, and walked down to the beach. Observing the glorious dawn rising over the listless palms, the scene was a direct contrast to my enormous plight. The dichotomy so very bizarre; feeling the utter calm of daybreak so peaceful in the buoyancy of paradise against the insuperable circumstances, the call of the ocean was unmistakable.

Shelli and Ramon were prompt, waiting with the car door open as I walked across the courtyard. Enroute they told me what was first on the agenda. I leant back against the head rest spacing out.

"Just try to follow along, keep up," I said to myself.

In a fog, I navigated one of the most grueling days of my life. The first stop, again the police station, gave us the official autopsy report. After waiting about a half hour, Ramon walked over to me, report in hand. He read it through the first time to himself. Beginning to hyperventilate, I hung onto the back of the chair as I rose struggling to keep my anxiety in check. Why was there no pulse, no response to resuscitation efforts? The surgeon had told me he detected no pulse whatsoever. I know Nick was the healthiest looking individual having an extremely physical job.

"Can't you read any damn faster, Ramon?" I thought.

I employed all of my faculties listening intently as Ramon began aloud, "asphyxia, that caused a major/massive coronary," while he pointed to each word in Spanish.

"Asphyxia?" I asked, astonished.

"Drowning," Ramon said.

"Drowned?" I asked, "Drowned?"

Ramon answered each question, trying to explain.

"How could he drown?" I stammered, "That caused a massive heart attack? Wouldn't it be the other way around?"

It didn't compute. Ramon tried to make sense of the report interpreting for me: salt water was in his lungs, salt water extremely toxic to lungs, blood and fluid from the body, flooding the lungs, cutting off oxygen, constriction, instant massive trauma. He asked whether I knew if Nick gulped any salt water at the end or any other time during the swim. None of it sunk in. The official conclusion was an absolute mystery that I had to accept, at least, for the time being. Yes, Nick was unquestionably gone. The fact was my strong, capable husband had talked to me and in less than five minutes he died from drowning! I stood there shaking my head.

Shelli walked me through the various agencies. At the ambulance station I signed off liability, putting the $700.00 ride on my credit card. My ignorance of our financial affairs, which I'd stubbornly refused to learn, compounded my stress. Time and again Nick had tried and failed to bring me up to speed. He would explain the economics in bits and pieces but I never took the time to gain a thorough knowledge or understanding of our situation. I didn't even know who his life insurance was with.

"I hate doing this," I'd whine to Nick, "you love it. I'll take care of other things. Division of labor," I'd argue, successfully sidestepping and exempting myself from financial issues.

How stupid that line of reasoning appeared to me at the present juncture. Why didn't he insist? Why didn't he make me sit down with him and teach me the essentials? I knew why. I was too damn belligerent. It wasn't worth the hassle.

Notarizing documents, hurrying around Playa del Carmen to wait in interminable lines, we had to break at 2:00p.m. while all business halted for siesta until 5:00. Dropped off at the hotel, I obsessed, intermittent thoughts churning with details not able to connect as if the synapses were live electrical wires flailing wildly in my brain. Getting clearance from the airlines and government allowing transport of Nick's body across the foreign border was the main obstacle. Having stumbled and muddled through the morning there wasn't any other option but to be patient and pray. All of the papers, information, documents and signatures were now being processed at the appropriate agencies. I knew in my heart that if the outcome wasn't positive, if the call at 5:00 delivered any more delays, if my kids had to wait any longer, their mom would unravel, and then we'd have another problem to deal with. I could feel the hysteria, the final breakdown just seconds away, so close, hovering behind my eyes like a dark shadow.

"But why can't we come down there?" Zelda asked. This was not acceptable to my take charge, in control daughter.

"Shelli said any more people, even one more, will compound the amount of details we have to deal with. It will mean another plane ticket home, more logistics to coordinate from Tulum to Cancun, possibly delaying my departure."

Much to their dismay, so frustrated and distraught, my kids complied, settling for phone conversations as we racked up hundreds of dollars in charges.

It was no use trying to lie down that afternoon. Instead, I walked around the mostly deserted complex during the extreme heat of the sun. The surgeon had said he was renting a condo along the beach so I walked, asking everyone I saw if they knew him. After half a dozen negatives I was directed to his place.

He was gone for the day but I was able to leave my name and room number with his roommate saying, "I'd appreciate talking with him."

There were so many questions, so many things that didn't add up. Could he somehow make me understand why my husband was dead?

Back in my room, drowning in rivers of tears, it was a relief to let it rip. I'd wail until I was out of breath, drifting off for a few minutes in exhausted sleep. Then I'd jolt awake with consciousness. At 5:15 the phone rang.

"Well, it looks like we've got clearance," Shelli related, stating the flight times in the morning, driving time, other particulars, ending with," So we're 80 percent sure we should have you home by tomorrow afternoon."

I asked, "What's the other 20 percent?"

"That's just the way things are in Mexico."

It rose up without warning as I screamed, "If it falls through, I can't stand it anymore, I'll lose it, I will, I know it!!"

She was doing everything humanly possible to expedite the matter and certainly didn't deserve the tongue lashing but my frazzled nerves blew.

Ending the conversation, I immediately relayed the 'good' news to Zelda who took it from there. The travel agency that Shelli worked for and the airline arranged for all of my needs, including front row seat, expedited check-in, and a private room on either end of the flight; one to await departure and one for the horrendous but wonderful reunion with my kids and Nick's mother. I proceeded to block out all doubts telling myself in 24 hours I'd be reunited with my precious loved ones.

I carefully placed Nick's belongings in the luggage knowing that would be the last time I'd ever do that, a final duty and labor of love. Taking the tan jersey polo, thinking how great he looked wearing it, gently folding it, with a kiss I laid it in. Closing my eyes, I could see him. God, what a handsome man.

His gentle hand on my shoulder, the slightest squeeze of affection, how he'd draw me into his chest, his face against my forehead. Gone. Forever. I continued with my clothes until everything was packed except my necessary morning toiletries. I wondered how I'd get through the night.

Calling the concierge, Liess, I said, "Would you see if you could locate the man who did chest compressions on Nick? I need to talk to him, if I can."

I wanted to thank him and get a picture to show the kids the man who tried to save their dad. It seemed paramount to me to get as many details as possible, to help them understand, make it real.

With the dusk, I tried to find respite in sleep placing five pillows all around me looking for a semblance of security. It didn't work. Lying there, the loneliness smothered me. His arms, long and strong, never to be around me, never to feel his lips, pressing, tasting, never to see his sparkling eyes. It couldn't be real. When would it stop being surreal? I should have been able to save him. Why couldn't I save you, my love? I'm so sorry, Babe.

The phone rang.

"Hi, Anne? I'm the one who did CPR on your husband."

"Would you be willing to come and talk to me?" I asked.

"Certainly, now?"

"Yes, thanks so much."

Our conversation was a godsend. Tom was a clinical psychologist who had dealt with this same situation, personally, and in his practice. I talked and talked, questioning him at length, gleaning whatever understanding achievable.

Having been in emergency scenarios, he stated, "Nick suffered a major, immediate trauma. I noticed, initially, his fingernails were all black and blue. All down the sides of his legs, they were mottled, meaning he was dead when he hit the sand."

"So then why did you even attempt reviving him?"

"Our training just sends us into auto pilot, going into resuscitation mode. I'm so very sorry for the outcome. I wish we could have altered it."

"It was out of our hands. It was his time, his number was up, we had no choice."

"You seem to have a clear understanding of where you're at."

"I believe, with all my heart, that I will see Nick again, that one day we will be together in some form. Don't ask me what that is, but it's the only thing keeping me sane."

"I've heard others talk like you. I've heard that faith lingo, a belief system. I may have thought that once, but when my brother was murdered, I said, fuck God."

His candor shocked me but I couldn't argue with his traumatic experience. Our conversation was interrupted by a knock at my door.

It was two complete strangers, "We represent a contingency from the bar that wish to express our sympathy and offers of help."

I was speechless, moved, and amazed by their caring and sincerity. Throughout the past grueling hours, I had been strengthened by and grateful for the protection and concern of the human family. Their proffered kindness brought hope to my battered psyche.

At 4:00a.m. I gave up lying down. Readying my bags, I took my tablet and camera down to the beach to memorialize our last day. Sitting alone, watching the sun rise, I desperately ached for home, going home, my family. I wanted to thank everyone who had been involved, all the many people that had witnessed my trauma. Seeing someone die would certainly have ruined my vacation. I wrote a note and left it at the desk for Liess to share with the guests.

My note read:

Here's my personal belief:

Love came through every one of you. I could feel that love holding me up, sustaining me through this most painful experience of my life. Thank you and God bless you all.

Liess placed my note next to a vase of flowers on a table in the courtyard along with my address for guests to send condolences.

At 7:00 Shelli and Ramon picked me up. She went over our itinerary as we drove to Cancun.

With all of my hopes fastened on the eighty percent, I prayed to myself, "God, make it happen."

"You can't reveal to anyone that Nick's body is onboard," Shelli's first admonition grabbed my attention.

"It's not like I'm going to be talking to anyone, but why?"

"People are very superstitious, even unreasonable when it comes to things like that," she explained.

It wasn't an issue, as far as I was concerned. If I could just be left alone, I could maintain.

At the airport a half hour before takeoff Shelli's phone rang (the twenty percent). There was an issue about the death certificate. The Mexican consulate didn't like the wording and wanted to alter it to simply read, heart attack, instead of asphyxia.

"I don't understand what they have to do with the medical examiner's report. They aren't certified in that area. They don't have any right to alter the facts," I argued with Shelli.

"Does it really make any difference? What if it prohibits your take-off?"

Adamant over the point, I wouldn't budge.

"Goddammit," raising my voice, "I can't let them just put in anything they like. I mean it, Shelli, I've had enough of this bullshit. I'm not taking any more of it," now yelling, "I'll take my chances. It's too much!"

Shelli walked several feet away, to a far corner but not out of earshot while the heated debate continued in Spanish.

In the meantime, Aaron called, "Mom, I rented a limo so we wouldn't have to split up into different vehicles."

"Thank you, Aaron," I choked out, "you're my sweetheart."

"They also have a private room where we can wait for you. They'll bring you to us when you land. They've really been helpful, Mom."

"We may have a glitch, Aaron. I don't know what's going on but Shelli is hassling with someone as we speak about the death certificate."

"What the hell is the problem now!?"

"Just a sec, hang on, here comes Shelli."

Shelli gave me the thumbs up and I exhaled loudly.

"We're on track, Aaron, you can check with the flight times to see when I'll be there."

"Are you okay, Mom?"

"Yeah, I'm almost there, honey. I'll make it. I'll see you soon. Give everyone my love. I love you."

"I love you, too, Mom."

20

Shelli walked me toward the gate as far as she could. Putting her arms around me, she whispered something I'll never forget, "I'm honored to have been involved with you, and if I had had a choice whether or not to be with you, I would gladly choose to do it again."

Profoundly moved, tears spilling over, I said, "Thank you, Shelli, I'll never forget you, your help. You kept me in this world."

I hugged her, desperately not wanting to let go. Proceeding through the line alone, so utterly alone, my wobbly legs responded to the row call. Operating on no sleep or sustenance for so long, somehow I was able to keep my wits. Rhythmically in and out, I willed myself to breathe through the panic, allowing me to regain sufficient equilibrium to board.

Finding my seat, I placed my bag in the overhead, keeping a watchful eye so that no one would trap it behind anything else. I anticipated running full speed, as soon as the plane touched down. As I detected the knowing look in the flight attendants, my best defense was to sit perfectly still imagining my arms around my four kids. The events of the past days drifted in and out like fragments.

My body twitched as I snapped out of my stupor hearing the captain's voice over the P.A. system, "We are beginning our descent into Minneapolis/St. Paul International airport."

With burning eyes, I squinted at the light.

He proceeded, "We ask all passengers to remain seated until we have turned off the 'fasten seat belts' sign."

Ignoring his direction, I leaned back to the young man seated behind me and asked, "Could you, please, reach my bag for me in the overhead?"

Nodding, he said, "Sure."

He just sat there, though, obedient to the pilot. The woman across the aisle from him either knew my situation or else sensed my imminent hysteria.

She yelled at him, "Now!"

In any other scenario, it would have cracked me up, watching him jump out of his seat. Grabbing my bag, he plopped it on my lap just as the wheels touched down. I let out an excruciating groan, gasping with deep, unearthly sobs doubling over in spasms. Two attendants instantly enveloped me in comforting arms, their tears mixed with mine, the awkward minutes stretching as we waited to deplane.

The couple next to me, agape in stunned silence, began crying as I offered haltingly, "My husband died on our anniversary trip."

"We ask that all passengers please remain in their seats while we escort a passenger off the plane," the captain announced.

No one moved a muscle as the attendant supported me down the aisle. I couldn't feel my legs, her arm around me. Apprised of the situation, the first checkpoint took less than a minute. At the second customs agent, I expected the same wave through.

"Hold it," the officer said, wanting a more thorough examination of my papers.

My legs gave way. The flight attendant grabbed me around the waist as I reached for the counter.

"Her husband died. The remains are on the plane," she explained, as succinctly as possible.

With a stunned look, "Go, go," he assented, getting it, handing my papers back.

Leaning heavily on the attendant, I began to run, letting her guide the way back behind the offices where my family waited. I saw the door. Reaching out my hand, turning the knob, the noise rumbled forth, erupting, exploding as we lunged for each other. Voices melded into one convulsive wail, screaming, crying as we wrapped our arms around, pulling tightly together in one embrace, one entwined person. This was the truth, the harsh reality of the last three days sinking in. This was **now**, the moment of such agony, and yet relief, that we were finally together. An incredible wrenching of the heart and soul. Along with our four children were Nick's mom, Violetta, Aaron's wife, Jillian, and Chloe's boyfriend, Steve. From the beginning to end, walking into the water, to the collapse on the beach, I recounted every detail, minute by minute, as it was burned into my brain. With hushed voice, I tried to somehow soften the impact. An hour later, when we finally emerged from the tiny room, the office workers had tactfully vacated.

Arrangements had been made with the funeral home to transport Nick's body from the airport. My psyche, my personality, my entire life, so altered; the visitation, the memorial, the ensuing processes a complete fog; I relied solely on my children and my closest friends to sort it all out. Shock kept me in a state of semi-consciousness until I saw Nick's picture in the obituary. There it was. My dead husband. Reality. Acceptance would require many more agonizing months.

Nick was so lucky to have gone so quickly, so effortlessly. A few gasps, his eyes glazed over, he was no longer cognizant. Gone. It took maybe 5 minutes in entirety. If we had the choice, wouldn't we all elect to go in that manner? I know I would. Blink, you're gone.

In the effort to keep our relationship not only surviving but thriving, Nick and I determined to block out all of our previous liaisons, especially one night stands. We felt like those experiences adulterated our unreserved, uncompromising devotion and we wanted to live as if we'd been each other's only lover. It was fantasy but erasing that part of our history enabled us to build together without past skeletons. He will always be my true love, faithful and committed all of our 31 years. I hold the beauty of our love for all time, believing Nick and I possessed what Aristotle spoke of, "What is a friend? A single soul dwelling in two bodies."

In the anniversary book that I compiled to surprise Nick with in Mexico, this is the final page, the last thing he read from me:

> My prayer, the longing of my heart
> is that we journey slowly,
> drifting easily,
> at the last,
> into eternity together.
> Happy Anniversary
> my one and only, forever.

Epilogue

The world of shock enveloping me in that first year after Nick died, where I hovered between insanity and despair, was truly hellish. The only thing that kept me in this world was my unwillingness to saddle my children with the additional trauma of suicide. As the first anniversary of Nick's death approached I wondered if I would feel any differently, any better.

Somewhere deep within my soul I wanted to recover but was powerless to achieve even the smallest semblance of wholeness. There is a plethora of material defining the one year benchmark as a watershed event. No such amelioration was noticeable. It took me all of two grueling years to be convinced I'd remain on the planet. Advice from one doctor was that if I wasn't back to my normal routine in three months I should get on medication. I envisioned leaping across his desk, pouncing on him and screaming while my fingers choked him to death. Rising from my chair without a word I simply walked out of his office. People say the first year is the hardest and in some ways that's true but for me the shock kept a lot of feelings at bay until that second year when depression and reality sunk in leaving me with this axiom:

> Your absence has gone through me
> like a thread through a needle.
> Everything I do is stitched with its color.
>
> W.S. Mervin

I believe this is an important book describing a period of time when anything seemed possible, peace & love were mixed with assholier-than-thous, and wars on everything began. It is a different slant on what Easy Rider does in describing cultures of the period.

Hippie at Heart is fun/frank/entertaining/tough and a great read about a singular free-ish period of time that I'd only witnessed from corporate-cog & academic treadmill vantage points; thus it filled in enough for me of the hippie life, making me more grateful for the paths I took. I must say, I first glossed over the childhood part and began really getting into the story after her high school. The parties, the communal aspects, building a log cabin from standing dead trees, living and birthing in primitive conditions way out in the boonies of northern New Mexico, finding God and hypocrisy, and finally experiencing what simply had to be the worst imaginable experience possible for the heroine. However, what a bittersweet ending for Nick. All up, it was seemingly his time to go, and he went mercifully quickly. Plus without his death this book would not have had such a powerful impact in terms of passion and posterity. By the way, on finishing the first read I immediately went back and reread the childhood part more carefully in order to assure I had gleaned every bit of the lives Anne describes so frankly and eloquently.

M.H. (Mack) McKinney, PhD

I read it straight through without stopping, and I loved it for several reasons. First and foremost, in its exquisite frankness it reminded me of my own hippie life, with the drugs, the casual sexual promiscuity, and "dropping out."

Second, the writing style is flawless, superb, wherein all the scenes come vividly to life. I'm thinking especially of the fights between Anne's mom and dad, summers at the farm, a pubescent near-rape by four boys. Taking the Pill for her menstrual cycle then using it to get laid, an attempted suicide, first LSD trip. Such wild days.

Third, a very real and deeply moving portrait is created of the relationship between Nick and Anne. We are drawn into this love from the very first line when Anne is flying her husband's body back to the States. And it stays with us right till the end, when we find out how he died. And how his death was a wound that would never really heal.

And finally, I love the title, *Hippie at Heart*, a three-word condensation of everything in this marvelous novel. In short, it's fantastic!

Ernest Brawley, PhD, Master of Arts, has published three novels, THE RAP, SELENA, and THE ALAMO TREE. His latest novel, BLOOD MOON, will soon be published by Little Machines Press/Roots Digital Media. Brawley has taught at the University of Hawaii, Hunter College, New York University and the Pantheon-Sorbonne. He has worked in Argentina, Spain, France, Italy, England, India, Thailand and Japan. He is a recipient of the Joseph Henry Jackson Award in Literature and served for several years on the Fiction Award Committee of the National Endowment for the Arts in Washington.

Printed in Great Britain
by Amazon

24711639R00176